THE COMPLETE GREEK TRAGEDIES

VOLUME I

AESCHYLUS

THE COMPLETE GREEK TRAGEDIES

Edited by David Grene and Richmond Lattimore

VOLUME I

AESCHYLUS

THE  UNIVERSITY OF CHICAGO PRESS
CHICAGO AND LONDON

The University of Chicago Press, Chicago 60637
The University of Chicago Press, Ltd., London

© 1942, 1953, 1956, 1960 by The University of Chicago

Agamemnon
  © 1947 by the Dial Press

Volume I published 1959. Fourth Impression 1974
Printed in the United States of America

International Standard Book Number: 0-226-30768-9

NOTE

The translation of *Agamemnon* which is here used first appeared in *Greek Plays in Modern Translation*, edited with an Introduction by Dudley Fitts (New York: Dial Press, 1947). It is used here by kind permission of The Dial Press, Inc. Some alterations have been made, chiefly in the matter of spelling Greek names. Two sections of *Agamemnon*, "The God of War, Money Changer of Dead Bodies," and "The Achaeans Have Got Troy, upon This Very Day," first published in *War and the Poet: A Comprehensive Anthology of the World's Great War Poetry*, edited by Richard Eberhart and Selden Rodman, are used by permission of the Devin-Adair Company.

The translation of all three plays is based on H. W. Smyth's "Loeb Classical Library" text (London and New York: William Heinemann, Ltd., and G. P. Putnam's Sons, 1926). A few deviations from this text occur where I have followed the manuscript readings instead of emendations accepted by Smyth.

Various editions of Greek drama divide the lines of lyric passages in various ways, but editors regularly follow the traditional line numbers whether their own line divisions tally with these numbers or not. This accounts for what may appear to be erratic line numbering in our translations, for instance, *The Eumenides* 360 and following. The line numbering in the translations in this volume is that of Smyth's text.

CONTENTS

INTRODUCTION TO THE *ORESTEIA*

The Life of Aeschylus

Aᴇꜱᴄʜʏʟᴜꜱ, the son of Euphorion, was born in the last quarter of the sixth century B.C., probably about 513 or 512 B.C. The great Persian Wars occurred during his early manhood, and he fought, certainly at Marathon (where his brother was killed in action) and probably also at Artemisium, Salamis, and Plataea. He is said to have begun at an early age to write tragedies; his first victory was in 484 B.C. In or about 476 B.C. he visited Sicily and, at the instance of Hieron of Syracuse, Pindar's friend, produced *The Women of Etna* at the new city of Etna which Hieron had founded. In 472 he produced his *Persians* at Athens, with Pericles as his choregus (or official sponsor) and re-produced it, presumably in the next year, in Sicily. Back in Athens in 468, he was defeated by the young Sophocles, but won again in 467 with a set of plays including *The Seven against Thebes*. In 458 he presented the *Oresteia* (*Agamemnon, The Libation Bearers, The Eumenides*). He died in Gela, Sicily, in 456 or 455 B.C., leaving behind him an epitaph which might be rendered as follows:

Under this monument lies Aeschylus the Athenian,
  Euphorion's son, who died in the wheatlands of Gela. The grove
of Marathon with its glories can speak of his valor in battle.
  The long-haired Persian remembers and can speak of it too.

He left behind more than seventy plays (the exact number is uncertain), of which seven have survived. They are *The Suppliants, The Persians, The Seven against Thebes, Prometheus Bound, Agamemnon, The Libation Bearers, The Eumenides*. He is said to have won first prize thirteen times while he lived, but after his death his tragedies were often produced again, and in competition with living poets he won more prizes still.

It would be interesting to know how old Aeschylus was when he wrote his known and dated plays. But the date of his birth is quite uncertain, though the year 525/4[1] is commonly given as if it were an established fact. It is true enough that apparently independent authorities give ages at the time of Marathon and at time of death which agree with this scheme. However, the birth date may very easily be accounted for by the rule-of-thumb method, favored by Greek chronologists, of taking an important event in a man's life and counting back forty years to an estimated date of birth. Thus the traditional birth date of Thucydides is 471 (from the outbreak of the war he recorded in 431); of Aristophanes, 445 (from the production of his masterpiece, *The Frogs*, in 405). Both these dates are bad (there are many parallels), and the one for Aeschylus is no more convincing. An age of forty at his first victory is suspect, not only because it tallies so neatly with a known method of reckoning, but because it is in itself unlikely that a man who utterly eclipsed his rivals in subsequent reputation, so that they are now very little more than bare names, should have had to wait so long before scoring his first success. A less popular but more attractive tradition would make him born in 513 or 512, but here also we may be dealing with estimates based on known and dated events, such as battles and dramatic productions.

Ancient authorities also tell us a few other things about Aeschylus which would be interesting if we could believe them. It is said that he left Athens for Sicily in chagrin because he was defeated by Simonides, the great lyric poet, in a competition for writing the epitaph of the dead at Marathon, or because he was defeated by Sophocles in dramatic competition, or because he disliked Athenian politics.[2]

1. Athenian dates are generally fixed by the term of the *archon*, or titular chief magistrate. Since the archons changed over some time in the summer, not at our new year, such dates overlap those of our calendar. Since, however, plays came out in the spring before the change-over, a play dated to an archonship of, for instance, 485/4 will *always* fall in 484.

2. Euripides, near the end of his life, left Athens in voluntary exile and died in Macedonia at the court of King Archelaus. There is reason to believe that he left because he had constantly failed to win critical approval in Athens and because he despaired of the hopeless course which his city had been following since the time of Pericles. The biographers doubtless applied the analogy of Euripides-Athens-Arche-

The defeats are real, but they do not tally, chronologically, with the visits to Sicily; on the contrary, after losing to Sophocles, Aeschylus stayed in Athens and won first prize with *The Seven against Thebes* and its related dramas the next year, which is quite different from going off to Sicily in a huff. If one may guess at why he went to Sicily, it was because Sicily was the America of that day, the new Greek world, rich, generous, and young, with its own artists but without the tradition of perfected culture which Old Greece had built up, and it attracted Pindar, Bacchylides, Simonides, and Aeschylus much as America has attracted English men of letters from Dickens, Thackeray, and Wilde down to the present day. We do not know much about the personal character of Aeschylus and can make little critical use of what we do know. The epitaph shows he was proud of his military record, but this scarcely helps us to understand *The Persians*, *The Seven against Thebes*, or *Agamemnon*. We must approach Aeschylus, not from the biographies, but from his own plays.

Early Tragedy

From the time of the almost legendary Thespis, a full generation before the earliest tragedy we possess, dramatic performances of some sort had been regularly produced at Athens. In origin, they must have been a special local development of the choral lyric—sacred, occasional, provincial, public—which was alive in all the cities of Greece. But the early phases of the course by which dramatic lyric was transformed into lyric drama are now invisible to us. We can recognize certain ingredients, or essential features. Early drama was choral, and the life of Attic tragedy shows the indispensable chorus to the end, though the actors steadily invade the preserves of the chorus until, at the close of the fifth century, Euripides is using it sometimes in a most perfunctory manner, as if it were a convention he could not get rid of but might otherwise have preferred to do without. Early drama was sacred, having to do with the

---

laus to Aeschylus-Athens-Hieron. But Euripides was a failure in his own lifetime, and it made him a defeatist and escapist. Of Aeschylus we can say with confidence that he was neither of these things.

cult of divinities, and particularly with the cult of Dionysus: on the formal side, it was performed to the end on ground devoted to that god and before his priest; but developed tragedy did not have to be *about* Dionysus, and seldom was. Like most choral lyric, it was given through the medium of a formal competition. The early tragic poets drew, for narrative material and for metrical forms, on an already rich and highly developed tradition of nondramatic poetry, epic and lyric. They also drew, no doubt, on the unwritten and almost inarticulate experience of a living people, on folk memory and folklore, cult and ritual and ceremony and passion play and mystery play. But tragedy did not grow out of such elements. It was made. Concerning the makers, we know little indeed about Thespis, Pratinas, Choerilus, Phrynichus. Tragedy, for us, begins with Aeschylus.

By or during the career of Aeschylus, the features of Greek tragedy become fixed. At an Athenian festival, three player-groups, each consisting of two (later three) actors and chorus, act out competitively four-drama sets. The material is based on stories told or indicated in previous Greek legend. Tragedy is heroic. The costumes are formal, physical action restrained and without violence; naturalism is neither achieved nor desired. Aeschylus himself, and his older contemporary Phrynichus before him, experimented with dramatic stories taken from contemporary history, and of these we have *The Persians*, dealing with the repulse of Xerxes and his forces. This was a success, but circumstances in this case were favorable to special occasional drama, for the defeat of Persia was the proudest achievement of Greek history. And, even here, the play is *about* the Persians, not the Greeks, the setting is Persia, and only Persian individuals are named. Remoteness from the immediate here-and-now, required by tragedy and guaranteed by legendary material, is here to a great extent achieved by placing the scene in the heart of Persia, so far away and guarded from Greeks that to the audience it might have seemed almost as legendary as the Troy of Hector or the Thebes of Oedipus.[3] A drama dealing directly with Themistocles and Pericles or

---

3. So Shakespeare drew on history and legend for his tragedies and romances, or, when these dealt with time not specifically antique, the place would be idealized by

with the war between Athens and Aegina would have been neither desired by the poet nor tolerated by his audience.

The body of legend on which Aeschylus and the other tragic poets drew was composed of the epic poems of Homer and his successors and constituted a loose and informal, but fairly comprehensive, history of the world as the Greeks knew it. Typical sources in this complex were the *Iliad* and the *Odyssey;* the "Epic Cycle," or series of subsequent epics which filled out the story of Troy and dealt in detail with its occasions and aftereffects; the epics that told the story of Thebes; and numerous other narratives either written down or transmitted through unwritten oral tradition. The dramatist rarely worked directly from the main body of the *Iliad* or the *Odyssey;* the less authoritative minor texts were more popular. The dramatist seems not to have felt free to invent his material outright, but he could—in fact, he must—choose among variants, expand or deepen and interpret character, generally shape the story on the trend of his own imagination. In the case of Aeschylus, this process can be best reconstructed in the *Oresteia,* the trilogy or sequence of three tragedies composed of *Agamemnon, The Libation Bearers,* and *The Eumenides.*

The Story of the House of Atreus

The version of the legend as Aeschylus used it runs as follows. Atreus and Thyestes, the sons of Pelops, quarreled because Thyestes had seduced his brother's wife, and disputed the throne of Argos. Thyestes, defeated and driven out, returned as a suppliant with his children, and Atreus in pretended reconciliation invited him and his children to a feast. There he slaughtered the children of Thyestes (all but one) and served them in a concealing dish to their father, who ate their flesh. When it was made known to him what he had been doing, Thyestes cursed the entire house and fled with his surviving son, Aegisthus. Agamemnon and Menelaus, the sons of Atreus, inherited the Kingdom of Argos, and married, respectively, Clytae-

---

distance and the vagueness of his audience's information: Italy, Bohemia, Illyria, Arden.

mestra and Helen, the daughters of Tyndareus the Spartan. Clytaemestra bore Agamemnon three children—Iphigeneia, Electra,
and Orestes. When Paris of Troy seduced Helen and carried her
away, the brothers organized a great expedition to win her back.
The armament, gathered at Aulis, was held there by wind and
weather; Calchas the prophet divined that this was due to the anger
of Artemis and, with the pressure of public opinion behind him,
forced Agamemnon to sacrifice his daughter, Iphigeneia, in order
to appease the goddess. Agamemnon with his forces sailed to Troy
and in the tenth year captured it, destroyed the city and its temples,
killed or enslaved the people, and set sail for home. On the sea, a
great storm struck the fleet, and Agamemnon, with a single galley,
made his way back to Argos, the rest of his ships being sunk or
driven out of sight and knowledge. With him he brought his mistress, Cassandra, captive princess and prophetess of Troy.

Meanwhile, in Argos, Aegisthus had returned and Clytaemestra
had taken him as her lover and sent Orestes out of the country.
Warned of the king's approach by signal flares through which he
had agreed to notify her of the fall of Troy, she made ready to receive him. She welcomed him into the house, but when he was un-
armed in his bath, she pinioned him in a robe and stabbed him to
death, and killed Cassandra as well. She defended her action before
the people of Argos, who were helpless against Aegisthus and his
bodyguard. But Orestes returned at last and was welcomed by his
sister Electra, who had remained rebellious against her mother but
without power to act. Orestes, disguised as a traveler and pretending
to bring news of his own death, won access to the house and killed
both Aegisthus and Clytaemestra. Portents and dreams had fore-
warned of this murder, and Orestes had been encouraged, even commanded, by Apollo to carry it through. Nevertheless, when he had
displayed the bodies and defended his act, the Furies (Eumenides),
or spirits of retribution, appeared to him and drove him out of Argos. Orestes took refuge with Apollo at Delphi and was at last
purified of the murder, but the Furies refused to acknowledge any
absolution and pursued him across the world until he took refuge on
the rock of Athens before the statue of Athene. There, in the pres-

ence of Athene, Apollo and the Furies appealed to her for a decision, and she, thinking the case too difficult to be judged by a single person, even her divine self, appointed a court of Athenian jurors to hear the arguments and judge the case. When the votes of these resulted in a tie, Athene herself cast the deciding ballot in favor of Orestes. Orestes, deeply grateful to Athene and her city, returned to Argos, while Athene found it necessary to propitiate the angry Eumenides by inducing them to accept an honorable place as tutelary spirits in Athens. The law court of the Areiopagus, which had judged the case, was perpetuated as a just tribunal for homicide down through the history of man.

Variations of the Legend

Such are the bare facts of the story, the raw stuff out of which Aeschylus forged three massive tragedies. The story of the murder of Agamemnon had been told by Homer in the *Odyssey*[4] and by the cyclic successors of Homer in the *Nostoi* ("Returns"), while the early part of the story appears in the *Cypria*. Stesichorus, the Sicilian poet, had made the fortunes of Orestes the subject of a long narrative in lyric form; and Pindar in his *Eleventh Pythian* had summarized the tale and reflected on the motives of Clytaemestra; and others, too, had touched on the story. On all these Aeschylus doubtless drew, and he had numerous variations from which to pick and choose.[5] The main difference between Aeschylus and Homer is to be found, however, not in details but in the whole approach to the

4. Piecemeal: the plot is constantly referred to by analogy with the plot of the *Odyssey*. The principal references are: i. 29–43, Zeus calls the vengeance of Orestes an example of just retribution; i. 298–300, Athene uses it as an encouragement to Telemachus; iii. 254–312, Nestor tells Telemachus of the beguiling of Clytaemestra, the wanderings of Menelaus, and the vengeance of Orestes; iv. 514–37, Menelaus tells how he heard from Proteus about the death of Agamemnon; xi. 405–34, the ghost of Agamemnon tells Odysseus how his wife and Aegisthus murdered him and Cassandra.

5. For example, Homer makes the scene of the murder (and consequently the palace of Agamemnon) Mycenae; Stesichorus and Simonides, Sparta; Pindar, Amyclae (which comes to the same thing); Aeschylus, Argos, doubtless for political reasons. Stesichorus called the nurse of Orestes Laodameia; Pindar, Arsinoë; Aeschylus, Cilissa; etc.

story, which, in turn, motivates selection, addition, or omission of detail. It is to be noted that Homer does not tell the story consecutively; he really does not tell it at all, but he draws on it for example and illustration. The homecoming of Agamemnon is played against the homecoming of Odysseus; the situations are analogous, but the characters are different and bring different results out of similar materials. The murderous suitors lurk in the house of Odysseus as did Aegisthus in that of Agamemnon, but Penelope has not joined the enemy as Clytaemestra did. Nevertheless, when Odysseus comes home, he has his warning from the ghost of Agamemnon and goes warily so as not to fall into a similar trap. As for Telemachus, the resolute activity of Orestes is set as an example against his own indecision. The parts of the story that bear on such an apposition come out, and the tendency of it varies accordingly. The story is a domestic tragedy, but, since the house is a king's house, the tragedy becomes dynastic also. It begins with the betrayal of a king and the alienation of his kingdom and ends with the rewinning of dynastic power by the rightful heir. Therefore, though the death of Agamemnon is tragic, the deaths of Aegisthus and Clytaemestra are nothing of the sort; no tragedy adheres to Orestes, he merits no compassion, only praise. It is, I think, because of this *approach* that Homer fails to mention certain aspects of the story which are prominent in Attic tragedy. Iphigeneia does not appear; her slaughter would have suggested some motive of justice mixed into the treachery of Clytaemestra. Nor do we hear of the wrongs inflicted by Atreus on Thyestes and his sons, for this would have made the murder of Agamemnon in some measure defensible as an act of retribution. Nowhere in Homer do we hear of an Orestes pursued by the Furies of his mother, whether these might be actual spirits or the remorse in his own memory. Did Homer, then, know nothing of how Orestes murdered Clytaemestra? The lines in which he speaks of her death betray him (*Od.* iii. 304-10), for, while Menelaus was still on his travels,

> Seven years Aegisthus was lord in golden Mycenae,
> but in the eighth the evil came on him when great Orestes
> came back from Athens and killed his father's slayer, the crafty

Aegisthus, who had murdered his glorious father. And after
he had killed him, in the Argives' presence he held a funeral
for his mother, who was hateful, and for the coward Aegisthus.

This unobtrusive notice is all we have, but it makes perfectly plain
the fact that the matricide was in Homer's tradition, and he could
not contradict it. But he was in a position to place the emphasis
wherever he chose and to tell only as much of the story, or as little,
as suited his purpose. It is surely no accident that the parts which he
leaves out are those which would complicate and confuse his simple
picture of Aegisthus as a conspiring villain, Orestes as an avenging
hero, and Clytaemestra as a woman who yielded to her weakness.

Aeschylus, on the other hand, told the whole story. *Agamemnon* takes us from the news of Troy's fall to the murder of Agamemnon and the confirmation of his murderers as despots in Argos.
The Libation Bearers begins with the return of Orestes and ends with
his flight from Argos, pursued by the Furies, after the murder of
Clytaemestra and Aegisthus. *The Eumenides* finds Orestes seeking
sanctuary at Delphi, takes him to Athens for his acquittal and absolution, and ends with the establishment of the Furies in their new home
at Athens. Further, particularly in the first play of the trilogy, there
are constant cutbacks which sweep into the drama much of the
foregoing material: the banquet of Thyestes, the sacrifice of Iphigeneia, the siege and fall of Troy. The simple narrative which we can
reconstruct from notices in Homer could not have carried the weight
of a tragic trilogy.

"Agamemnon"

Agamemnon is, first of all, a domestic tragedy. The dominant figure, Clytaemestra, is a wife estranged through the wrong her husband committed on their daughter; love for Iphigeneia, acting
through the murder of Agamemnon, is on its way toward driving
her to fight her love for her surviving daughter and for her son.
Her paramour and partner is her husband's cousin. Behind them all
is the figure of Helen, Clytaemestra's sister, wife of Agamemnon's
brother, whose treachery caused the Trojan War, Iphigeneia's death,
and all the estrangement and broken faith that followed. The theme

here is the *philos-aphilos* or hate-in-love; its drive is the dynamic force of contradiction.

Behind the domestic tragedy lies the tragedy of war. For the sake of Helen, whose beauty was unforgettable but whose worth could not be demonstrated by reason or defended by argument, Agamemnon drained Greece of its manhood and involved the innocent in the miseries of a bitter campaign. The Trojans welcomed Helen and her captor and so were guilty; but their punishment—the total destruction of their city, their temples, and their men; the enslavement and defiling of their women and children—was out of all proportion to any harm they had done to Greece. Neither Troy nor Greece deserved what the idea of Helen made Agamemnon do to them. For he destroyed his own country as well as Troy; many died in the years before Ilium, the survivors were drowned or scattered in the great storm on the way back; and the pomp of his entrance thinly disguises the fact that he brought home the crew of a single ship.

Because of this, with the war tragedy goes political tragedy as well. The means by which this is communicated is through the chorus, who, in so far as they function as characters in the play, represent the solid elders of Argos. These are king's men, since the king in the heroic period stands for lawful authority; they have seen that Agamemnon's expedition was wrong, and they tell him so (799-804), but they would still be loyal to him if he were a much worse man than he is. It is these sturdy citizens who tell how, as the death reports and the urns full of ashes came in from the front, the people at home began to mutter against the king and ask why the war was fought; and, though the chorus cannot take their part, they cannot deny that there is cause for such mutterings. But the people did find a champion, or so they thought, at least a leader, Aegisthus, the king's cousin. He took advantage of the disaffection among those who hated the king he hated, and so returned from exile; he won the throne by winning the queen, confirmed his seizure by contriving the murder of Agamemnon, and defended it with his tyrant's personal bodyguard.[6]

6. The word *tyrannos* ("tyrant") was used by the Greek prose writers in a semi-technical sense, and it only gradually became a term of reproach. The tyrant was a

Thus we come about once more to the dynastic tragedy of Homer. But the interpretations of Agamemnon's murder do not exclude one another. Aeschylus can work on several levels at once. The war tragedy and the political tragedy do not contradict, they cohere with and deepen the tragedy of persons.

On the personal level, *Agamemnon* works through a complex of collisions, not so much right against wrong as right against right, each person insisting on his right with the force of passion. Agamem-

---

self-appointed despot whose career was characteristic in various places at various times in Greek history, but especially in the seventh and sixth centuries B.C. The Athenian using the word would think at once of his own tyrants, Peisistratus and his son Hippias; the restoration of the latter was still a political issue when Aeschylus was a young man. The following may serve as a general description of the typical early tyrant. He was an aristocrat, but one who was likely not to be in power while the government remained stable. He posed as a representative of the underprivileged and won and used their support, but generally got his position by unconstitutional means. His policy was generally to hold more than royal power without assuming any formal title, through influence and threat. He nevertheless always attempted to found a permanent dynasty through his sons, but hardly ever succeeded. His championship of the poorer classes was generally more than a pose, and he frequently worked toward broadening the base of democracy. Thus his most persistent enemies were not the masses but his fellow-aristocrats, except for the few he could win over into his own personal following; but, because, in spite of all the good he might do, his very existence flouted all legality, those who loved law and liberty hated him too. He had to guard himself, and infallible signs of his presence were the bodyguard of professionals and the spy system. Tyranny was one of the great growing pains in the life of young democracy, and history has been unkind to the tyrant, but for solid reasons.

Tyranny actually came later than Homeric or heroic kingship, and Aeschylus probably knew very well that it was anachronistic to see in Aegisthus' usurpation a tyrant's *coup de main*. Yet he seems to have committed that anachronism. When the chorus hear Agamemnon's death cries and sense murder by the queen and her lover, one of them says (1354-55; see also 1365): "Anyone can see it, by these first steps they have taken, they purpose to be tyrants here upon our city." In speaking of tyranny (*tyrannis*) here, either Aeschylus is using the word strictly, or he is not. He might use "tyrant" loosely, as a synonym for *basileus*, "king" (Euripides does this). But then the statement would have no point whatever, for what could the chorus expect other than that the murderer would make himself king? Plainly, they fear life not only under the wrong ruler but under the wrong kind of government. Historically, the tyrant overthrew a republic (the lawful constitution), but, in the heroic age on which tragedy drew, there was no republic; the lawful constitution was kingship; therefore, the tyrant overthrew this. When Aegisthus at last appears, he has his tyrant's bodyguard. It is impossible not to connect Aegisthus' *coup de main* with the rebellious murmuring of the masses against the king and his war. But the political pattern is a submotif, not fully worked out; its main effect is to shadow the character of Aegisthus—seducer, murderer, usurper already—with the dark memory of the hated historical tyrant.

uon, the king, with a king's power and pride in arms, appears briefly and is relatively simple. Pride would have driven him without hesitation to undertake the recovery of Helen, and this decision sets in motion a chain of events which becomes increasingly inescapable. The sacrifice of Iphigeneia, the persistence in besieging Troy, even the intrigue with Cassandra, follow necessarily; his pride grows on its own acts, until just before death he is a swollen vanity. He himself began the series of acts which pile up to overwhelm him, but, looking back, one cannot see where a proud king could have chosen otherwise. Clytaemestra's motives are far more complex. Homer had made her act in simple surrender and consequent betrayal. But Pindar speculated on motives which would, if admitted by Homer, have spoiled the cast of his version:

> Was it Iphigeneia, who at the Euripos crossing
> was slaughtered far from home,
> that vexed her to drive in anger the hand of violence?
> Or was it couching in a strange bed
> by night that broke her will and set her awry—for young wives
> a sin most vile.[7]

Two motives to choose from: Iphigeneia or Aegisthus. But Pindar has already mentioned Cassandra and so implied a third alternative, mother-resentment, guilty love, or jealousy. After Pindar, we could choose A or B or C. Aeschylus ignores the "or" and takes them all. Clytaemestra has loved Agamemnon, Iphigeneia has made her hate him, she loves Aegisthus. But her love for Agamemnon was real, and enough of that love remains to waken perfectly real jealousy at the sight of Agamemnon's lovely captive. This also moves her enormous pride, which amounts to unprecedented ambition for dynastic power. The women of the heroic age are represented as people of character, with will and temper of their own; but if their men insist, they must give way. Force them and they love. Cassandra, Clytaemestra's foil and rival, has seen her city and people wiped out by Agamemnon, her father and brothers butchered by his followers, but she clings to him. So Briseis in the *Iliad* clings to Achilles, who has personally killed her husband, and so Sophocles makes his Tecmessa protest to Aias

7. Pindar *Pyth.* 11. 22-25, trans. Lattimore.

that she loves him, for she has no one else, since he has destroyed her home.[8] Not so Clytaemestra, who, like Helen her sister, chooses her own loves. Again, the code obviously allowed the warlord, married or unmarried, to have the comforts of a captive mistress on campaign. But if Clytaemestra did not like a code, she would smash it. With her "male strength of heart in its high confidence," she steps boldly from the sphere of women's action into that of men;[9] like a king, she handles the city in her lord's absence, and to her the hostile and suspicious chorus turns with unwilling admiration. When the chorus doubts her intelligences, again when after the murder they openly challenge her, she faces them down and silences them; and it is only on the appearance of Aegisthus, whom they despise as they cannot despise Clytaemestra, that they break out rebelliously again. Even in deceit, as in shameless defiance, she is stately (855–88, 1667). She is the born aristocrat, heiress by birth as by marriage to the power and wealth of kings, and so contemptuous of the *nouveau riche* (1042–46). Everything she does and says is in the grand manner. The chain of beacon fires linking Argos and Troy, defeating distance and time, is a characteristically grand gesture, and worthy of it are the arrogant lines in which she concludes her story of relayed signal flares (315–16):

> By such proof and such symbol I announce to you
> my lord at Troy has sent his messengers to me.

Such is the spirit of her grandiose welcome to Agamemnon, the purple carpet on which he is forced to walk to his butchery, and the words in which such lavish outlay is defended, "the sea is there," with its plain implication that "the sea is ours."

Such characteristics give Clytaemestra stature, but in no sense justify her. It is not only that, in asserting her right, or at least determination, to act as freely as a man, she has taken to her bed the

8. The most detailed Attic study of the womanly woman in the heroic age is Euripides' Andromache in the play named after her. It is she who says (213–14): "A wife, even if she is given to a worthless man, should cling to him, not set her will up against his." It is noteworthy that her definitions of a woman's duties occur in debate with her Spartan rival, Hermione, daughter of Menelaus and Helen.

9. When she refers to herself as "a mere woman," it is with massive sarcasm (348, 590–97, 1661).

"womanish" Aegisthus. The whole house has been wrong since the quarrel of Atreus and Thyestes. Atreus was hideous in murder, but this does not justify Aegisthus in murdering Agamemnon, any more than the sins of Agamemnon justified his murder by Clytaemestra, or the sins of Paris and Helen justified the obliteration of Troy. All the executioners plead that they act for just retribution, but the chain of murder has got out of hand and is perpetuating itself, until it seems no longer to come from personal purpose but has grown into a Curse, a Thing. Every correction is a blood-bath which calls for new correction.

> The truth stands ever beside God's throne
> eternal: he who has wrought shall pay; that is law.
> Then who shall tear the curse from their blood?
> The seed is stiffened to ruin.

Clytaemestra answers, over the corpse of Agamemnon, that she has been bloody but the house is clean. No more evil need be done. Orestes is to make the same claim over the corpse of Clytaemestra herself. Both are mistaken.

The tragedy is no simple matter of right and wrong, of pride and fall, though these enter in. It is a matter of love and hate working simultaneously to force distorted action, and the situation is given depth by cross-characterization. Clytaemestra imagines before the chorus the scene in captured Troy, opening with savage satisfaction in the thought of what is going on and closing with a prayer for peace, that her husband and his men may use their victory temperately, so that no fresh wrong may follow. As she speaks these words, she is herself plotting the fresh wrong she deprecates. There is surface contradiction, but under it lies not only the fact that Clytaemestra is intensely proud of the husband she is about to murder but also the lyric imagination, akin to the diviner's gift, by which the character's mind can transcend time and distance and penetrate to a sphere of objective truth which is beyond the character's own desire and prejudice. When she tells Agamemnon and the public of the torments she went through in his absence at Troy, she is flattering him and misleading all, but by means of truth, not fiction. This is the past, and this is real.

It is evil and a thing of terror when a wife
sits in the house forlorn with no man by.

Flattery, confession, reproach combine (through how much longing
for the memory-ghost, as with Menelaus for Helen, might Clytaemestra have gone before she took Aegisthus as a lover; or even
after?). Agamemnon, on the point of being entangled by flattery
and dragged to his death, soberly describes himself as proof against
flatterers. In a sense this is irony; it corresponds to his entrance full
of the pride of capture on the heels of a warning by the chorus against
pride; to the gloomy speculations of the chorus on sackers of cities
that presages the return of the herald to tell of Troy's obliteration.
But that is mainly a matter of timing; here the point is that Agamemnon's intelligence is partly engaged with the course he does not
mean to take. He is proof against illusions except at the one point
where they will be fatal to him. When Aegisthus, in the height of
his dispute with the challenging chorus (1668), says of Orestes,

Exiles feed on empty dreams of hope. I know it. I was one,

the jibe turns into a flash of instantly forgotten sympathy. The actors, in particular Clytaemestra and the chorus, do not collide with
purely external forces but act always against a part of their own will
or sympathy which is committed to the other side, and what they kill
is what they love.

The action of the play in itself, of the trilogy as a whole, is thus
bound inward upon itself. Its course is not logical, not even strictly
dramatic sequence. After the fashion of choral lyric, it is both united
to itself and given inward dimension through persistent ideas and
a complex of symbols.

Idea and Symbol

By "idea" I mean motive, theme of subject, or type of situation
which is dominant in the dramatic action. By "symbol" I mean a
particular thing, usually material, which may be taken to represent
the idea. And by a "complex of symbols" I mean a group of such
objects which are related to one another in their nature or use.

The exhaustive study of this technique and the detailing of its uses is a proper study for a monograph, not for a segment of the introduction to a translation.[10] I will content myself with illustrating the principle through the symbol-complex of the net.

A central motive in the *Oresteia* is the idea of entanglement: the taming of wild things, the subjugation of the powerful, the involvement of innocent creatures as well. It is expressed in the *curb* forged to subdue Troy (132) or Cassandra (1066); the *bit* that gags Iphigeneia (234); the *yoke* of circumstance that forces Agamemnon to his crime; the *yoke* of slavery forced on Troy (529), on Cassandra (953, 1071, 1226), on the defiant citizens (1635), even the yoke of teammates (842); the *snare* of the huntsman, in which Agamemnon captures Troy (358, 821) and Cassandra (1048) and in which he is presently captured (1115, 1375, 1611).[11] Curb, yoke, snare—different objects for related purposes—might have been no more than persistent and thematic metaphor, but they have one embodiment which is not metaphorical, and this is the robe or shawl in which Clytaemestra actually entangles Agamemnon in order to strike him down and which is to be displayed on stage as a murder exhibit by Orestes in *The Libation Bearers* (980–84, 997–1004). Clytaemestra anticipates herself when she tells of her dreams and imaginations of terror in Agamemnon's long absence (866–68):

> Had Agamemnon taken all
> the wounds the tale whereof was carried home to me,
> he had been cut full of gashes like a fishing net,

and returns to her imagery in her challenging confession of murder (1382–83):

> as fishermen cast their huge circling nets, I spread
> deadly abundance of rich robes and caught him fast.

This is the idea seen in the thing and the thing embodying the idea, both in metaphor and in action. There are numerous other symbols and other ideas. Symbols are the snake (specially the viper) and the poison of the snake; the archer; the house; the ship; gold.

10. Miss Barbara Hughes is at present working on such a monograph as a doctoral dissertation.

11. The idea of the manhunt appears in the retributive expedition against Troy (127, 695), and in *The Eumenides* it characterizes the Furies' pursuit of Orestes.

Ideas are (in addition to entanglement) persuasion (flattery); recurrent sickness; hate-in-love; blood and sex; light in the dark; sound (of terror) in the night; dream and memory. The bare lists are not complete, and, in particular, neither symbols nor ideas are exclusive, nor does a given symbol stand toward a given idea in a one-to-one relation. The viper, who turns against his own family, whose mating is murder, stands principally for the idea of hate-in-love and, as such, might be called the prime symbol of the *Oresteia*, but its poison is involved also in the idea of recurrent sickness,[12] and its coils in the idea of entanglement (elsewhere signified by yoke, net, etc., as we have seen). So *The Libation Bearers*, 246–49:

> Behold
> the orphaned children of the eagle-father, now
> that he has died entangled in the binding coils
> of the deadly viper.

The spider web in which Agamemnon was trapped (1492) is one more variation of entanglement, spun by another creature who murders in marriage. Entanglement may come by outright force or by seduction and surprise. Clytaemestra lures Agamemnon into it by flattery, persuasion, by her sex (1116):

> Or is the trap the woman there, the murderess?

Cross-binding and coherence of idea in symbol is seen where Agamemnon recoils (he is soon to surrender) from stepping on the gorgeous robe Clytaemestra has spread at his feet (922–27)

> Such state becomes the gods, and none beside.
> I am a mortal, a man; I cannot trample down
> these tinted splendors without fear thrown in my path.
> I tell you, as a man, not god, to reverence me.
> Discordant is the murmur at such treading down
> of lovely things.

On the level of discourse, the speech is moral. The male rationalism is fighting against the irrational persuasion of the woman, the Greek defends his code ("as if I were some Asiatic"), the king deprecates the

12. The word *palinkotos* might signify a sickness or poisoning which lies hidden in the system, seemingly gone, then *recurs*; or the viper, which *re*-coils upon itself, or those so close to it that they form a part of itself.

subjects' disapproval; this is colored also by lyric memory. The "tread-ing down of lovely things" recalls Paris, who "trampled down the delicacy of things inviolable" (371) and on whom Persuasion also worked (385). Agamemnon, who punished the barbarians, is being turned barbarian in order to be punished. He is a victim of his wife's flattery and the magnificence of his own possessions. Lastly, the robe itself on which he walks prefigures the robe in which he is to be entangled and killed.

Cut anywhere into the play, and you will find such a nexus of in-tercrossing motives and properties. The system gives the play its inner dimension and strength. An analogous but separable principle dominates the larger structure.

Dramatic Structure and Lyric Dimension

As theater, *Agamemnon* and its companion pieces are simple. The scene of *Agamemnon* is the familiar fixed position before the doors of a house, which is, as most often in subsequent drama and in the nature of things, a palace. The same setting serves for *The Libation Bearers; The Eumenides* has one of those shifts of scene which are relatively rare in extant Greek tragedy, for we begin before the doors of Phoebus at Delphi and end before the doors of Athene in Athens, but this shift can easily be signified by addition or subtraction of a very few properties.

Characters are used sparingly. Aeschylus has at his disposal the three actors who were by now allotted to each poet or producer; but, far from reveling in this sober allowance, he is most reluctant to use all three at once in speaking action. Cassandra is on stage with Agamemnon and Clytaemestra, but does not speak until the other actors (not counting the chorus or chorus leader) have gone out.[13] Dialogue is, for the most part, just that, a passage between

13. Clytaemestra, apparently on stage at 83, does not respond to the chorus at that point and remains silent through their stasimon (ode); she speaks only when, 258-63, they address her again. In *The Libation Bearers* Pylades, present almost through the entire play, speaks only three lines (900-902); these have critical force in the action. In *Prometheus*, the titan is silent all through the first scene, where he is being fastened to the rock. We know also that Aeschylus exploited the silent character in many of

two persons, one of whom may be the chorus leader, at a time, not as in modern drama a complex in which three, four, or a dozen speaking persons participate. There are supernumeraries to be sure, handmaidens attending Clytaemestra and soldiers returning with Agamemnon, the significant bodyguard of Aegisthus; and at the close of *The Eumenides* the stage is quite full of people, and the exodus takes on the dignity of a processional. Agamemnon clearly must enter with Cassandra beside him in a horse-drawn chariot. The unrolling of the robe for Agamemnon's feet is an effective use of showy gesture. Yet, on the whole, the trilogy is physically unpretentious, relying less on staging and properties than *Prometheus* appears to do. Also, it is physically static; not much physical activity or motion is called for. The use made of materials, of what might appeal to the eye, is measured and temperate.

There is a corresponding simplicity in plot. Considering the length of *Agamemnon*, there are few events that take place, nor are the major events displayed against any variety of subplot. It therefore takes dramatic time for these events to happen. The return of Aga-

---

his lost plays. On the silent characters of Aeschylus, see the scene in the *Frogs* of Aristophanes, where the ghost of Euripides challenges that of Aeschylus in the presence of Dionysus and Hades (911–22):

"*Eur.:* First of all he would cover a character's face and make him sit on the stage there,
Achilles, maybe, or Niobe, but never show their features.
They made his tragedy look fine, but didn't mutter a syllable.

"*Dion.:* By god, you know, they didn't at that.

"*Eur.:* The chorus would pound out long chains of poetry, four one after another. The characters said nothing.

"*Dion.:* You know, I liked them quiet that way. They gave me as much pleasure as the ones that gabble at us now.

"*Eur.:* Of course. You were a half-wit and that's a fact. .

"*Dion.:* I know, I know. Tell me then, why did he do it?

"*Eur.:* To lead you on, and keep the audience in suspense. They were waiting for Niobe to speak. Meanwhile his play was getting over.

"*Dion.:* The dirty rat! So all that time he was cheating us out of our drama. (*To Aesch.*) Why are you frowning and looking so cross?

"*Eur.:* I'm exposing him. He doesn't like it."

memnon, assured from the watchman's opening speech (25), does not take place until line 782.[14] The only other *event* of the play is his murder, which does not take place until line 1344. Audience and actors occupy the times preceding these events in a growing strain of suspense, which gives the events redoubled impact when at last they do take place. The means by which the anomaly of many lines–little action is solved are the same as the means by which action and motive are deepened. The simplicity is on the surface. As, on its major plane, the action of the tragedy moves deliberately forward, in another dimension lyric memory and forecast take us, by association of ideas rather than in obedience to order in time, deep away into the past, the future, and the elsewhere.

Memory and forecast are a part of imagination, that divining spirit which takes men beyond the limits of what their senses can perceive. He who habitually, and under patronage of a god, so divines is the *mantis* or prophet. The prophet knew "all things that

14. Much unnecessary ingenuity has been wasted on the problem of "real" time in *Agamemnon*. By means of her beacons, Clytaemestra is understood to learn of Troy's capture just after the event, almost within the hour (320). The return voyage from Troy to Argos is a three or four days' sailing, hardly shortened by the hurricane that wrecked the fleet; and, further, Homer and the other sources on which tragedy drew make it plain that the Achaeans did not pick up and go home the moment Troy fell but understandably took some time getting off. Therefore, the arrival of the herald, followed by Agamemnon, comes days after the first scene of the play. This is true, but creates a problem only for those unduly preoccupied with the Aristotelian unities. "Tragedy tries as far as practicable to fall within the scope of a single day, or exceeds it by only a little" (*Poetics* v. 8). The statement of Aristotle is not made as if he meant to press it very hard. Also it should not be necessary, but apparently is, to point out that Aeschylus had never heard of Aristotle. To Aeschylus, the next thing that happened *in the plot*, after the arrival of the news, was the arrival of the Achaeans. It would have been, to him, as pointless as it would have been ugly to have the chorus solemnly quit the stage and return after the posting of a placard saying "six days later." What he does put in is a long choral lyric in which the choristers muse on the whole train of action (though not in chronological order) from the flight of Helen to the fall of Troy; thus giving in lyric form the illusion that far more time has passed than the real time it has actually taken them to deliver their ode. At l. 475, after the lyric closes, they begin to speak "in character." Their mood has changed; before the ode they were utterly convinced by Clytaemestra's beacons; now they are unconvinced and sarcastic. After the herald's speeches, they inform Clytaemestra that she has been right all along, and she tells them she has done *her* rejoicing *long ago*. By now, we are plainly meant to understand that a lapse of time has occurred, but *not* encouraged to figure out just how much, or how it could have happened.

were, the things to come, and the things past" (*Iliad* i. 70); that is, he knew not only past and future, but *present*, what is occurring right now beyond that fragmentary point of space where he stands. Calchas the prophet of the Achaeans is remembered in the first ode, Cassandra the prophetess of Troy appears in person. But, apart from these formal prophets, the chorus assumes divining powers ("still by God's grace there surges within me singing magic": "why this strain unwanted, unrepaid, thus prophetic?"), and the imaginations of Clytaemestra, the herald, Agamemnon, and Aegisthus range far away. Calchas, in the memory of the chorus, goes deep into the past in order to make predictions which will be fulfilled, years away, in the subsequent action of the tragedy. Cassandra, who knows of a past she never witnessed, sees in its light the invisible network of treachery that waits for Agamemnon and her. The swan, who sings in the face of death and is helplessly dedicated to Apollo, is her symbol.

The choristers remember in their entrance chant the departure of the armament ten years ago (40–59), and it makes them see the struggle going on in Troy (60–68). They remember the portents that attended the gathering of the ships, the predictions of Calchas, and the sacrifice of Iphigeneia that was their sequel (104–257). Clytaemestra's living imagination follows the course of her beacon system, itself a device to defeat space and diminish time, as it breaks out from peak to peak on its way to her (281–316), and she sees the Achaeans in captured Troy, now, though far away (320–37). The chorus broods on the moral that Troy fallen conveys, but they think in pictures; of a man secure in wealth kicking over an altar (the audience will remember the golden Persians, their pride, sacrilege, and defeat); of Persuasion as a siren; of false fires and spurious metal gilded; of a greedy innocent child trying to catch a bird—the images, not the propositions, of delusion (367–95). This is Paris, and they fall at once to re-creating in imagination the flight of Helen (403–8). And there were *prophets* there, to be sure, who imagined the loneliness to follow for Menelaus with an empty bed and empty-eyed images of his wife, whose loveliness eluded him in dreams (408–26). But dream image is memory image, and there are others who remember too. The families of the common soldiers see brought back to them the ashes of their dead, transubstantiated by the money-changer, who is the god of war. They murmur against the king; their muttering is inarticulate and not clearly heard in high places but may be the symptom of a storm that waits for the returning king (427–74). *Te deum laudamus* has been transformed into fore-boding, not through logical succession of ground and consequent but through a lyric succession of images whose forms melt into one another. Agamemnon's herald remembers the campaigning before Troy (551–81). At first, it is the dirty and brutal details of war-business that come out of the mist, but the sense of achievement infects him with Agamemnon's fatal pride, so that at the end the wings of his imagination take him out of the past across the present and far into the future and the days when the capture of Troy will be an antique glory of Argos. He is shaken out of this mood, however, by the questioning of the chorus leader, who wants to know what happened to the rest of the army and to Menelaus. He tells of the storm (650–70) in terms that make living things out of fire, wind, water, and rocks, and shows the wide seascape on which at dawn lay the wreckage of the Achaean fleet, torn flowers on the water.

The chorus, far now from the momentary exaltation they felt at news of the victory, now chant in terms of disaster: the sinister name of Helen, with the imagination once again of her flight to Troy (681–98); the lion's cub, the pet turned murderous (716–36), who is fatal Helen beguiling the Trojans (737–49). We remember Iphigeneia when Helen's eyes, like Iphigeneia's, sweep the beholder with soft arrows, and the victorious and guileful charmer recalls the innocent charmer who failed. The moralities which follow to prelude Agamemnon's entrance, the terms in which he is greeted, work again through images: houses gilded to hide dust, false coin, the smile of the charmer. Action follows in the public encounter of Clytaemestra and Agamemnon, but the wife's welcome brings back out of the past the fears that attended her during the years of separation (858–94). When he has gone into the house, the chorus turn uneasily from memory to forecast, and their gloom is abetted by Cassandra, who has vision on vision of the past, of the present (the intention behind

Clytaemestra's face and words, the scene preparing behind closed doors), and the far future on the day when the avengers shall punish for the crime not yet committed (1069-1330). The death cry tells the chorus only what they already know. We do not see the murder take place, but we are told what happened (1381-92). In the scene that follows, where Clytaemestra faces the people, neither side can escape the memory of the hideous past which has forced these things to happen. Aegisthus' defense is a recounting of the crime of Atreus (1583-1611). At the end, Clytaemestra speaks as if all were over, but we know it is not, that the future holds more violence and it is the past which has made this so.

Lyric Tragedy

The brief dramatic time of the play is a point of convergence for actions that come from deep in the past and project far into the future. The limited stage is a pivotal point from which we can be transported far away. The tragedy of Agamemnon, Cassandra, and Clytaemestra is involved with and opens into the tragedy of the children of Thyestes, of Iphigeneia, of Troy and all the Achaean army; and its action, in return, is partly dictated by the figures never enacted, remote but always present in memory, of Atreus, Iphigeneia, Paris, and Helen.[15]

This is the form of lyric tragedy, perfected here and never since so completely realized. Its manner is due partly to the historical accident in which two forms of fiction were combined: drama, still relatively primitive and naïve, with choral lyric, now, after generations of mature practice, brought to its highest point of development by Simonides and Pindar. But the direction taken by this form is due also to deliberate choice. The desire is to transcend the limitations of dramatic presentation, even before these limitations have been firmly established. The spirit is that of Shakespeare's chorus in *Henry V:*

15. We may compare *The Persians.* The cast of actors consists only of Darius, his queen, Xerxes, messenger, and chorus. The visible scene in Persia is static. But the scene of the action which the play is *about* is Salamis, and then all the water and land between; the persons of this action are all the vast army of the Persians, and all the Greeks. *The Persians* is the great messenger-play.

> But pardon, gentles all,
> The flat unraised spirits that have dared
> On this unworthy scaffold to bring forth
> So great an object: can this cockpit hold
> The vasty fields of France? Or may we cram
> Within this wooden O the very casques
> That did affright the air at Agincourt?

It is true that Shakespeare intends to take us to the actual field of Agincourt, but principally he is aware of the impossibility of *staging* expeditions and battles adequately, and the appeal is to the imagination of the audience:

> For 'tis your thoughts that now must deck our kings,
> Carry them here and there; jumping o'er times,
> Turning the accomplishment of many years
> Into an hour-glass.

> Thus with imagined wing our swift scene flies
> In motion of no less celerity
> Than that of thought.

Shakespeare and Aeschylus alike forecast combinations which only the motion picture can realize visually—flashback, imaginary scene, pictorial dramatization of history, and messenger's account. Shakespeare's concern in this particular play with the fragmentary nature of staged action gives his chorus a brilliant part, but it is only a ghost of Aeschylus, for in Aeschylus the past and the elsewhere dominate present action.

But the direction in which he steered tragedy was not generally followed. Sophoclean drama prevailed, since Euripides, under protest, framed tragedy in accordance with Sophocles, not Aeschylus. Sophocles turned tragedy inward upon the principal actors, and drama becomes drama of character. His plays may open with public scenes, but, as they progress, the interest focuses hard on the hero. *Oedipus Tyrannus* begins with the plague in Thebes, but its ending is all Oedipus, and Thebes is as good as forgotten. It is true that the dead hand reaches out of the past to strike down Oedipus, Antigone, Aias, Heracles. But this is their tragedy, and theirs alone. *Agamemnon* is a play about the Trojan War, but *Antigone* is not a play about the

Theban War, though that lies in the background. In Sophocles, the choruses are commentaries on the action, not part of the larger action, and their imagery is functional to the choruses themselves but not to the tragedy as a whole. Trilogy gives way to single drama. The enormous background becomes mainly irrelevant and is screened out. Lyric tragedy gives way to actor's tragedy.

Agamemnon is, in fact, the culmination of lyric tragedy, because the action narrows in *The Libation Bearers*, and when in *The Eumenides* it opens out again, it is with a new kind of meaning and composition.

"The Libation Bearers"

The second play of the trilogy takes place some years after the close of *Agamemnon*. The usurpers have grown secure in power. Orestes, sequestered in Phocis, is now a young man, and his sister Electra, resentful and bitter, awaits his return. The opening event is simple recognition, the identification of Orestes and the confirmation of the fact that, as Electra and the chorus hope, he means to avenge his father and regain his throne. Recognition is thus at once transformed into conspiracy. The children, with their faithful chorus, gather at Agamemnon's tomb, where Electra has gone on her mother's behalf, but without sympathy for her, to propitiate the dead king by reason of terrifying dreams which had shaken Clytaemestra in the night. The dead king is now a hero; his arrogance and his mistakes have been annulled by death, and his grave is a center of power. Therefore, the children with the chorus turn to him, invoke his ghost to anger against his murderers, with twofold driving intention: to enchant actual power out of the spirit and the grave and to incite themselves and arm themselves with the anger that will make them do what they must do. They then plot the means for assassination. Orestes poses as a traveling merchant who brings news of the death of Orestes; Clytaemestra, with archaic and stately courtesy, invites him in and sends for Aegisthus. As the messenger who is sent to summon him (she happens to be the slave who nursed Orestes when he was little) goes out on her errand, she encounters the chorus, who tell her not to suggest that Aegisthus should bring his bodyguard. Orestes and Pylades kill the king, and Clytaemestra stands at their mercy. She dares Orestes to kill her, and he stands irresolute until a word from Pylades solidifies his will. The bodies are brought out and displayed, with the robe in which Agamemnon had been entrapped, and Orestes declares publicly, as Clytaemestra had done, that this act is his own and that it is justice. But his wits are going, he sees the Furies, the avenging spirits of his mother (no one else can see them), and leaves in flight. This time, even before the play is over, the assassin knows that his act was not final but has created more suffering yet to come.

Once again the plot is simple, and the dramatic actions are few. Once again, despite these facts, the texture is saved from thinness, but the factors are different from those that give *Agamemnon* its coherence. First, this is a far shorter play. Second, the emphasis and direction have changed. We have, in a sense, more plot; there is intrigue, a practical problem. In *Agamemnon* the king's murder is felt by the witnessing chorus in their bones; it happens, is mourned, and defended. The problems of Clytaemestra, *whether* she can kill the husband she has loved and *how* she will do it, are implicit, but we are not present while she is solving them. But in *The Libation Bearers*, we are present at the deliberations of Orestes as he decides whether he can kill his mother, and how the assassination is to be effected. In recognition, decision, conspiracy, and climactic action we have, in fact, the mechanism, in naïve or even crude form, of that drama of revenge or play of successful action which we found in the Homeric story.

But *The Libation Bearers* is only superficially a drama of intrigue, and, in so far as it is one, it is hardly a significant specimen of its kind. The mechanism of the assassin's plot is simple, as the mechanism of recognition and identification is primitive. The emphasis lies on the mood in which the characters act.

For this is not a simple revenge play in which the young hero, long lost, returns to his sister and his kingdom to strike down the murderous and usurping villains. Orestes hardly gets a sight of his kingship before he must leave, haunted, driven, and alone. It is not until much later, near the close of *The Eumenides*, that he can speak

as a king with subjects. Also, here the emotions of Orestes and Electra are, like those of Clytaemestra, half-committed to the side against
which they act; and Clytaemestra, in turn, loves the son whom she
fears, who kills her, and whom she would kill if she could. It is the
philos-aphilos still, or love-in-hate, the murder committed not against
an external enemy but against a part of the self.[16] The hate gains in-
tensity from the strength of the original love when that love has
been stopped or rejected. Electra ("the unmarried") has love to
lavish, but her mother has turned it aside. The chorus, like the captive women they are, cling to the memory of Agamemnon, who enslaved them. Orestes, together with the sense of outrage over the
loss of his rightful inheritance (the dynastic motive), nurses a deep
sense of jealousy against his mother for having sacrificed not only
Agamemnon but *Orestes* to her love for Aegisthus. The children
were the price for which she bought herself this man (132–34). It is
the venom of such jealousy that spills out in the bitterly salacious
mockery of the dead lovers, and jealousy on his father's behalf and
his own is the theme of his last sharp dispute with his mother. Clytaemestra, when she hears the false news of her son's death, is in a
temper where relief and sorrow cross, though relief wins. Her very
dream of bearing and nursing the snake (symbol of ingratitude), who
fixes his poisonous fangs in her breast, enacts terror through a gesture of love. Aegisthus, at the word that Orestes is dead, goes soberly
back to the image of the poison and the snake:

> For our house, already bitten
> and poisoned, to take this new load upon itself
> would be a thing of dripping fear and blood.

The chorus consider that both the tyrants are hypocrites, but even
such hypocrites know what they are doing, and to whom.

This mood of tangled motivation means that the conspirators
must work strongly upon themselves before they can act. Between
the recognition and the resolve to act comes a scene of incantation.

---

16. So *Hamlet* is transformed from the vigorous revenge-intrigue drama it might
have been into the tragedy it is, because Hamlet is emotionally involved with the queen
and Ophelia, who are on the side of the enemy. Even the arch-enemy is close in blood
and perhaps once admired.

Sister, brother, and chorus turn to invoke dead Agamemnon. They implore his blessings and aid, they set forth their grievances and his, they challenge and taunt him to action:

Orestes
Think of that bath, father, where you were stripped of life.

Electra
Think of the casting-net that they contrived for you.

Orestes
They caught you like a beast in toils no bronzesmith made.

Electra
Rather, hid you in shrouds that were thought out in shame.

Orestes
Will you not waken, father to these challenges?

Electra
Will you not rear upright that best beloved head?

But, while they are invoking a power and a tradition whose force is felt but only dimly believed, they are also lashing themselves into the fury of self-pity that will make them do what they have to do. So the theme of lyric prophecy which was at work in *Agamemnon* is altered here. There is dealing in both cases with what lies beyond the powers of perception, but there it was lyric memory and vision on the part of those who were to witness, and to suffer from, the ugly act; here those who are themselves about to commit the ugly act manipulate the unseen, in a mood more of witchcraft than of prophecy.

For this reason and because the drama focuses on the will to act, *The Libation Bearers* ties back to *Agamemnon*, but *Agamemnon* ties back to the whole world of action latent behind the beginning of the tragedy. The symbols of the earlier play are caught up and intensified, particularly viper and net. But the emphasis is changed, because we see things from the point of view of the murderers. In *Agamemnon*, vice was alluring, wearing all the captivating graces of Helen and her attendant symbols; in *The Libation Bearers*, duty becomes repulsive. Both tragedies are carried on a strong underdrift of sex, but in the second play the sex impulse, though it works, has lost its charm. Orestes at the end has done a brutal, necessary job.

Like Clytaemestra at the close of *Agamemnon*, Orestes defends his position in terms of: "I have cleared my house. It was bloody, but necessary. Now we can have peace." As for Clytaemestra, his claim is no better than a desperate challenge flung at circumstances. The blood-bath was no cleaning-out, and it means more blood. Clytaemestra had to reckon with resentment in the state and the younger generation to come. The enlightenment of Orestes, the defeat of his hollow optimism, comes without delay. "The house has been rid of snakes": and at once, on the heads of his mother's Furies, more snakes appear.

"The Eumenides" (The Furies)

As we have seen (see above, p. 6), the last act of the trilogy finds Orestes cleared by Apollo but still pursued by the Furies. Is he clear, or not? Plainly, one divine decision has clashed with another decision which is also unquestionably divine. The fate of Orestes is referred to Athens and to a third divinity, Athene, who, reserving for herself the casting ballot, refers it to a jury of mortal men. When their vote is even and Athene has cast her deciding vote in his favor, the Furies must be propitiated by a new cult, as a new kind of goddess, in Athens. It is this episode that closes the play and the trilogy of the House of Atreus. The chorus has returned to its archaic part as chief character in the drama.

Who are the Furies, and what do they mean? And, since they stand up and identify themselves and protest their rights in the face of Apollo and Athene, we must also ask, What do these better-known Olympians represent for the purposes of Aeschylus?

As seen in the grand perspective, Agamemnon was only an unwilling agent in a chain of action far bigger than the fortunes of a single man. From the seduction of Atreus' wife, the murder of the children of Atreus, the sacrifice of Iphigeneia and the youth of Hellas, claim and counterclaim have been fiercely sustained, each act of blood has been avenged in a new act of blood. The problems of public good have been solved through private murder, which is no solution, until the situation has become intolerable to the forces that rule the world, and these must intervene to see that the contestants and the impulses in nature which drive the contestants become reconciled and find their places in a scheme that will be harmonious and progressive, not purely destructive.

Behind the personal motivations in the two first dramas of the trilogy, we can, if we choose, discern a conflict of related forces: of the younger against the elder generation; of male against female; of Greek against barbarian. As the gods step out of the darkness, where, before, they could be reached only in fitful visions of the prophetic mind, and take their place on the stage, they personify these general forces, and, because they are divine and somewhat abstract, they can carry still further dimensions of meaning. The Furies are older than Apollo and Athene, and, being older, they are childish and barbarous; attached to Clytaemestra as mother, they are themselves female and represent the woman's claim to act which Clytaemestra has sustained from the beginning; in a Greek world they stand for the childhood of the race before it won Hellenic culture, the barbarian phase of pre-Hellenism, the dark of the race and of the world; they have archaic uprightness and strictness in action, with its attendant cruelty; they insist on the fact against the idea; they ignore the justifications of Orestes, for the blood on his hands means far more than the reasons why the blood is there. Apollo stands for everything which the Furies are not: Hellenism, civilization, intellect, and enlightenment. He is male and young. He despises cruelty for the fun of cruelty, and the thirst for blood, but he is as ruthless as the Furies. The commonwealth of the gods—therefore the universe—is in a convulsion of growth; the young Olympians are fighting down their own barbaric past.

But they must not fight it out of existence. In the impasse, Apollo uses every threat of arrogant force, but Athene, whose nature reconciles female with male, has a wisdom deeper than the intelligence of Apollo. She clears Orestes but concedes to the detested Furies what they had not known they wanted, a place in the affections of a civilized community of men, as well as in the divine hierarchy. There, gracious and transformed though they are, their place in the world is still made potent by the unchanged base of their character.

The new city cannot progress by exterminating its old order of life; it must absorb and use it. Man cannot obliterate, and should not repress, the unintelligible emotions. Or again, in different terms, man's nature being what it is and Fury being a part of it, Justice must go armed with Terror before it can work.

Thus, through the dilemma of Orestes and its solution, the drama of the House of Atreus has been transformed into a grand parable of progress. Persuasion (flattery), the deadly magic of the earlier plays, has been turned to good by Athene as she wins the Furies to accept of their own free will a new and better place in the world. By the time Orestes leaves the stage, he has become an issue, a Dred Scott or Dreyfus, more important for what he means than for what he is; and, when he goes, the last human personality is gone, and with it vanish the bloody entanglements of the House of Atreus, as the anonymous citizens of Athens escort their protecting divinities into the beginning of a new world.

It is appropriate, and characteristic of Aeschylus, that this final parable, with its tremendous burden of thought, should be enacted on the frame of a naïve dramatic structure, where the basis of decision on matricide is as crude as the base of Portia's decision against Shylock. The magnificence of *The Eumenides* is different from that of *Agamemnon*. The imagery—the lyric imagination in memory and magic—is gone, because we are not now merely to see but to understand. The final act comes down into the present day and seals within itself the wisdom, neither reactionary nor revolutionary, of a great man. But in its own terms *The Eumenides* is the necessary conclusion of a trilogy whose special greatness lies in the fact that it transcends the limitations of dramatic enactment on a scale never achieved before or since.

AGAMEMNON

Translated by

RICHMOND LATTIMORE

CHARACTERS

Watchman

Clytaemestra

Herald

Agamemnon

Cassandra

Aegisthus

Chorus of Argive Elders

*Attendants of Clytaemestra: of Agamemnon: bodyguard
of Aegisthus (all silent parts)*

Time, directly after the fall of Troy.

AGAMEMNON

SCENE: *Argos, before the palace of King Agamemnon. The Watchman,*
who speaks the opening lines, is posted on the roof of the palace.
Clytaemestra's entrances are made from a door in the center of the
stage; all others, from the wings.

(The Watchman, alone.)

I ask the gods some respite from the weariness
of this watchtime measured by years I lie awake
elbowed upon the Atreidae's roof dogwise to mark
the grand processionals of all the stars of night
burdened with winter and again with heat for men,   5
dynasties in their shining blazoned on the air,
these stars, upon their wane and when the rest arise.

I wait; to read the meaning in that beacon light,
a blaze of fire to carry out of Troy the rumor
and outcry of its capture; to such end a lady's   10
male strength of heart in its high confidence ordains.
Now as this bed stricken with night and drenched with dew
I keep, nor ever with kind dreams for company:
since fear in sleep's place stands forever at my head
against strong closure of my eyes, or any rest: 15
I mince such medicine against sleep failed: I sing,
only to weep again the pity of this house
no longer, as once, administered in the grand way.
Now let there be again redemption from distress,
the flare burning fróm the blackness in good augury.   20

(A light shows in the distance.)

Oh hail, blaze of the darkness, harbinger of day's
shining, and of processionals and dance and choirs
of multitudes in Argos for this day of grace.
Ahoy!
I cry the news aloud to Agamemnon's queen,   25

that she may rise up from her bed of state with speed
to raise the rumor of gladness welcoming this beacon,
and singing rise, if truly the citadel of Ilium
has fallen, as the shining of this flare proclaims.
I also, I, will make my choral prelude, since   30
my lord's dice cast aright are counted as my own,
and mine the tripled sixes of this torchlit throw.

May it only happen. May my king come home, and I
take up within this hand the hand I love. The rest
I leave to silence; for an ox stands huge upon   35
my tongue. The house itself, could it take voice, might speak
aloud and plain. I speak to those who understand,
but if they fail, I have forgotten everything.

                        (*Exit. The Chorus enters, speaking.*)

Ten years since the great contestants   40
of Priam's right,
Menelaus and Agamemnon, my lord,
twin throned, twin sceptered, in twofold power
of kings from God, the Atreidae,
put forth from this shore   45
the thousand ships of the Argives,
the strength and the armies.
Their cry of war went shrill from the heart,
as eagles stricken in agony
for young perished, high from the nest   50
eddy and circle
to bend and sweep of the wings' stroke,
lost far below
the fledgelings, the nest, and the tendance.
Yet someone hears in the air, a god,   55
Apollo, Pan, or Zeus, the high
thin wail of these sky-guests, and drives
late to its mark
the Fury upon the transgressors.

So drives Zeus the great guest god   60

the Atreidae against Alexander:
for one woman's promiscuous sake
the struggling masses, legs tired,
knees grinding in dust,
spears broken in the onset.   65
Danaans and Trojans
they have it alike. It goes as it goes
now. The end will be destiny.
You cannot burn flesh or pour unguents,
not innocent cool tears,   70
that will soften the gods' stiff anger.

But we; dishonored, old in our bones,
cast off even then from the gathering horde,
stay here, to prop up
on staves the strength of a baby.   75
Since the young vigor that urges
inward to the heart
is frail as age, no warcraft yet perfect,
while beyond age, leaf
withered, man goes three footed   80
no stronger than a child is,
a dream that falters in daylight.

    (*Clytaemestra enters quietly. The Chorus continues to speak.*)
But you, lady,
daughter of Tyndareus, Clytaemestra, our queen:
What is there to be done? What new thing have you heard?   85
In persuasion of what
report do you order such sacrifice?
To all the gods of the city,
the high and the deep spirits,
to them of the sky and the market places,   90
the altars blaze with oblations.
The staggered flame goes sky high
one place, then another,
drugged by the simple soft

persuasion of sacred unguents,   95
the deep stored oil of the kings.
Of these things what can be told
openly, speak.
Be healer to this perplexity
that grows now into darkness of thought,   100
while again sweet hope shining from the flames
beats back the pitiless pondering
of sorrow that eats my heart.

I have mastery yet to chant the wonder at the wayside
given to kings. Still by God's grace there surges within me   105
singing magic
grown to my life and power,
how the wild bird portent
hurled forth the Achaeans'
twin-stemmed power single hearted,   110
lords of the youth of Hellas,
with spear and hand of strength
to the land of Teucrus.
Kings of birds to the kings of the ships,
one black, one blazed with silver,   115
clear seen by the royal house
on the right, the spear hand,
they lighted, watched by all
tore a hare, ripe, bursting with young unborn yet,
stayed from her last fleet running.   120
Sing sorrow, sorrow: but good win out in the end.

Then the grave seer of the host saw through to the hearts divided,
knew the fighting sons of Atreus feeding on the hare
with the host, their people.
Seeing beyond, he spoke: 125
"With time, this foray
shall stalk the castle of Priam.
Before then, under
the walls, Fate shall spoil

in violence the rich herds of the people.   130
Only let no doom of the gods darken
upon this huge iron forged to curb Troy—
from inward. Artemis the undefiled
is angered with pity
at the flying hounds of her father   135
eating the unborn young in the hare and the shivering mother.
She is sick at the eagles' feasting.
Sing sorrow, sorrow: but good win out in the end.

Lovely you are and kind   140
to the tender young of ravening lions.
For sucklings of all the savage
beasts that lurk in the lonely places you have sympathy.
Grant meaning to these appearances
good, yet not without evil.   145
Healer Apollo, I pray you
let her not with cross winds
bind the ships of the Danaans
to time-long anchorage   150
forcing a second sacrifice unholy, untasted,
working bitterness in the blood
and faith lost. For the terror returns like sickness to lurk in the
    house;
the secret anger remembers the child that shall be avenged."   155
Such, with great good things beside, rang out in the voice of
    Calchas,
these fatal signs from the birds by the way to the house of the
    princes,
wherewith in sympathy
sing sorrow, sorrow: but good win out in the end.

Zeus: whatever he may be, if this name   160
pleases him in invocation,
thus I call upon him.
I have pondered everything
yet I cannot find a way,

only Zeus, to cast this dead weight of ignorance 165
finally from out my brain.

He who in time long ago was great,
throbbing with gigantic strength,
shall be as if he never were, unspoken. 170
He who followed him has found
his master, and is gone.
Cry aloud without fear the victory of Zeus,
you will not have failed the truth: 175

Zeus, who guided men to think,
who has laid it down that wisdom
comes alone through suffering.
Still there drips in sleep against the heart
grief of memory; against 180
our pleasure we are temperate.
From the gods who sit in grandeur
grace comes somehow violent.

On that day the elder king
of the Achaean ships, no more
strict against the prophet's word, 185
turned with the crosswinds of fortune,
when no ship sailed, no pail was full,
and the Achaean people sulked
fast against the shore at Aulis
facing Chalcis, where the tides ebb and surge: 190

and winds blew from the Strymon, bearing
sick idleness, ships tied fast, and hunger,
distraction of the mind, carelessness
for hull and cable; 195
with time's length bent to double measure
by delay crumbled the flower and pride
of Argos. Then against the bitter wind
the seer's voice clashed out
another medicine 200

more hateful yet, and spoke of Artemis, so that the kings
dashed their staves to the ground and could not hold their tears.

The elder lord spoke aloud before them: 205
"My fate is angry if I disobey these,
but angry if I slaughter
this child, the beauty of my house,
with maiden blood shed staining
these father's hands beside the altar.   210
What of these things goes now without disaster?
How shall I fail my ships
and lose my faith of battle?
For them to urge such sacrifice of innocent blood   215
angrily, for their wrath is great—it is right. May all be well yet."

But when necessity's yoke was put upon him
he changed, and from the heart the breath came bitter
and sacrilegious, utterly infidel,   220
to warp a will now to be stopped at nothing.
The sickening in men's minds, tough,
reckless in fresh cruelty brings daring. He endured then
to sacrifice his daughter
to stay the strength of war waged for a woman,   225
first offering for the ships' sake.

Her supplications and her cries of father
were nothing, nor the child's lamentation
to kings passioned for battle.   230
The father prayed, called to his men to lift her
with strength of hand swept in her robes aloft
and prone above the altar, as you might lift
a goat for sacrifice, with guards
against the lips' sweet edge, to check   235
the curse cried on the house of Atreus
by force of bit and speech drowned in strength.

Pouring then to the ground her saffron mantle
she struck the sacrificers with   240
the eyes' arrows of pity,

lovely as in a painted scene, and striving
to speak—as many times
at the kind festive table of her father
she had sung, and in the clear voice of a stainless maiden   245
with love had graced the song
of worship when the third cup was poured.

What happened next I saw not, neither speak it.
The crafts of Calchas fail not of outcome.
Justice so moves that those only learn   250
who suffer; and the future
you shall know when it has come; before then, forget it.
It is grief too soon given.
All will come clear in the next dawn's sunlight.
Let good fortune follow these things as   255
she who is here desires,
our Apian land's singlehearted protectress.

(*The Chorus now turns toward Clytaemestra, and the leader
speaks to her.*)

I have come in reverence, Clytaemestra, of your power.
For when the man is gone and the throne void, his right
falls to the prince's lady, and honor must be given.   260
Is it some grace—or otherwise—that you have heard
to make you sacrifice at messages of good hope?
I should be glad to hear, but must not blame your silence.

Clytaemestra

As it was said of old, may the dawn child be born
to be an angel of blessing from the kindly night.   265
You shall know joy beyond all you ever hoped to hear.
The men of Argos have taken Priam's citadel.

Chorus

What have you said? Your words escaped my unbelief.

Clytaemestra

The Achaeans are in Troy. Is that not clear enough?

Chorus

    This slow delight steals over me to bring forth tears.   270

Clytaemestra

    Yes, for your eyes betray the loyal heart within.

Chorus

    Yet how can I be certain? Is there some evidence?

Clytaemestra

    There is, there must be; unless a god has lied to me.

Chorus

    Is it dream visions, easy to believe, you credit?

Clytaemestra

    I accept nothing from a brain that is dull with sleep.   275

Chorus

    The charm, then, of some rumor, that made rich your hope?

Clytaemestra

    Am I some young girl, that you find my thoughts so silly?

Chorus

    How long, then, is it since the citadel was stormed?

Clytaemestra

    It is the night, the mother of this dawn I hailed.

Chorus

    What kind of messenger could come in speed like this?   280

Clytaemestra

    Hephaestus, who cast forth the shining blaze from Ida.
    And beacon after beacon picking up the flare
    carried it here; Ida to the Hermaean horn
    of Lemnos, where it shone above the isle, and next
    the sheer rock face of Zeus on Athos caught it up;   285
    and plunging skyward to arch the shoulders of the sea
    the strength of the running flare in exultation,
    pine timbers flaming into gold, like the sunrise,

brought the bright message to Macistus' sentinel cliffs,
who, never slow nor in the carelessness of sleep   290
caught up, sent on his relay in the courier chain,
and far across Euripus' streams the beacon flare
carried to signal watchmen on Messapion.
These took it again in turn, and heaping high a pile
of silvery brush flamed it to throw the message on.   295
And the flare sickened never, but grown stronger yet
outleapt the river valley of Asopus like
the very moon for shining, to Cithaeron's scaur
to waken the next station of the flaming post.
These watchers, not contemptuous of the far-thrown blaze,   300
kindled another beacon vaster than commanded.
The light leaned high above Gorgopis' staring marsh,
and striking Aegyplanctus' mountain top, drove on
yet one more relay, lest the flare die down in speed.
Kindled once more with stintless heaping force, they send   305
the beard of flame to hugeness, passing far beyond
the promontory that gazes on the Saronic strait
and flaming far, until it plunged at last to strike
the steep rock of Arachnus near at hand, our watchtower.
And thence there fell upon this house of Atreus' sons   310
the flare whose fathers mount to the Idaean beacon.
These are the changes on my torchlight messengers,
one from another running out the laps assigned.
The first and the last sprinters have the victory.
By such proof and such symbol I announce to you   315
my lord at Troy has sent his messengers to me.

Chorus

The gods, lady, shall have my prayers and thanks straightway.
And yet to hear your story till all wonder fades
would be my wish, could you but tell it once again.

Clytaemestra

The Achaeans have got Troy, upon this very day.   320
I think the city echoes with a clash of cries.

Pour vinegar and oil into the selfsame bowl,
you could not say they mix in friendship, but fight on.
Thus variant sound the voices of the conquerors
and conquered, from the opposition of their fates.   325
Trojans are stooping now to gather in their arms
their dead, husbands and brothers; children lean to clasp
the aged who begot them, crying upon the death
of those most dear, from lips that never will be free.
The Achaeans have their midnight work after the fighting   330
that sets them down to feed on all the city has,
ravenous, headlong, by no rank and file assigned,
but as each man has drawn his shaken lot by chance.
And in the Trojan houses that their spears have taken
they settle now, free of the open sky, the frosts   335
and dampness of the evening; without sentinels set
they sleep the sleep of happiness the whole night through.
And if they reverence the gods who hold the city
and all the holy temples of the captured land,
they, the despoilers, might not be despoiled in turn.   340
Let not their passion overwhelm them; let no lust
seize on these men to violate what they must not.
The run to safety and home is yet to make; they must turn
the pole, and run the backstretch of the double course.
Yet, though the host come home without offence to high   345
gods, even so the anger of these slaughtered men
may never sleep. Oh, let there be no fresh wrong done!

Such are the thoughts you hear from me, a woman merely.
Yet may the best win through, that none may fail to see.
Of all good things to wish this is my dearest choice.   350

Chorus

My lady, no grave man could speak with better grace.
I have listened to the proofs of your tale, and I believe,
and go to make my glad thanksgivings to the gods.
This pleasure is not unworthy of the grief that gave it.

O Zeus our lord and Night beloved,   355
bestower of power and beauty,
you slung above the bastions of Troy
the binding net, that none, neither great
nor young, might outleap
the gigantic toils   360
of enslavement and final disaster.
I gaze in awe on Zeus of the guests
who wrung from Alexander such payment.
He bent the bow with slow care, that neither
the shaft might hurdle the stars, nor fall   365
spent to the earth, short driven.

They have the stroke of Zeus to tell of.
This thing is clear and you may trace it.
He acted as he had decreed. A man thought
the gods deigned not to punish mortals   370
who trampled down the delicacy of things
inviolable. That man was wicked.
The curse on great daring
shines clear; it wrings atonement   375
from those high hearts that drive to evil,
from houses blossoming to pride
and peril. Let there be
wealth without tears; enough for
the wise man who will ask no further.   380
There is not any armor
in gold against perdition
for him who spurns the high altar
of Justice down to the darkness.

Persuasion the persistent overwhelms him,   385
she, strong daughter of designing Ruin.
And every medicine is vain; the sin
smolders not, but burns to evil beauty.
As cheap bronze tortured   390
at the touchstone relapses

to blackness and grime, so this man
tested shows vain
as a child that strives to catch the bird flying .
and wins shame that shall bring down his city.   395
No god will hear such a man's entreaty,
but whoso turns to these ways
they strike him down in his wickedness.
This was Paris: he came
to the house of the sons of Atreus,   400
stole the woman away, and shamed
the guest's right of the board shared.

She left among her people the stir and clamor
of shields and of spearheads,   405
the ships to sail and the armor.
She took to Ilium her dowry, death.
She stepped forth lightly between the gates
daring beyond all daring. And the prophets
about the great house wept aloud and spoke:
"Alas, alas for the house and for the champions,   410
alas for the bed signed with their love together.
Here now is silence, scorned, unreproachful.
The agony of his loss is clear before us.
Longing for her who lies beyond the sea
he shall see a phantom queen in his household.   415
Her images in their beauty
are bitterness to her lord now
where in the emptiness of eyes
all passion has faded."

Shining in dreams the sorrowful   420
memories pass; they bring him
vain delight only.
It is vain, to dream and to see splendors,
and the image slipping from the arms' embrace
escapes, not to return again,   425
on wings drifting down the ways of sleep.

Such have the sorrows been in the house by the hearthside;
such have there been, and yet there are worse than these.
In all Hellas, for those who swarmed to the host
the heartbreaking misery   430
shows in the house of each.
Many are they who are touched at the heart by these things.
Those they sent forth they knew;
now, in place of the young men
urns and ashes are carried home   435
to the houses of the fighters.

The god of war, money changer of dead bodies,
held the balance of his spear in the fighting,
and from the corpse-fires at Ilium   440
sent to their dearest the dust
heavy and bitter with tears shed
packing smooth the urns with
ashes that once were men.
They praise them through their tears, how this man   445
knew well the craft of battle, how another
went down splendid in the slaughter:
and all for some strange woman.
Thus they mutter in secrecy,
and the slow anger creeps below their grief   450
at Atreus' sons and their quarrels.
There by the walls of Ilium
the young men in their beauty keep
graves deep in the alien soil
they hated and they conquered.   455

The citizens speak: their voice is dull with hatred.
The curse of the people must be paid for.
There lurks for me in the hooded night
terror of what may be told me.   460
The gods fail not to mark
those who have killed many.
The black Furies stalking the man

fortunate beyond all right
wrench back again the set of his life   465
and drop him to darkness. There among
the ciphers there is no more comfort
in power. And the vaunt of high glory
is bitterness; for God's thunderbolts
crash on the towering mountains.   470
Let me attain no envied wealth,
let me not plunder cities,
neither be taken in turn, and face
life in the power of another.

      (Various members of the Chorus, speaking severally.)

From the beacon's bright message   475
the fleet rumor runs
through the city. If this be real
who knows? Perhaps the gods have sent some lie to us.

Who of us is so childish or so reft of wit
that by the beacon's messages   480
his heart flamed must despond again
when the tale changes in the end?

It is like a woman indeed
to take the rapture before the fact has shown for true.

They believe too easily, are too quick to shift   485
from ground to ground; and swift indeed
the rumor voiced by a woman dies again.

Now we shall understand these torches and their shining,
the beacons, and the interchange of flame and flame.   490
They may be real; yet bright and dreamwise ecstasy
in light's appearance might have charmed our hearts awry.
I see a herald coming from the beach, his brows
shaded with sprigs of olive; and upon his feet
the dust, dry sister of the mire, makes plain to me   495
that he will find a voice, not merely kindle flame
from mountain timber, and make signals from the smoke,

but tell us outright, whether to be happy, or—
but I shrink back from naming the alternative.
That which appeared was good; may yet more good be given.   500

And any man who prays that different things befall
the city, may he reap the crime of his own heart.

                    (*The Herald enters, and speaks.*)
Soil of my fathers, Argive earth I tread upon,
in daylight of the tenth year I have come back to you.
All my hopes broke but one, and this I have at last.   505
I never could have dared to dream that I might die
in Argos, and be buried in this beloved soil.
Hail to the Argive land and to its sunlight, hail
to its high sovereign, Zeus, and to the Pythian king.
May you no longer shower your arrows on our heads.   510
Beside Scamandrus you were grim; be satisfied
and turn to savior now and healer of our hurts,
my lord Apollo. Gods of the market place assembled,
I greet you all, and my own patron deity
Hermes, beloved herald, in whose right all heralds   515
are sacred; and you heroes that sent forth the host,
propitiously take back all that the spear has left.
O great hall of the kings and house beloved; seats
of sanctity; divinities that face the sun:
if ever before, look now with kind and glowing eyes   520
to greet our king in state after so long a time.
He comes, lord Agamemnon, bearing light in gloom
to you, and to all that are assembled here.
Salute him with good favor, as he well deserves,
the man who has wrecked Ilium with the spade of Zeus   525
vindictive, whereby all their plain has been laid waste.
Gone are their altars, the sacred places of the gods
are gone, and scattered all the seed within the ground.
With such a yoke as this gripped to the neck of Troy
he comes, the king, Atreus' elder son, a man   530

fortunate to be honored far above all men
alive; not Paris nor the city tied to him
can boast he did more than was done him in return.
Guilty of rape and theft, condemned, he lost the prize
captured, and broke to sheer destruction all the house   535
of his fathers, with the very ground whereon it stood.
Twice over the sons of Priam have atoned their sins.

Chorus

Hail and be glad, herald of the Achaean host.

Herald

I am happy; I no longer ask the gods for death.

Chorus

Did passion for your country so strip bare your heart?   540

Herald

So that the tears broke in my eyes, for happiness.

Chorus

You were taken with that sickness, then, that brings delight.

Herald

How? I cannot deal with such words until I understand.

Chorus

Struck with desire of those who loved as much again.

Herald

You mean our country longed for us, as we for home?   545

Chorus

So that I sighed, out of the darkness of my heart.

Herald

Whence came this black thought to afflict the mind with fear?

Chorus

Long since it was my silence kept disaster off.

Herald

But how? There were some you feared when the kings went
    away?

Chorus

So much that as you said now, even death were grace.   550

Herald

Well: the end has been good. And in the length of time
part of our fortune you could say held favorable,
but part we cursed again. And who, except the gods,
can live time through forever without any pain?
Were I to tell you of the hard work done, the nights   555
exposed, the cramped sea-quarters, the foul beds—what part
of day's disposal did we not cry out loud?
Ashore, the horror stayed with us and grew. We lay
against the ramparts of our enemies, and from
the sky, and from the ground, the meadow dews came out   560
to soak our clothes and fill our hair with lice. And if
I were to tell of winter time, when all birds died,
the snows of Ida past endurance she sent down,
or summer heat, when in the lazy noon the sea
fell level and asleep under a windless sky—   565
but why live such grief over again? That time is gone
for us, and gone for those who died. Never again
need they rise up, nor care again for anything.
Why must a live man count the numbers of the slain,
why grieve at fortune's wrath that fades to break once more?   570
I call a long farewell to all our unhappiness.
For us, survivors of the Argive armament,
the pleasure wins, pain casts no weight in the opposite scale.
And here, in this sun's shining, we can boast aloud,
whose fame has gone with wings across the land and sea: 575
"Upon a time the Argive host took Troy, and on
the houses of the gods who live in Hellas nailed
the spoils, to be the glory of days long ago."
And they who hear such things shall call this city blest
and the leaders of the host; and high the grace of God   580
shall be exalted, that did this. You have the story.

Chorus

I must give way; your story shows that I was wrong.
Old men are always young enough to learn, with profit.

But Clytaemestra and her house must hear, above
others, this news that makes luxurious my life.   585

(Clytaemestra comes forward and speaks.)

I raised my cry of joy, and it was long ago
when the first beacon flare of message came by night
to speak of capture and of Ilium's overthrow.
But there was one who laughed at me, who said: "You trust   590
in beacons so, and you believe that Troy has fallen?
How like a woman, for the heart to lift so light."
Men spoke like that; they thought I wandered in my wits;
yet I made sacrifice, and in the womanish strain
voice after voice caught up the cry along the city   595
to echo in the temples of the gods and bless
and still the fragrant flame that melts the sacrifice.

Why should you tell me then the whole long tale at large
when from my lord himself I shall hear all the story?
But now, how best to speed my preparation to   600
receive my honored lord come home again—what else
is light more sweet for woman to behold than this,
to spread the gates before her husband home from war
and saved by God's hand?—take this message to the king:
Come, and with speed, back to the city that longs for him,   605
and may he find a wife within his house as true
as on the day he left her, watchdog of the house
gentle to him alone, fierce to his enemies,
and such a woman in all her ways as this, who has
not broken the seal upon her in the length of days.   610
With no man else have I known delight, nor any shame
of evil speech, more than I know how to temper bronze.

(Clytaemestra goes to the back of the stage.)

Herald

A vaunt like this, so loaded as it is with truth,
it well becomes a highborn lady to proclaim.

Chorus

    Thus has she spoken to you, and well you understand,   615
    words that impress interpreters whose thought is clear.
    But tell me, herald; I would learn of Menelaus,
    that power beloved in this land. Has he survived
    also, and come with you back to his home again?

Herald

    I know no way to lie and make my tale so fair   620
    that friends could reap joy of it for any length of time.

Chorus

    Is there no means to speak us fair, and yet tell the truth?
    It will not hide, when truth and good are torn asunder.

Herald

    He is gone out of the sight of the Achaean host,
    vessel and man alike. I speak no falsehood there.   625

Chorus

    Was it when he had put out from Ilium in your sight,
    or did a storm that struck you both whirl him away?

Herald

    How like a master bowman you have hit the mark
    and in your speech cut a long sorrow to brief stature.

Chorus

    But then the rumor in the host that sailed beside,   630
    was it that he had perished, or might yet be living?

Herald

    No man knows. There is none could tell us that for sure
    except the Sun, from whom this earth has life and increase.

Chorus

    How did this storm, by wrath of the divinities,
    strike on our multitude at sea? How did it end?   635

Herald

    It is not well to stain the blessing of this day
    with speech of evil weight. Such gods are honored apart.

And when the messenger of a shaken host, sad faced,
brings to his city news it prayed never to hear,
this scores one wound upon the body of the people;   640
and that from many houses many men are slain
by the two-lashed whip dear to the War God's hand, this turns
disaster double-bladed, bloodily made two.
The messenger so freighted with a charge of tears
should make his song of triumph at the Furies' door.   645
But, carrying the fair message of our hopes' salvation,
come home to a glad city's hospitality,
how shall I mix my gracious news with foul, and tell
of the storm on the Achaeans by God's anger sent?
For they, of old the deepest enemies, sea and fire,   650
made a conspiracy and gave the oath of hand
to blast in ruin our unhappy Argive army.
At night the sea began to rise in waves of death.
Ship against ship the Thracian stormwind shattered us,
and gored and split, our vessels, swept in violence   655
of storm and whirlwind, beaten by the breaking rain,
drove on in darkness, spun by the wicked shepherd's hand.
But when the sun came up again to light the dawn,
we saw the Aegaean Sea blossoming with dead men,
the men of Achaea, and the wreckage of their ships.   660
For us, and for our ship, some god, no man, by guile
or by entreaty's force prevailing, laid his hand
upon the helm and brought us through with hull unscarred.
Life-giving fortune deigned to take our ship in charge
that neither riding in deep water she took the surf   665
nor drove to shoal and break upon some rocky shore.
But then, delivered from death at sea, in the pale day,
incredulous of our own luck, we shepherded
in our sad thoughts the fresh disaster of the fleet
so pitifully torn and shaken by the storm.   670
Now of these others, if there are any left alive
they speak of us as men who perished, must they not?
Even as we, who fear that they are gone. But may

it all come well in the end. For Menelaus: be sure
if any of them come back that he will be the first. 675
If he is still where some sun's gleam can track him down,
alive and open-eyed, by blessed hand of God
who willed that not yet should his seed be utterly gone,
there is some hope that he will still come home again.
You have heard all; and be sure, you have heard the truth. 680

(*The Herald goes out.*)

Chorus

Who is he that named you so
fatally in every way?
Could it be some mind unseen
in divination of your destiny
shaping to the lips that name 685
for the bride of spears and blood,
Helen, which is death? Appropriately
death of ships, death of men and cities
from the bower's soft curtained 690
and secluded luxury she sailed then,
driven on the giant west wind,
and armored men in their thousands came,
huntsmen down the oar blade's fading footprint 695
to struggle in blood with those
who by the banks of Simoeis
beached their hulls where the leaves break.

And on Ilium in truth
in the likeness of the name 700
the sure purpose of the Wrath drove
marriage with death: for the guest board
shamed, and Zeus kindly to strangers,
the vengeance wrought on those men
who graced in too loud voice the bride-song 705
fallen to their lot to sing,
the kinsmen and the brothers.
And changing its song's measure

the ancient city of Priam   710
chants in high strain of lamentation,
calling Paris him of the fatal marriage;
for it endured its life's end
in desolation and tears
and the piteous blood of its people.   715

Once a man fostered in his house
a lion cub, from the mother's milk
torn, craving the breast given.
In the first steps of its young life   720
mild, it played with children
and delighted the old.
Caught in the arm's cradle
they pampered it like a newborn child,
shining eyed and broken to the hand   725
to stay the stress of its hunger.

But it grew with time, and the lion
in the blood strain came out; it paid
grace to those who had fostered it
in blood and death for the sheep flocks,   730
a grim feast forbidden.
The house reeked with blood run
nor could its people beat down the bane,
the giant murderer's onslaught.
This thing they raised in their house was blessed   735
by God to be priest of destruction.

And that which first came to the city of Ilium,
call it a dream of calm
and the wind dying,
the loveliness and luxury of much gold,   740
the melting shafts of the eyes' glances,
the blossom that breaks the heart with longing.
But she turned in mid-step of her course to make
bitter the consummation,   745

whirling on Priam's people
to blight with her touch and nearness.
Zeus hospitable sent her,
a vengeance to make brides weep.

It has been made long since and grown old among men,   750
this saying: human wealth
grown to fulness of stature
breeds again nor dies without issue.
From high good fortune in the blood   755
blossoms the quenchless agony.
Far from others I hold my own
mind; only the act of evil
breeds others to follow,
young sins in its own likeness.   760
Houses clear in their right are given
children in all loveliness.

But Crime aging is made
in men's dark actions
ripe with the young pride   765
late or soon when the dawn of destiny
comes and birth is given
to the spirit none may fight nor beat down,
sinful Daring; and in those halls
the black visaged Disasters stamped   770
in the likeness of their fathers.

And Righteousness is a shining in
the smoke of mean houses.
Her blessing is on the just man.
From high halls starred with gold by reeking hands   775
she turns back
with eyes that glance away to the simple in heart,
spurning the strength of gold
stamped false with flattery.   780
And all things she steers to fulfilment.

(Agamemnon enters in a chariot, with Cassandra beside
him. The Chorus speaks to him.)

Behold, my king: sacker of Troy's citadel,
own issue of Atreus.
How shall I hail you? How give honor   785
not crossing too high nor yet bending short
of this time's graces?
For many among men are they who set high
the show of honor, yet break justice.
If one be unhappy, all else are fain   790
to grieve with him: yet the teeth of sorrow
come nowise near to the heart's edge.
And in joy likewise they show joy's semblance,
and torture the face to the false smile.
Yet the good shepherd, who knows his flock,   795
the eyes of men cannot lie to him,
that with water of feigned
love seem to smile from the true heart.
But I: when you marshalled this armament
for Helen's sake, I will not hide it,   800
in ugly style you were written in my heart
for steering aslant the mind's course
to bring home by blood
sacrifice and dead men that wild spirit.
But now, in love drawn up from the deep heart,   805
not skimmed at the edge, we hail you.
You have won, your labor is made gladness.
Ask all men: you will learn in time
which of your citizens have been just
in the city's sway, which were reckless.   810

Agamemnon

To Argos first, and to the gods within the land,
I must give due greeting; they have worked with me to bring
me home; they helped me in the vengeance I have wrought
on Priam's city. Not from the lips of men the gods
heard justice, but in one firm cast they laid their votes   815

within the urn of blood that Ilium must die
and all her people; while above the opposite vase
the hand hovered and there was hope, but no vote fell.
The stormclouds of their ruin live; the ash that dies
upon them gushes still in smoke their pride of wealth.   820
For all this we must thank the gods with grace of much
high praise and memory, we who fenced within our toils
of wrath the city; and, because one woman strayed,
the beast of Argos broke them, the fierce young within
the horse, the armored people who marked out their leap   825
against the setting of the Pleiades. A wild
and bloody lion swarmed above the towers of Troy
to glut its hunger lapping at the blood of kings.

This to the gods, a prelude strung to length of words.
But, for the thought you spoke, I heard and I remember   830
and stand behind you. For I say that it is true.
In few men is it part of nature to respect
a friend's prosperity without begrudging him,
as envy's wicked poison settling to the heart
piles up the pain in one sick with unhappiness,   835
who, staggered under sufferings that are all his own,
winces again to the vision of a neighbor's bliss.
And I can speak, for I have seen, I know it well,
this mirror of companionship, this shadow's ghost,
these men who seemed my friends in all sincerity.   840
One man of them all, Odysseus, he who sailed unwilling,
once yoked to me carried his harness, nor went slack.
Dead though he be or living, I can say it still.

Now in the business of the city and the gods
we must ordain full conclave of all citizens   845
and take our counsel. We shall see what element
is strong, and plan that it shall keep its virtue still.
But that which must be healed—we must use medicine,
or burn, or amputate, with kind intention, take
all means at hand that might beat down corruption's pain.   850

So to the King's house and the home about the hearth
I take my way, with greeting to the gods within
who sent me forth, and who have brought me home once more.
My prize was conquest; may it never fail again.

(Clytaemestra comes forward and speaks.)

Grave gentlemen of Argolis assembled here,   855
I take no shame to speak aloud before you all
the love I bear my husband. In the lapse of time
modesty fades; it is human.
                What I tell you now
I learned not from another; this is my own sad life
all the long years this man was gone at Ilium.   860
It is evil and a thing of terror when a wife
sits in the house forlorn with no man by, and hears
rumors that like a fever die to break again,
and men come in with news of fear, and on their heels
another messenger, with worse news to cry aloud   865
here in this house. Had Agamemnon taken all
the wounds the tale whereof was carried home to me,
he had been cut full of gashes like a fishing net.
If he had died each time that rumor told his death,
he must have been some triple-bodied Geryon   870
back from the dead with threefold cloak of earth upon
his body, and killed once for every shape assumed.
Because such tales broke out forever on my rest,
many a time they cut me down and freed my throat   875
from the noose overslung where I had caught it fast.
And therefore is your son, in whom my love and yours
are sealed and pledged, not here to stand with us today,
Orestes. It were right; yet do not be amazed.
Strophius of Phocis, comrade in arms and faithful friend   880
to you, is keeping him. He spoke to me of peril
on two counts; of your danger under Ilium,
and here, of revolution and the clamorous people
who might cast down the council—since it lies in men's

nature to trample on the fighter already down. 885
Such my excuse to you, and without subterfuge.

For me: the running springs that were my tears have dried
utterly up, nor left one drop within. I keep
the pain upon my eyes where late at night I wept
over the beacons long ago set for your sake, 890
untended left forever. In the midst of dreams
the whisper that a gnat's thin wings could winnow broke
my sleep apart. I thought I saw you suffer wounds
more than the time that slept with me could ever hold.

Now all my suffering is past, with griefless heart 895
I hail this man, the watchdog of the fold and hall;
the stay that keeps the ship alive; the post to grip
groundward the towering roof; a father's single child;
land seen by sailors after all their hope was gone;
splendor of daybreak shining from the night of storm; 900
the running spring a parched wayfarer strays upon.
Oh, it is sweet to escape from all necessity!

Such is my greeting to him, that he well deserves.
Let none bear malice; for the harm that went before
I took, and it was great.
                              Now, my beloved one, 905
step from your chariot; yet let not your foot, my lord,
sacker of Ilium, touch the earth. My maidens there!
Why this delay? Your task has been appointed you,
to strew the ground before his feet with tapestries.
Let there spring up into the house he never hoped 910
to see, where Justice leads him in, a crimson path.

In all things else, my heart's unsleeping care shall act
with the gods' aid to set aright what fate ordained.

               (Clytaemestra's handmaidens spread a bright carpet
                              between the chariot and the door.)

Agamemnon

Daughter of Leda, you who kept my house for me,
there is one way your welcome matched my absence well. 915

You strained it to great length. Yet properly to praise
me thus belongs by right to other lips, not yours.
And all this—do not try in woman's ways to make
me delicate, nor, as if I were some Asiatic
bow down to earth and with wide mouth cry out to me,   920
nor cross my path with jealousy by strewing the ground
with robes. Such state becomes the gods, and none beside.
I am a mortal, a man; I cannot trample upon
these tinted splendors without fear thrown in my path.
I tell you, as a man, not god, to reverence me.   925
Discordant is the murmur at such treading down
of lovely things; while God's most lordly gift to man
is decency of mind. Call that man only blest
who has in sweet tranquillity brought his life to close.
If I could only act as such, my hope is good.   930

Clytaemestra

  Yet tell me this one thing, and do not cross my will.

Agamemnon

  My will is mine. I shall not make it soft for you.

Clytaemestra

  It was in fear surely that you vowed this course to God.

Agamemnon

  No man has spoken knowing better what he said.

Clytaemestra

  If Priam had won as you have, what would he have done?   935

Agamemnon

  I well believe he might have walked on tapestries.

Clytaemestra

  Be not ashamed before the bitterness of men.

Agamemnon

  The people murmur, and their voice is great in strength.

Clytaemestra

Yet he who goes unenvied shall not be admired.

Agamemnon

Surely this lust for conflict is not womanlike?   940

Clytaemestra

Yet for the mighty even to give way is grace.

Agamemnon

Does such a victory as this mean so much to you?

Clytaemestra

Oh yield! The power is yours. Give way of your free will.

Agamemnon

Since you must have it—here, let someone with all speed
take off these sandals, slaves for my feet to tread upon.   945
And as I crush these garments stained from the rich sea
let no god's eyes of hatred strike me from afar.
Great the extravagance, and great the shame I feel
to spoil such treasure and such silver's worth of webs.

So much for all this. Take this stranger girl within   950
now, and be kind. The conqueror who uses softly
his power, is watched from far in the kind eyes of God,
and this slave's yoke is one no man will wear from choice.
Gift of the host to me, and flower exquisite
from all my many treasures, she attends me here.   955

Now since my will was bent to listen to you in this
my feet crush purple as I pass within the hall.

Clytaemestra

The sea is there, and who shall drain its yield? It breeds
precious as silver, ever of itself renewed,
the purple ooze wherein our garments shall be dipped.   960
And by God's grace this house keeps full sufficiency
of all. Poverty is a thing beyond its thought.
I could have vowed to trample many splendors down

had such decree been ordained from the oracles
those days when all my study was to bring home your life.   965
For when the root lives yet the leaves will come again
to fence the house with shade against the Dog Star's heat,
and now you have come home to keep your hearth and house
you bring with you the symbol of our winter's warmth;
but when Zeus ripens the green clusters into wine   970
there shall be coolness in the house upon those days
because the master ranges his own halls once more.

Zeus, Zeus accomplisher, accomplish these my prayers.
Let your mind bring these things to pass. It is your will.

> (*Agamemnon and Clytaemestra enter the house. Cassandra*
> *remains in the chariot. The Chorus speaks.*)

Why must this persistent fear   975
beat its wings so ceaselessly
and so close against my mantic heart?
Why this strain unwanted, unrepaid, thus prophetic?
Nor can valor of good hope   980
seated near the chambered depth
of the spirit cast it out
as dreams of dark fancy; and yet time
has buried in the mounding sand
the sea cables since that day   985
when against Ilium
the army and the ships put to sea.

Yet I have seen with these eyes
Agamemnon home again.
Still the spirit sings, drawing deep   990
from within this unlyric threnody of the Fury.
Hope is gone utterly,
the sweet strength is far away.
Surely this is not fantasy.   995
Surely it is real, this whirl of drifts
that spin the stricken heart.
Still I pray; may all this

expectation fade as vanity
into unfulfilment, and not be.   1000

Yet it is true: the high strength of men
knows no content with limitation. Sickness
chambered beside it beats at the wall between.
Man's fate that sets a true   1005
course yet may strike upon
the blind and sudden reefs of disaster.
But if before such time, fear
throw overboard some precious thing
of the cargo, with deliberate cast,   1010
not all the house, laboring
with weight of ruin, shall go down,
nor sink the hull deep within the sea.
And great and affluent the gift of Zeus
in yield of ploughed acres year on year   1015
makes void again sick starvation.

But when the black and mortal blood of man
has fallen to the ground before his feet, who then   1020
can sing spells to call it back again?
Did Zeus not warn us once
when he struck to impotence
that one who could in truth charm back the dead men?
Had the gods not so ordained   1025
that fate should stand against fate
to check any man's excess,
my heart now would have outrun speech
to break forth the water of its grief.
But this is so; I murmur deep in darkness   1030
sore at heart; my hope is gone now
ever again to unwind some crucial good
from the flames about my heart.

(*Clytaemestra comes out from the house again
and speaks to Cassandra.*)

Cassandra, you may go within the house as well,   1035
since Zeus in no unkindness has ordained that you

must share our lustral water, stand with the great throng
of slaves that flock to the altar of our household god.
Step from this chariot, then, and do not be so proud.
And think—they say that long ago Alcmena's son   1040
was sold in bondage and endured the bread of slaves.
But if constraint of fact forces you to such fate,
be glad indeed for masters ancient in their wealth.
They who have reaped success beyond their dreams of hope
are savage above need and standard toward their slaves.   1045
From us you shall have all you have the right to ask.

Chorus

What she has spoken is for you, and clear enough.
Fenced in these fatal nets wherein you find yourself
you should obey her if you can; perhaps you can not.

Clytaemestra

Unless she uses speech incomprehensible,   1050
barbarian, wild as the swallow's song, I speak
within her understanding, and she must obey.

Chorus

Go with her. What she bids is best in circumstance
that rings you now. Obey, and leave this carriage seat.

Clytaemestra

I have no leisure to stand outside the house and waste   1055
time on this woman. At the central altarstone
the flocks are standing, ready for the sacrifice
we make to this glad day we never hoped to see.
You: if you are obeying my commands at all, be quick.
But if in ignorance you fail to comprehend,   1060
speak not, but make with your barbarian hand some sign.

Chorus

I think this stranger girl needs some interpreter
who understands. She is like some captive animal.

Clytaemestra

No, she is in the passion of her own wild thoughts.
Leaving her captured city she has come to us   1065

untrained to take the curb, and will not understand
until her rage and strength have foamed away in blood.
I shall throw down no more commands for her contempt.

(*Clytaemestra goes back into the house.*)

Chorus

I, though, shall not be angry, for I pity her.
Come down, poor creature, leave the empty car. Give way   1070
to compulsion and take up the yoke that shall be yours.

(*Cassandra descends from the chariot and cries out loud.*)

Oh shame upon the earth!
Apollo, Apollo!

Chorus

You cry on Loxias in agony? He is not
of those immortals the unhappy supplicate.   1075

Cassandra

Oh shame upon the earth!
Apollo, Apollo!

Chorus

Now once again in bitter voice she calls upon
this god, who has not part in any lamentation.

Cassandra

Apollo, Apollo!   1080
Lord of the ways, my ruin.
You have undone me once again, and utterly.

Chorus

I think she will be prophetic of her own disaster.
Even in the slave's heart the gift divine lives on.

Cassandra

Apollo, Apollo!   1085
Lord of the ways, my ruin.
Where have you led me now at last? What house is this?

Chorus

>The house of the Atreidae. If you understand
>not that, I can tell you; and so much at least is true.

Cassandra

>No, but a house that God hates, guilty within   1090
>of kindred blood shed, torture of its own,
>the shambles for men's butchery, the dripping floor.

Chorus

>The stranger is keen scented like some hound upon
>the trail of blood that leads her to discovered death.

Cassandra

>Behold there the witnesses to my faith.   1095
>The small children wail for their own death
>and the flesh roasted that their father fed upon.

Chorus

>We had been told before of this prophetic fame
>of yours: we want no prophets in this place at all.

Cassandra

>Ah, for shame, what can she purpose now?   1100
>What is this new and huge
>stroke of atrocity she plans within the house
>to beat down the beloved beyond hope of healing?
>Rescue is far away.

Chorus

>I can make nothing of these prophecies. The rest   1105
>I understood; the city is full of the sound of them.

Cassandra

>So cruel then, that you can do this thing?
>The husband of your own bed
>to bathe bright with water—how shall I speak the end?
>This thing shall be done with speed. The hand gropes now, and
>>   the other   1110
>hand follows in turn.

Chorus

> No, I am lost. After the darkness of her speech
> I go bewildered in a mist of prophecies.

Cassandra

> No, no, see there! What is that thing that shows?
> Is it some net of death?
> Or is the trap the woman there, the murderess?   1115
> Let now the slakeless fury in the race
> rear up to howl aloud over this monstrous death.

Chorus

> Upon what demon in the house do you call, to raise
> the cry of triumph? All your speech makes dark my hope.   1120
> And to the heart below trickles the pale drop
> as in the hour of death
> timed to our sunset and the mortal radiance.
> Ruin is near, and swift.

Cassandra

> See there, see there! Keep from his mate the bull.
> Caught in the folded web's   1125
> entanglement she pinions him and with the black horn
> strikes. And he crumples in the watered bath.
> Guile, I tell you, and death there in the caldron wrought.

Chorus

> I am not proud in skill to guess at prophecies,   1130
> yet even I can see the evil in this thing.
> From divination what good ever has come to men?
> Art, and multiplication of words
> drifting through tangled evil bring
> terror to them that hear.   1135

Cassandra

> Alas, alas for the wretchedness of my ill-starred life.
> This pain flooding the song of sorrow is mine alone.
> Why have you brought me here in all unhappiness?
> Why, why? Except to die with him? What else could be?

Chorus

You are possessed of God, mazed at heart   1140
to sing your own death
song, the wild lyric as
in clamor for Itys, Itys over and over again
her long life of tears weeping forever grieves
the brown nightingale.   1145

Cassandra

Oh for the nightingale's pure song and a fate like hers.
With fashion of beating wings the gods clothed her about
and a sweet life gave her and without lamentation.
But mine is the sheer edge of the tearing iron.

Chorus

Whence come, beat upon beat, driven of God,   1150
vain passions of tears?
Whence your cries, terrified, clashing in horror,
in wrought melody and the singing speech?
Whence take you the marks to this path of prophecy
and speech of terror?   1155

Cassandra

Oh marriage of Paris, death to the men beloved!
Alas, Scamandrus, water my fathers drank.
There was a time I too at your springs
drank and grew strong. Ah me,
for now beside the deadly rivers, Cocytus   1160
and Acheron, I must cry out my prophecies.

Chorus

What is this word, too clear, you have uttered now?
A child could understand.
And deep within goes the stroke of the dripping fang
as mortal pain at the trebled song of your agony   1165
shivers the heart to hear.

Cassandra

O sorrow, sorrow of my city dragged to uttermost death.
O sacrifices my father made at the wall.

Flocks of the pastured sheep slaughtered there.
And no use at all   1170
to save our city from its pain inflicted now.
And I too, with brain ablaze in fever, shall go down.

Chorus

This follows the run of your song.
Is it, in cruel force of weight,
some divinity kneeling upon you brings   1175
the death song of your passionate suffering?
I can not see the end.

Cassandra

No longer shall my prophecies like some young girl
new-married glance from under veils, but bright and strong
as winds blow into morning and the sun's uprise   1180
shall wax along the swell like some great wave, to burst
at last upon the shining of this agony.
Now I will tell you plainly and from no cryptic speech;
bear me then witness, running at my heels upon
the scent of these old brutal things done long ago.   1185
There is a choir that sings as one, that shall not again
leave this house ever; the song thereof breaks harsh with menace.
And drugged to double fury on the wine of men's
blood shed, there lurks forever here a drunken rout
of ingrown vengeful spirits never to be cast forth.   1190
Hanging above the hall they chant their song of hate
and the old sin; and taking up the strain in turn
spit curses on that man who spoiled his brother's bed.
Did I go wide, or hit, like a real archer? Am I
some swindling seer who hawks his lies from door to door?   1195
Upon your oath, bear witness that I know by heart
the legend of ancient wickedness within this house.

Chorus

And how could an oath, though cast in rigid honesty,
do any good? And still we stand amazed at you,

reared in an alien city far beyond the sea,   1200
how can you strike, as if you had been there, the truth.

Cassandra

Apollo was the seer who set me to this work.

Chorus

Struck with some passion for you, and himself a god?

Cassandra

There was a time I blushed to speak about these things.

Chorus

True; they who prosper take on airs of vanity.   1205

Cassandra

Yes, then; he wrestled with me, and he breathed delight.

Chorus

Did you come to the getting of children then, as people do?

Cassandra

I promised that to Loxias, but I broke my word.

Chorus

Were you already ecstatic in the skills of God?

Cassandra

Yes; even then I read my city's destinies.   1210

Chorus

So Loxias' wrath did you no harm? How could that be?

Cassandra

For this my trespass, none believed me ever again.

Chorus

But we do; all that you foretell seems true to us.

Cassandra

But this is evil, see!
Now once again the pain of grim, true prophecy   1215
shivers my whirling brain in a storm of things foreseen.

Look there, see what is hovering above the house,
so small and young, imaged as in the shadow of dreams,
like children almost, killed by those most dear to them,
and their hands filled with their own flesh, as food to eat.   1220
I see them holding out the inward parts, the vitals,
oh pitiful, that meat their father tasted of. . . .
I tell you: There is one that plots vengeance for this,
the strengthless lion rolling in his master's bed,
who keeps, ah me, the house against his lord's return;   1225
my lord too, now that I wear the slave's yoke on my neck.
King of the ships, who tore up Ilium by the roots,
what does he know of this accursed bitch, who licks
his hand, who fawns on him with lifted ears, who like
a secret death shall strike the coward's stroke, nor fail?   1230
No, this is daring when the female shall strike down
the male. What can I call her and be right? What beast
of loathing? Viper double-fanged, or Scylla witch
holed in the rocks and bane of men that range the sea;
smoldering mother of death to smoke relentless hate   1235
on those most dear. How she stood up and howled aloud
and unashamed, as at the breaking point of battle,
in feigned gladness for his salvation from the sea!
What does it matter now if men believe or no?
What is to come will come. And soon you too will stand   1240
beside, to murmur in pity that my words were true.

Chorus

Thyestes' feast upon the flesh of his own children
I understand in terror at the thought, and fear
is on me hearing truth and no tale fabricated.
The rest: I heard it, but wander still far from the course.   1245

Cassandra

I tell you, you shall look on Agamemnon dead.

Chorus

Peace, peace, poor woman; put those bitter lips to sleep.

Cassandra

Useless; there is no god of healing in this story.

Chorus

Not if it must be; may it somehow fail to come.

Cassandra

Prayers, yes; they do not pray; they plan to strike, and kill.   1250

Chorus

What man is it who moves this beastly thing to be?

Cassandra

What man? You did mistake my divination then.

Chorus

It may be; I could not follow through the schemer's plan.

Cassandra

Yet I know Greek; I think I know it far too well.

Chorus

And Pythian oracles are Greek, yet hard to read.   1255

Cassandra

Oh, flame and pain that sweeps me once again! My lord,
Apollo, King of Light, the pain, aye me, the pain!
This is the woman-lioness, who goes to bed
with the wolf, when her proud lion ranges far away,
and she will cut me down; as a wife mixing drugs   1260
she wills to shred the virtue of my punishment
into her bowl of wrath as she makes sharp the blade
against her man, death that he brought a mistress home.
Why do I wear these mockeries upon my body,
this staff of prophecy, these flowers at my throat?   1265
At least I will spoil you before I die. Out, down,
break, damn you! This for all that you have done to me.
Make someone else, not me, luxurious in disaster. . . .
Lo now, this is Apollo who has stripped me here
of my prophetic robes. He watched me all the time   1270

wearing this glory, mocked of all, my dearest ones
who hated me with all their hearts, so vain, so wrong;
called like some gypsy wandering from door to door
beggar, corrupt, half-starved, and I endured it all.
And now the seer has done with me, his prophetess,   1275
and led me into such a place as this, to die.
Lost are my father's altars, but the block is there
to reek with sacrificial blood, my own. We two
must die, yet die not vengeless by the gods. For there
shall come one to avenge us also, born to slay   1280
his mother, and to wreak death for his father's blood.
Outlaw and wanderer, driven far from his own land,
he will come back to cope these stones of inward hate.
For this is a strong oath and sworn by the high gods,
that he shall cast men headlong for his father felled.   1285
Why am I then so pitiful? Why must I weep?
Since once I saw the citadel of Ilium
die as it died, and those who broke the city, doomed
by the gods, fare as they have fared accordingly,
I will go through with it. I too will take my fate.   1290
I call as on the gates of death upon these gates
to pray only for this thing, that the stroke be true,
and that with no convulsion, with a rush of blood
in painless death, I may close up these eyes, and rest.

Chorus

O woman much enduring and so greatly wise,   1295
you have said much. But if this thing you know be true,
this death that comes upon you, how can you, serene,
walk to the altar like a driven ox of God?

Cassandra

Friends, there is no escape for any longer time.

Chorus

Yet longest left in time is to be honored still.   1300

Cassandra

The day is here and now; I can not win by flight.

Chorus

Woman, be sure your heart is brave; you can take much.

Cassandra

None but the unhappy people ever hear such praise.

Chorus

Yet there is a grace on mortals who so nobly die.

Cassandra

Alas for you, father, and for your lordly sons.   1305
Ah!

Chorus

What now? What terror whirls you backward from the door?

Cassandra

Foul, foul!

Chorus

What foulness then, unless some horror in the mind?

Cassandra

That room within reeks with blood like a slaughter house.

Chorus

What then? Only these victims butchered at the hearth.   1310

Cassandra

There is a breath about it like an open grave.

Chorus

This is no Syrian pride of frankincense you mean.

Cassandra

So. I am going in, and mourning as I go
my death and Agamemnon's. Let my life be done.
Ah friends,   1315
truly this is no wild bird fluttering at a bush,
nor vain my speech. Bear witness to me when I die,
when falls for me, a woman slain, another woman,

and when a man dies for this wickedly mated man.
Here in my death I claim this stranger's grace of you.   1320

Chorus

Poor wretch, I pity you the fate you see so clear.

Cassandra

Yet once more will I speak, and not this time my own
death's threnody. I call upon the Sun in prayer
against that ultimate shining when the avengers strike
these monsters down in blood, that they avenge as well   1325
one simple slave who died, a small thing, lightly killed.

Alas, poor men, their destiny. When all goes well
a shadow will overthrow it. If it be unkind
one stroke of a wet sponge wipes all the picture out;
and that is far the most unhappy thing of all.   1330

(Cassandra goes slowly into the house.)

Chorus

High fortune is a thing slakeless
for mortals. There is no man who shall point
his finger to drive it back from the door
and speak the words: "Come no longer."
Now to this man the blessed ones have given   1335
Priam's city to be captured
and return in the gods' honor.
Must he give blood for generations gone,
die for those slain and in death pile up
more death to come for the blood shed,   1340
what mortal else who hears shall claim
he was born clear of the dark angel?

(Agamemnon, inside the house.)

Ah, I am struck a deadly blow and deep within!

Chorus

Silence: who cried out that he was stabbed to death within
the house?

Agamemnon

Ah me, again, they struck again. I am wounded twice.   1345

Chorus

How the king cried out aloud to us! I believe the thing is done.
Come, let us put our heads together, try to find some safe way
out.

> (*The members of the Chorus go about distractedly,*
> *each one speaking in turn.*)

Listen, let me tell you what I think is best to do.
Let the herald call all citizens to rally here.

No, better to burst in upon them now, at once,   1350
and take them with the blood still running from their blades.

I am with this man and I cast my vote to him.
Act now. This is the perilous and instant time.

Anyone can see it, by these first steps they have taken,
they purpose to be tyrants here upon our city.   1355

Yes, for we waste time, while they trample to the ground
deliberation's honor, and their hands sleep not.

I can not tell which counsel of yours to call my own.
It is the man of action who can plan as well.

I feel as he does; nor can I see how by words   1360
we shall set the dead man back upon his feet again.

Do you mean, to drag our lives out long, that we must yield
to the house shamed, and leadership of such as these?

No, we can never endure that; better to be killed.
Death is a softer thing by far than tyranny.   1365

Shall we, by no more proof than that he cried in pain,
be sure, as by divination, that our lord is dead?

Yes, we should know what is true before we break our rage.
Here is sheer guessing and far different from sure knowledge.

From all sides the voices multiply to make me choose   1370
this course; to learn first how it stands with Agamemnon.

(The doors of the palace open, disclosing the bodies of
Agamemnon and Cassandra, with Clytaemestra
standing over them.)

Clytaemestra

Much have I said before to serve necessity,
but I will take no shame now to unsay it all.
How else could I, arming hate against hateful men
disguised in seeming tenderness, fence high the nets   1375
of ruin beyond overleaping? Thus to me
the conflict born of ancient bitterness is not
a thing new thought upon, but pondered deep in time.
I stand now where I struck him down. The thing is done.
Thus have I wrought, and I will not deny it now.   1380
That he might not escape nor beat aside his death,
as fishermen cast their huge circling nets, I spread
deadly abundance of rich robes, and caught him fast.
I struck him twice. In two great cries of agony
he buckled at the knees and fell. When he was down   1385
I struck him the third blow, in thanks and reverence
to Zeus the lord of dead men underneath the ground.
Thus he went down, and the life struggled out of him;
and as he died he spattered me with the dark red
and violent driven rain of bitter savored blood   1390
to make me glad, as gardens stand among the showers
of God in glory at the birthtime of the buds.

These being the facts, elders of Argos assembled here,
be glad, if it be your pleasure; but for me, I glory.
Were it religion to pour wine above the slain,   1395
this man deserved, more than deserved, such sacrament.
He filled our cup with evil things unspeakable
and now himself come home has drunk it to the dregs.

Chorus

We stand here stunned. How can you speak this way, with mouth
so arrogant, to vaunt above your fallen lord?   1400

Clytaemestra

You try me out as if I were a woman and vain;
but my heart is not fluttered as I speak before you.
You know it. You can praise or blame me as you wish;
it is all one to me. That man is Agamemnon,
my husband; he is dead; the work of this right hand   1405
that struck in strength of righteousness. And that is that.

Chorus

Woman, what evil thing planted upon the earth
or dragged from the running salt sea could you have tasted now
to wear such brutality and walk in the people's hate?
You have cast away, you have cut away. You shall go homeless
    now,   1410
crushed with men's bitterness.

Clytaemestra

Now it is I you doom to be cast out from my city
with men's hate heaped and curses roaring in my ears.
Yet look upon this dead man; you would not cross him once
when with no thought more than as if a beast had died,   1415
when his ranged pastures swarmed with the deep fleece of flocks,
he slaughtered like a victim his own child, my pain
grown into love, to charm away the winds of Thrace.
Were you not bound to hunt him then clear of this soil
for the guilt stained upon him? Yet you hear what I   1420
have done, and lo, you are a stern judge. But I say to you:
go on and threaten me, but know that I am ready,
if fairly you can beat me down beneath your hand,
for you to rule; but if the god grant otherwise,
you shall be taught—too late, for sure—to keep your place.   1425

Chorus

Great your design, your speech is a clamor of pride.
Swung to the red act drives the fury within your brain
signed clear in the splash of blood over your eyes.
Yet to come is stroke given for stroke
vengeless, forlorn of friends.   1430

Clytaemestra

Now hear you this, the right behind my sacrament:
By my child's Justice driven to fulfilment, by
her Wrath and Fury, to whom I sacrificed this man,
the hope that walks my chambers is not traced with fear
while yet Aegisthus makes the fire shine on my hearth,   1435
my good friend, now as always, who shall be for us
the shield of our defiance, no weak thing; while he,
this other, is fallen, stained with this woman you behold,
plaything of all the golden girls at Ilium;
and here lies she, the captive of his spear, who saw   1440
wonders, who shared his bed, the wise in revelations
and loving mistress, who yet knew the feel as well
of the men's rowing benches. Their reward is not
unworthy. He lies there; and she who swanlike cried
aloud her lyric mortal lamentation out   1445
is laid against his fond heart, and to me has given
a delicate excitement to my bed's delight.

Chorus

O that in speed, without pain
and the slow bed of sickness
death could come to us now, death that forever   1450
carries sleep without ending, now that our lord is down,
our shield, kindest of men,
who for a woman's grace suffered so much,
struck down at last by a woman.

Alas, Helen, wild heart   1455
for the multitudes, for the thousand lives
you killed under Troy's shadow,
you alone, to shine in man's memory
as blood flower never to be washed out. Surely a demon then   1460
of death walked in the house, men's agony.

Clytaemestra

No, be not so heavy, nor yet draw down
in prayer death's ending,

neither turn all wrath against Helen
for men dead, that she alone killed   1465
all those Danaan lives, to work
the grief that is past all healing.

Chorus

Divinity that kneel on this house and the two
strains of the blood of Tantalus,
in the hands and hearts of women you steer   1470
the strength tearing my heart.
Standing above the corpse, obscene
as some carrion crow she sings
the crippled song and is proud.

Clytaemestra

Thus have you set the speech of your lips   1475
straight, calling by name
the spirit thrice glutted that lives in this race.
From him deep in the nerve is given
the love and the blood drunk, that before
the old wound dries, it bleeds again.   1480

Chorus

Surely it is a huge
and heavy spirit bending the house you cry;
alas, the bitter glory
of a doom that shall never be done with;
and all through Zeus, Zeus,   1485
first cause, prime mover.
For what thing without Zeus is done among mortals?
What here is without God's blessing?

O king, my king
how shall I weep for you?   1490
What can I say out of my heart of pity?
Caught in this spider's web you lie,
Your life gasped out in indecent death,
struck prone to this shameful bed

by your lady's hand of treachery   1495
and the stroke twin edged of the iron.

Clytaemestra

  Can you claim I have done this?
  Speak of me never
  more as the wife of Agamemnon.
  In the shadow of this corpse's queen   1500
  the old stark avenger
  of Atreus for his revel of hate
  struck down this man,
  last blood for the slaughtered children.

Chorus

  What man shall testify   1505
  your hands are clean of this murder?
  How? How? Yet from his father's blood
  might swarm some fiend to guide you.
  The black ruin that shoulders
  through the streaming blood of brothers   1510
  strides at last where he shall win requital
  for the children who were eaten.

  O king, my king
  how shall I weep for you?
  What can I say out of my heart of pity?   1515
  Caught in this spider's web you lie,
  your life gasped out in indecent death,
  struck prone to this shameful bed
  by your lady's hand of treachery
  and the stroke twin edged of the iron.   1520

Clytaemestra

  No shame, I think, in the death given
  this man. And did he not
  first of all in this house wreak death
  by treachery?
  The flower of this man's love and mine,   1525

Iphigeneia of the tears
he dealt with even as he has suffered.
Let his speech in death's house be not loud.
With the sword he struck,
with the sword he paid for his own act.

Chorus

My thoughts are swept away and I go bewildered.   1530
Where shall I turn the brain's
activity in speed when the house is falling?
There is fear in the beat of the blood rain breaking
wall and tower. The drops come thicker.
Still fate grinds on yet more stones the blade   1535
for more acts of terror.

Earth, my earth, why did you not fold me under
before ever I saw this man lie dead
fenced by the tub in silver?   1540
Who shall bury him? Who shall mourn him?
Shall you dare this who have killed
your lord? Make lamentation,
render the graceless grace to his soul   1545
for huge things done in wickedness?
Who over this great man's grave shall lay
the blessing of tears
worked soberly from a true heart?   1550

Clytaemestra

Not for you to speak of such tendance.
Through us he fell,
by us he died; we shall bury.
There will be no tears in this house for him.
It must be Iphigeneia   1555
his child, who else,
shall greet her father by the whirling stream
and the ferry of tears
to close him in her arms and kiss him.

Chorus

Here is anger for anger. Between them   1560
who shall judge lightly?
The spoiler is robbed; he killed, he has paid.
The truth stands ever beside God's throne
eternal: he who has wrought shall pay; that is law.
Then who shall tear the curse from their blood?   1565
The seed is stiffened to ruin.

Clytaemestra

You see truth in the future
at last. Yet I wish
to seal my oath with the Spirit
in the house: I will endure all things as they stand   1570
now, hard though it be. Hereafter
let him go forth to make bleed with death
and guilt the houses of others.
I will take some small
measure of our riches, and be content
that I swept from these halls   1575
the murder, the sin, and the fury.

*(Aegisthus enters, followed at a little distance by his
armed bodyguard.)*

Aegisthus

O splendor and exaltation of this day of doom!
Now I can say once more that the high gods look down
on mortal crimes to vindicate the right at last,
now that I see this man—sweet sight—before me here   1580
sprawled in the tangling nets of fury, to atone
the calculated evil of his father's hand.
For Atreus, this man's father, King of Argolis—
I tell you the clear story—drove my father forth,
Thyestes, his own brother, who had challenged him   1585
in his king's right—forth from his city and his home.
Yet sad Thyestes came again to supplicate
the hearth, and win some grace, in that he was not slain

nor soiled the doorstone of his fathers with blood spilled.
Not his own blood. But Atreus, this man's godless sire,   1590
angrily hospitable set a feast for him,
in seeming a glad day of fresh meat slain and good
cheer; then served my father his own children's flesh
to feed on. For he carved away the extremities,
hands, feet, and cut the flesh apart, and covered them   1595
served in a dish to my father at his table apart,
who with no thought for the featureless meal before him ate
that ghastly food whose curse works now before your eyes.
But when he knew the terrible thing that he had done,
he spat the dead meat from him with a cry, and reeled   1600
spurning the table back to heel with strength the curse:
"Thus crash in ruin all the seed of Pleisthenes."
Out of such acts you see this dead man stricken here,
and it was I, in my right, who wrought this murder, I
third born to my unhappy father, and with him   1605
driven, a helpless baby in arms, to banishment.
Yet I grew up, and justice brought me home again,
till from afar I laid my hands upon this man,
since it was I who pieced together the fell plot.
Now I can die in honor again, if die I must,   1610
having seen him caught in the cords of his just punishment.

Chorus

Aegisthus, this strong vaunting in distress is vile,
You claim that you deliberately killed the king,
you, and you only, wrought the pity of this death.
I tell you then: There shall be no escape, your head   1615
shall face the stones of anger from the people's hands.

Aegisthus

So loud from you, stooped to the meanest rowing bench
with the ship's masters lordly on the deck above?
You are old men; well, you shall learn how hard it is
at your age, to be taught how to behave yourselves.   1620
But there are chains, there is starvation with its pain,

excellent teachers of good manners to old men,
wise surgeons and exemplars. Look! Can you not see it?
Lash not at the goads for fear you hit them, and be hurt.

Chorus

So then you, like a woman, waited the war out   1625
here in the house, shaming the master's bed with lust,
and planned against the lord of war this treacherous death?

Aegisthus

It is just such words as these will make you cry in pain.
Not yours the lips of Orpheus, no, quite otherwise,
whose voice of rapture dragged all creatures in his train.   1630
You shall be dragged, for baby whimperings sobbed out
in rage. Once broken, you will be easier to deal with.

Chorus

How shall you be lord of the men of Argos, you
who planned the murder of this man, yet could not dare
to act it out, and cut him down with your own hand?   1635

Aegisthus

No, clearly the deception was the woman's part,
and I was suspect, that had hated him so long.
Still with his money I shall endeavor to control
the citizens. The mutinous man shall feel the yoke
drag at his neck, no cornfed racing colt that runs   1640
free traced; but hunger, grim companion of the dark
dungeon shall see him broken to the hand at last.

Chorus

But why, why then, you coward, could you not have slain
your man yourself? Why must it be his wife who killed,
to curse the country and the gods within the ground?   1645
Oh, can Orestes live, be somewhere in sunlight still?
Shall fate grown gracious ever bring him back again
in strength of hand to overwhelm these murderers?

Aegisthus

You shall learn then, since you stick to stubbornness of mouth
    and hand.
Up now from your cover, my henchmen: here is work for you
    to do.   1650

Chorus

Look, they come! Let every man clap fist upon his hilted sword.

Aegisthus

I too am sword-handed against you; I am not afraid of death.

Chorus

Death you said and death it shall be; we take up the word of
    fate.

Clytaemestra

No, my dearest, dearest of all men, we have done enough. No
    more
violence. Here is a monstrous harvest and a bitter reaping time.   1655
There is pain enough already. Let us not be bloody now.
Honored gentlemen of Argos, go to your homes now and give
    way
to the stress of fate and season. We could not do otherwise
than we did. If this is the end of suffering, we can be content
broken as we are by the brute heel of angry destiny.   1660
Thus a woman speaks among you. Shall men deign to under-
    stand?

Aegisthus

Yes, but think of these foolish lips that blossom into leering gibes,
think of the taunts they spit against me daring destiny and power,
sober opinion lost in insults hurled against my majesty.

Chorus

It was never the Argive way to grovel at a vile man's feet.   1665

Aegisthus

I shall not forget this; in the days to come I shall be there.

Chorus

Nevermore, if God's hand guiding brings Orestes home again.

Aegisthus

Exiles feed on empty dreams of hope. I know it. I was one.

Chorus

Have your way, gorge and grow fat, soil justice, while the power is yours.

Aegisthus

You shall pay, make no mistake, for this misguided insolence.   1670

Chorus

Crow and strut, brave cockerel by your hen; you have no threats to fear.

Clytaemestra

These are howls of impotent rage; forget them, dearest; you and I

have the power; we two shall bring good order to our house at least.

(*They enter the house. The doors close. All persons leave the stage.*)

THE

LIBATION

BEARERS

Translated by

RICHMOND LATTIMORE

CHARACTERS

Orestes, son of Agamemnon and Clytaemestra

Pylades, his friend

Electra, his sister

Chorus, of foreign serving-women

A servant (doorkeeper)

Clytaemestra, now wife of Aegisthus, queen of Argos

Cilissa, the nurse

Aegisthus, now king of Argos

A follower of Aegisthus

Various attendants of Orestes, Clytaemestra, Aegisthus (silent parts)

THE LIBATION BEARERS

SCENE: *Argos. The first part of the play (1–651) takes place at the tomb of Agamemnon: the last part (652 to the end) before the door of Clytaemestra's palace. No mechanical change of scene is necessary. The altar or tomb of Agamemnon should be well down stage. The door to the house should be in the center, back..*

(Enter, as travelers, Orestes and Pylades.)

Orestes

 Hermes, lord of the dead, who watch over the powers
 of my fathers, be my savior and stand by my claim.
 Here is my own soil that I walk. I have come home;
 and by this mounded gravebank I invoke my sire
 to hear, to listen.   5
 Here is a lock of hair for Inachus, who made
 me grow to manhood. Here a strand to mark my grief.
 I was not by, my father, to mourn for your death
 nor stretched my hand out when they took your corpse away.

(The chorus, with Electra, enter from the side.)

 But what can this mean that I see, this group that comes   10
 of women veiled in dignities of black? At what
 sudden occurrence can I guess? Is this some new
 wound struck into our house? I think they bring these urns
 to pour, in my father's honor, to appease the powers
 below. Can I be right? Surely, I think I see   15
 Electra, my own sister, walk in bitter show
 of mourning. Zeus, Zeus, grant me vengeance for my father's
 murder. Stand and fight beside me, of your grace.

 Pylades, stand we out of their way. So may I learn
 the meaning of these women; what their prayer would ask.   20

Chorus

 I came in haste out of the house
 to carry libations, hurt by the hard stroke of hands.

My cheek shows bright, ripped in the bloody furrows
of nails gashing the skin.   25
This is my life: to feed the heart on hard-drawn breath.
And in my grief, with splitting weft
of ragtorn linen across my heart's
brave show of robes
came sound of my hands' strokes   30
in sorrows whence smiles are fled.

Terror, the dream diviner of
this house, belled clear, shuddered the skin, blew wrath
from sleep, a cry in night's obscure watches,
a voice of fear deep in the house,   35
dropping deadweight in women's inner chambers.
And they who read the dream meanings
and spoke under guarantee of God
told how under earth
dead men held a grudge still   40
and smoldered at their murderers.

On such grace without grace, evil's turning aside
(Earth, Earth, kind mother!)
bent, the godless woman   45
sends me forth. But terror
is on me for this word let fall.
What can wash off the blood once spilled upon the ground?
O hearth soaked in sorrow,
o wreckage of a fallen house.   50
Sunless and where men fear to walk
the mists huddle upon this house
where the high lords have perished.

The pride not to be warred with, fought with, not to be beaten
      down   55
of old, sounded in all men's
ears, in all hearts sounded,
has shrunk away. A man
goes in fear. High fortune,

this in man's eyes is god and more than god is this.   60
But, as a beam balances, so
sudden disasters wait, to strike
some in the brightness, some in gloom
of half dark in their elder time.
Desperate night holds others.   65

Through too much glut of blood drunk by our fostering ground
the vengeful gore is caked and hard, will not drain through.
The deep-run ruin carries away
the man of guilt. Swarming infection boils within.   70

For one who handles the bridal close, there is no cure.
All the world's waters running in a single drift
may try to wash blood from the hand
of the stained man; they only bring new blood guilt on.   75

But as for me: gods have forced on my city
resisted fate. From our fathers' houses
they led us here, to take the lot of slaves.
And mine it is to wrench my will, and consent
to their commands, right or wrong,   80
to beat down my edged hate.
And yet under veils I weep
the vanities that have killed
my lord; and freeze with sorrow in the secret heart.

Electra

Attendant women, who order our house, since you
are with me in this supplication and escort   85
me here, be also my advisers in this rite.
What shall I say, as I pour out these outpourings
of sorrow? How say the good word, how make my prayer
to my father? Shall I say I bring it to the man
beloved, from a loving wife, and mean my mother? I   90
have not the daring to say this, nor know what else
to say, as I pour this liquid on my father's tomb.
Shall I say this sentence, regular in human use:

"Grant good return to those who send to you these flowers
of honor: gifts to match the . . . evil they have done."   95

Or, quiet and dishonored, as my father died
shall I pour out this offering for the ground to drink,
and go, like one who empties garbage out of doors,
and turn my eyes, and throw the vessel far away.

Dear friends, in this deliberation stay with me.   100
We hold a common hatred in this house. Do not
for fear of any, hide your thought inside your heart.
The day of destiny waits for the free man as well
as for the man enslaved beneath an alien hand.
If you know any better course than mine, tell me.   105

Chorus

In reverence for your father's tomb as if it were
an altar, I will speak my heart's thought, as you ask.

Electra

Tell me then, please, as you respect my father's grave.

Chorus

Say words of grace for those of good will, as you pour.

Electra

Whom of those closest to me can I call my friend?   110

Chorus

Yourself first; all who hate Aegisthus after that.

Electra

You mean these prayers shall be for you, and for myself?

Chorus

You see it now; but it is you whose thought this is.

Electra

Is there some other we should bring in on our side?

Chorus

Remember Orestes, though he wanders far away.   115

Electra

That was well spoken; you did well reminding me.

Chorus

Remember, too, the murderers, and against them . . .

Electra

What shall I say? Guide and instruct my ignorance.

Chorus

Invoke the coming of some man, or more than man.

Electra

To come to judge them, or to give them punishment?   120

Chorus

Say simply: "one to kill them, for the life they took."

Electra

I can ask this, and not be wrong in the gods' eyes?

Chorus

May you not hurt your enemy, when he struck first?

Electra

Almighty herald of the world above, the world
below: Hermes, lord of the dead, help me; announce
my prayers to the charmed spirits underground, who watch   125
over my father's house, that they may hear. Tell Earth
herself, who brings all things to birth, who gives them strength,
then gathers their big yield into herself at last.
I myself pour these lustral waters to the dead,
and speak, and call upon my father: Pity me;   130
pity your own Orestes. How shall we be lords
in our house? We have been sold, and go as wanderers
because our mother bought herself, for us, a man,
Aegisthus, he who helped her hand to cut you down.
Now I am what a slave is, and Orestes lives   135
outcast from his great properties, while they go proud
in the high style and luxury of what you worked

to win. By some good fortune let Orestes come
back home. Such is my prayer, my father. Hear me; hear.
And for myself, grant that I be more temperate   140
of heart than my mother; that I act with purer hand.

Such are my prayers for us; but for our enemies,
father, I pray that your avenger come, that they
who killed you shall be killed in turn, as they deserve.
Between my prayer for good and prayer for good I set   145
this prayer for evil; and I speak it against Them.
For us, bring blessings up into the world. Let Earth
and conquering Justice, and all gods beside, give aid.

Such are my prayers; and over them I pour these drink
offerings. Yours the strain now, yours to make them flower   150
with mourning song, and incantation for the dead.

Chorus

Let the tear fall, that clashes as it dies
as died our fallen lord;
die on this mound that fences good from evil,
washing away the death stain accursed   155
of drink offerings shed. Hear me, oh hear, my lord,
majesty hear me from your dark heart; oh hear.
Let one come, in strength
of spear, some man at arms who will set free the house   160
holding the Scythian bow backbent in his hands,
a barbarous god of war spattering arrows
or closing to slash, with sword hilted fast to his hand.

Electra

Father, the earth has drunk my offerings poured to you.
Something has happened here, my women. Help me now.   165

Chorus

Speak, if you will. My heart is in a dance of fear.

Electra

Someone has cut a strand of hair and laid it on
the tomb.

Chorus

What man? Or was it some deep-waisted girl?

Electra

There is a mark, which makes it plain for any to guess.   170

Chorus

Explain, and let your youth instruct my elder age.

Electra

No one could have cut off this strand, except myself.

Chorus

Those others, whom it would have become, are full of hate.

Electra

Yet here it is, and for appearance matches well . . .

Chorus

With whose hair? Tell me. This is what I long to know. . . .   175

Electra

With my own hair. It is almost exactly like.

Chorus

Can it then be a secret gift from Orestes?

Electra

It seems that it must be nobody's hair but his.

Chorus

Did Orestes dare to come back here? How could this be?

Electra

He sent this severed strand, to do my father grace.   180

Chorus

It will not stop my tears if you are right. You mean
that he can never again set foot upon this land.

Electra

The bitter wash has surged upon my heart as well.
I am struck through, as by the cross-stab of a sword,

and from my eyes the thirsty and unguarded drops   185
burst in a storm of tears like winter rain, as I
look on this strand of hair. How could I think some other
man, some burgess, could ever go grand in hair like this?
She never could have cut it, she who murdered him
and is my mother, but no mother in her heart   190
which has assumed God's hate and hates her children. No.
And yet, how can I say in open outright confidence
this is a treasured token from the best beloved
of men to me, Orestes? Does hope fawn on me?
Ah
I wish it had the kind voice of a messenger   195
so that my mind would not be torn in two, I not
shaken, but it could tell me plain to throw this strand
away as vile, if it was cut from a hated head,
or like a brother could have mourned with me, and been
a treasured splendor for my father, and his grave.   200

The gods know, and we call upon the gods; they know
how we are spun in circles like seafarers, in
what storms. But if we are to win, and our ship live,
from one small seed could burgeon an enormous tree.

But see, here is another sign. Footprints are here.   205
The feet that made them are alike, and look like mine.
There are two sets of footprints: of the man who gave
his hair, and one who shared the road with him. I step
where he has stepped, and heelmarks, and the space between
his heel and toe are like the prints I make. Oh, this   210
is torment, and my wits are going.

(*Orestes comes from his place of concealment.*)

Orestes

Pray for what is to come, and tell the gods that they
have brought your former prayers to pass. Pray for success.

Electra

Upon what ground? What have I won yet from the gods?

Orestes

You have come in sight of all you long since prayed to see. 215

Electra

How did you know what man was subject of my prayer?

Orestes

I know about Orestes, how he stirred your heart.

Electra

Yes; but how am I given an answer to my prayers?

Orestes

Look at me. Look for no one closer to you than I.

Electra

Is this some net of treachery, friend, you catch me in? 220

Orestes

Then I must be contriving plots against myself.

Electra

It is your pleasure to laugh at my unhappiness.

Orestes

I only mock my own then, if I laugh at you.

Electra

Are you really Orestes? Can I call you by that name?

Orestes

You see my actual self and are slow to learn. And yet 225
you saw this strand of hair I cut in sign of grief
and shuddered with excitement, for you thought you saw
me, and again when you were measuring my tracks.
Now lay the severed strand against where it was cut
and see how well your brother's hair matches my head. 230
Look at this piece of weaving, the work of your hand
with its blade strokes and figured design of beasts. No, no,
control yourself, and do not lose your head for joy.
I know those nearest to us hate us bitterly.

Electra

O dearest, treasured darling of my father's house,   235
hope of the seed of our salvation, wept for, trust
your strength of hand, and win your father's house again.
O bright beloved presence, you bring back four lives
to me. To call you father is constraint of fact,
and all the love I could have borne my mother turns   240
your way, while she is loathed as she deserves; my love
for a pitilessly slaughtered sister turns to you.
And now you were my steadfast brother after all.
You alone bring me honor; but let Force, and Right,
and Zeus almighty, third with them, be on your side.   245

Orestes

Zeus, Zeus, direct all that we try to do. Behold
the orphaned children of the eagle-father, now
that he has died entangled in the binding coils
of the deadly viper, and the young he left behind
are worn with hunger of starvation, not full grown   250
to bring their shelter slain food, as their father did.
I, with my sister, whom I name, Electra here,
stand in your sight, children whose father is lost. We both
are driven from the house that should be ours. If you
destroy these fledgelings of a father who gave you   255
sacrifice and high honor, from what hand like his
shall you be given the sacred feast which is your right?
Destroy the eagle's brood, and you have no more means
to send your signs to mortals for their strong belief;
nor, if the stump rot through on this baronial tree,   260
shall it sustain your altars on sacrificial days.
Safe keep it: from a little thing you can raise up
a house to grandeur, though it now seem overthrown.

Chorus

O children, silence! Saviors of your father's house,
be silent, children. Otherwise someone may hear   265
and for mere love of gossip carry news of all

you do, to those in power, to those I long to see
some day as corpses in the leaking pitch and flame.

Orestes

The big strength of Apollo's oracle will not
forsake me. For he charged me to win through this hazard,   270
with divination of much, and speech articulate,
the winters of disaster under the warm heart
were I to fail against my father's murderers;
told me to cut them down in their own fashion, turn
to the bull's fury in the loss of my estates.   275
He said that else I must myself pay penalty
with my own life, and suffer much sad punishment;
spoke of the angers that come out of the ground from those
beneath who turn against men; spoke of sicknesses,
ulcers that ride upon the flesh, and cling, and with   280
wild teeth eat away the natural tissue, how on this
disease shall grow in turn a leprous fur. He spoke
of other ways again by which the avengers might
attack, brought to fulfilment from my father's blood.
For the dark arrow of the dead men underground   285
from those within my blood who fell and turn to call
upon me; madness and empty terror in the night
on one who sees clear and whose eyes move in the dark,
must tear him loose and shake him until, with all his bulk
degraded by the bronze-loaded lash, he lose his city.   290
And such as he can have no share in the communal bowl
allowed them, no cup filled for friends to drink. The wrath
of the father comes unseen on them to drive them back
from altars. None can take them in nor shelter them.
Dishonored and unloved by all the man must die   295
at last, shrunken and wasted away in painful death.

Shall I not trust such oracles as this? Or if
I do not trust them, here is work that must be done.
Here numerous desires converge to drive me on:
the god's urgency and my father's passion, and   300

with these the loss of my estates wears hard on me;
the thought that these my citizens, most high renowned
of men, who toppled Troy in show of courage, must
go subject to this brace of women; since his heart
is female; or, if it be not, that soon will show.   305

Chorus

Almighty Destinies, by the will
of Zeus let these things
be done, in the turning of Justice.
For the word of hatred spoken, let hate
be a word fulfilled. The spirit of Right   310
cries out aloud and extracts atonement
due: blood stroke for the stroke of blood
shall be paid. Who acts, shall endure. So speaks
the voice of the age-old wisdom.

Orestes

Father, o my dread father, what thing   315
can I say, can I accomplish
from this far place where I stand, to mark
and reach you there in your chamber
with light that will match your dark?
Yet it is called an action   320
of grace to mourn in style for the house,
once great, of the sons of Atreus.

Chorus

Child, when the fire burns
and tears with teeth at the dead man
it can not wear out the heart of will.   325
He shows his wrath in the after-
days. One dies, and is dirged.
Light falls on the man who killed him.
He is hunted down by the deathsong
for sires slain and for fathers,   330
disturbed, and stern, and enormous.

Electra

    Hear me, my father; hear in turn
    all the tears of my sorrows.
    Two children stand at your tomb to sing
    the burden of your death chant.   335
    Your grave is shelter to suppliants,
    shelter to the outdriven.
    What here is good; what escape from grief?
    Can we outwrestle disaster?

Chorus

    Yet from such as this the god, if he will,   340
    can work out strains that are fairer.
    For dirges chanted over the grave
    the winner's song in the lordly house;
    bring home to new arms the beloved.

Orestes

    If only at Ilium,   345
    father, and by some Lycian's hands
    you had gone down at the spear's stroke,
    you would have left high fame in your house,
    in the going forth of your children
    eyes' admiration;   350
    founded the deep piled bank of earth
    for grave by the doubled water
    with light lift for your household;

Chorus

    loved then by those he loved
    down there beneath the ground   355
    who died as heroes, he would have held
    state, and a lord's majesty,
    vassal only to those most great,
    the Kings of the under darkness.
    For he was King on earth when he lived   360
    over those whose hands held power of life
    and death, and the staff of authority.

Electra

> No, but not under Troy's
> ramparts, father, should you have died,
> nor, with the rest of the spearstruck hordes   365
> have found your grave by Scamandrus' crossing.
> Sooner, his murderers
> should have been killed, as he was,
> by those they loved, and have found their death,
> and men remote from this outrage   370
> had heard the distant story.

Chorus

> Child, child, you are dreaming, since dreaming is a light
> pastime, of fortune more golden than gold
> or the Blessed Ones north of the North Wind.
> But the stroke of the twofold lash is pounding   375
> close, and powers gather under ground
> to give aid. The hands of those who are lords
> are unclean, and these are accursed.
> Power grows on the side of the children.

Orestes

> This cry has come to your ear   380
> like a deep driven arrow.
> Zeus, Zeus, force up from below
> ground the delayed destruction
> on the hard heart and the daring
> hand, for the right of our fathers.   385

Chorus

> May I claim right to close the deathsong
> chanted in glory across
> the man speared and the woman
> dying. Why darken what deep within me forever
> flitters? Long since against the heart's   390
> stem a bitter wind has blown
> thin anger and burdened hatred.

Electra

> May Zeus, from all shoulder's strength,
> pound down his fist upon them,   395
> ohay, smash their heads.
> Let the land once more believe.
> There has been wrong done. I ask for right.
> Hear me, Earth. Hear me, grandeurs of Darkness.

Chorus

> It is but law that when the red drops have been spilled   400
> upon the ground they cry aloud for fresh
> blood. For the death act calls out on Fury
> to bring out of those who were slain before
> new ruin on ruin accomplished.

Orestes

> Hear me, you lordships of the world below.   405
> Behold in assembled power, curses come from the dead,
> behold the last of the sons of Atreus, foundering
> lost, without future, cast
> from house and right. O god, where shall we turn?

Chorus

> The heart jumped in me once again   410
> to hear this unhappy prayer.
> I was disconsolate then
> and the deep heart within
> darkened to hear you speak it.
> But when strength came back hope lifted   415
> me again, and the sorrow
> was gone and the light was on me.

Electra

> Of what thing can we speak, and strike more close,
> than of the sorrows they who bore us have given?
> So let her fawn if she likes. It softens not.   420
> For we are bloody like the wolf
> and savage born from the savage mother.

Chorus

> I struck my breast in the stroke-style of the Arian,
> the Cissian mourning woman,
> and the hail-beat of the drifting fists was there to see   425
> as the rising pace went in a pattern of blows
> downward and upward until the crashing strokes
> played on my hammered, my all-stricken head.

Electra

> O cruel, cruel
> all daring mother, in cruel processional   430
> with all his citizens gone,
> with all sorrow for him forgotten
> you dared bury your unbewept lord.

Orestes

> O all unworthy of him, that you tell me.
> Shall she not pay for this dishonor   435
> for all the immortals,
> for all my own hands can do?
> Let me but take her life and die for it.

Chorus

> Know then, they hobbled him beneath the armpits,
> with his own hands. She wrought so, in his burial   440
> to make his death a burden
> beyond your strength to carry.
> The mutilation of your father. Hear it.

Electra

> You tell of how my father was murdered. Meanwhile I   445
> stood apart, dishonored, nothing worth,
> in the dark corner, as you would kennel a vicious dog,
> and burst in an outrush of tears, that came that day
> where smiles would not, and hid the streaming of my grief.
> Hear such, and carve the letters of it on your heart.   450

Chorus

    Let words such as these
    drip deep in your ears, but on a quiet heart.
    So far all stands as it stands;
    what is to come, yourself burn to know.
    You must be hard, give no ground, to win home.   455

Orestes

    I speak to you. Be with those you love, my father.

Electra

    And I, all in my tears, ask with him.

Chorus

    We gather into murmurous revolt. Hear
    us, hear. Come back into the light.
    Be with us against those we hate.   460

Orestes

    Warstrength shall collide with warstrength; right with right.

Electra

    O gods, be just in what you bring to pass.

Chorus

    My flesh crawls as I listen to them pray.
    The day of doom has waited long.
    They call for it. It may come.   465

    O pain grown into the race
    and blood-dripping stroke
    and grinding cry of disaster,
    moaning and impossible weight to bear.
    Sickness that fights all remedy.   470

    Here in the house there lies
    the cure for this, not to be brought
    from outside, never from others
    but in themselves, through the fierce wreck and bloodshed.
    Here is a song sung to the gods beneath us.   475

Hear then, you blessed ones under the ground,
and answer these prayers with strength on our side,
free gift for your children's conquest.

Orestes

Father, o King who died no kingly death, I ask
the gift of lordship at your hands, to rule your house.   480

Electra

I too, my father, ask of you such grace as this:
to murder Aegisthus with strong hand, and then go free.

Orestes

So shall your memory have the feasts that men honor
in custom. Otherwise when feasts are gay, and portions
burn for the earth, you shall be there, and none give heed.   485

Electra

I too out of my own full dowership shall bring
libations for my bridal from my father's house.
Of all tombs, yours shall be the lordliest in my eyes.

Orestes

O Earth, let my father emerge to watch me fight.

Electra

Persephone, grant still the wonder of success.   490

Orestes

Think of that bath, father, where you were stripped of life.

Electra

Think of the casting net that they contrived for you.

Orestes

They caught you like a beast in toils no bronzesmith made.

Electra

Rather, hid you in shrouds that were thought out in shame.

Orestes

Will you not waken, father, to these challenges?   495

Electra

Will you not rear upright that best beloved head?

Orestes

Send out your right to battle on the side of those
you love, or give us holds like those they caught you in.
For they threw you. Would you not see them thrown in turn?

Electra

Hear one more cry, father, from me. It is my last.   500
Your nestlings huddle suppliant at your tomb: look forth
and pity them, female with the male strain alike.
Do not wipe out this seed of the Pelopidae.
So, though you died, you shall not yet be dead, for when
a man dies, children are the voice of his salvation   505
afterward. Like corks upon the net, these hold
the drenched and flaxen meshes, and they will not drown.
Hear us, then. Our complaints are for your sake, and if
you honor this our argument, you save yourself.

Chorus

None can find fault with the length of this discourse you drew   510
out, to show honor to a grave and fate unwept
before. The rest is action. Since your heart is set
that way, now you must strike and prove your destiny.

Orestes

So. But I am not wandering from my strict course
when I ask why she sent these libations, for what cause   515
she acknowledges, too late, a crime for which there is
no cure. Here was a wretched grace brought to a man
dead and unfeeling. This I fail to understand.
The offerings are too small for the act done. Pour out
all your possessions to atone one act of blood,   520
you waste your work, it is all useless, reason says.
Explain me this, for I would learn it, if you know.

Chorus

> I know, child, I was there. It was the dreams she had.
> The godless woman had been shaken in the night
> by floating terrors, when she sent these offerings.   525

Orestes

> Do you know the dream, too? Can you tell it to me right?

Chorus

> She told me herself. She dreamed she gave birth to a snake.

Orestes

> What is the end of the story then? What is the point?

Chorus

> She laid it swathed for sleep as if it were a child.

Orestes

> A little monster. Did it want some kind of food?   530

Chorus

> She herself, in the dream, gave it her breast to suck.

Orestes

> How was her nipple not torn by such a beastly thing?

Chorus

> It was. The creature drew in blood along with the milk.

Orestes

> No void dream this. It is the vision of a man.

Chorus

> She woke screaming out of her sleep, shaky with fear,   535
> as torches kindled all about the house, out of
> the blind dark that had been on them, to comfort the queen.
> So now she sends these mourning offerings to be poured
> and hopes they are medicinal for her disease.

Orestes

> But I pray to the earth and to my father's grave   540
> that this dream is for me and that I will succeed.

See, I divine it, and it coheres all in one piece.
If this snake came out of the same place whence I came,
if she wrapped it in robes, as she wrapped me, and if
its jaws gaped wide around the breast that suckled me, 545
and if it stained the intimate milk with an outburst
of blood, so that for fright and pain she cried aloud,
it follows then, that as she nursed this hideous thing
of prophecy, she must be cruelly murdered. I
turn snake to kill her. This is what the dream portends. 550

Chorus

I choose you my interpreter to read these dreams.
So may it happen. Now you must rehearse your side
in their parts. For some, this means the parts they must not play.

Orestes

Simple to tell them. My sister here must go inside.
I charge her to keep secret what we have agreed, 555
so that, as they by treachery killed a man of high
degree, by treachery tangled in the self same net
they too shall die, in the way Loxias has ordained,
my lord Apollo, whose word was never false before.
Disguised as an outlander, for which I have all gear, 560
I shall go to the outer gates with Pylades
whom you see here. He is hereditary friend
and companion-in-arms of my house. We two shall both assume
the Parnassian dialect and imitate the way
they talk in Phocis. If none at the door will take us in 565
kindly, because the house is in a curse of ills,
we shall stay there, till anybody who goes by
the house will wonder why we are shut out, and say:
"why does Aegisthus keep the suppliant turned away
from his gates, if he is hereabouts and knows of this?" 570
But if I once cross the doorstone of the outer gates
and find my man seated upon my father's throne,
or if he comes down to confront me, and uplifts
his eyes to mine, then lets them drop again, be sure,

before he can say: "where does the stranger come from?" I   575
shall plunge my sword with lightning speed, and drop him dead.
Our Fury who is never starved for blood shall drink
for the third time a cupful of unwatered blood.

Electra, keep a careful eye on all within
the house, so that our plans will hold together. You,   580
women: I charge you, hold your tongues religiously.
Be silent if you must, or speak in the way that will
help us. And now I call upon the god who stands
close, to look on, and guide the actions of my sword.

(*Exeunt Orestes and Pylades. Exit separately, Electra.*)

Chorus

Numberless, the earth breeds   585
dangers, and the sober thought of fear.
The bending sea's arms swarm
with bitter, savage beasts.
Torches blossom to burn along
the high space between ground and sky.   590
Things fly, and things walk the earth.
Remember too
the storm and wrath of the whirlwind.

But who can recount all
the high daring in the will   595
of man, and in the stubborn hearts of women
the all-adventurous passions
that couple with man's overthrow.
The female force, the desperate
love crams its resisted way   600
on marriage and the dark embrace
of brute beasts, of mortal men.

Let him, who goes not on flimsy wings
of thought, learn from her,
Althaea, Thestius'
daughter: who maimed her child, and hard   605
of heart, in deliberate guile

set fire to the bloody torch, her own son's
agemate, that from the day he emerged
from the mother's womb crying
shared the measure of all his life   610
down to the marked death day.

And in the legends there is one more, a girl
of blood, figure of hate
who, for the enemy's   615
sake killed one near in blood, seduced by the wrought
golden necklace from Crete,
wherewith Minos bribed her. She sundered
from Nisus his immortal hair
as he all unsuspecting   620
breathed in a tranquil sleep. Foul wretch,
Hermes of death has got her now.

Since I recall cruelties from quarrels long
ago, in vain, and married love turned to bitterness
a house would fend far away   625
by curse; the guile, treacheries of the woman's heart
against a lord armored in
power, a lord his enemies revered,
I prize the hearth not inflamed within the house,
the woman's right pushed not into daring.   630

Of all foul things legends tell the Lemnian
outranks, a vile wizard's charm, detestable
so that man names a hideous
crime "Lemnian" in memory of their wickedness.
When once the gods loathe a breed   635
of men they go outcast and forgotten.
No man respects what the gods have turned against.
What of these tales I gather has no meaning?

The sword edges near the lungs.
It stabs deep, bittersharp,   640
and right drives it. For that which had no right

lies not yet stamped into the ground, although
one in sin transgressed Zeus' majesty.   645

Right's anvil stands staunch on the ground
and the smith, Destiny, hammers out the sword.
Delayed in glory, pensive from
the murk, Vengeance brings home at last   650
a child, to wipe out the stain of blood shed long ago.

(Enter Orestes and Pylades.)

Orestes

In there! Inside! Does anyone hear me knocking at
the gate? I will try again. Is anyone at home?
Try a third time. I ask for someone to come from the house,   655
if Aegisthus lets it welcome friendly visitors.

Servant (inside)

All right, I hear you. Where does the stranger come from, then?

Orestes

Announce me to the masters of the house. It is
to them I come, and I have news for them to hear.
And be quick, for the darkening chariot of night   660
leans to its course; the hour for wayfarers to drop
anchor in some place that entertains all travelers.
Have someone of authority in the house come out,
the lady of the place or, more appropriately,
its lord, for then no delicacy in speaking blurs   665
the spoken word. A man takes courage and speaks out
to another man, and makes clear everything he means.

(Enter Clytaemestra.)

Clytaemestra

Friends, tell me only what you would have, and it is yours.
We have all comforts that go with a house like ours,
hot baths, and beds to charm away your weariness   670
with rest, and the regard of temperate eyes. But if
you have some higher business, more a matter of state,
that is the men's concern, and I will tell them of it.

Orestes

I am a Daulian stranger out of Phocis. As
I traveled with my pack and my own following   675
making for Argos, where my feet are rested now,
I met a man I did not know, nor did he know
me, but he asked what way I took, and told me his.
It was a Phocian, Strophius; for he told me his name
and said: "Friend, since in any case you make for Argos,   680
remember carefully to tell Orestes' parents
that he is dead; please do not let it slip your mind.
Then, if his people decide to have him brought back home,
or bury him where he went to live, all outlander
forever, carry their requests again to me.   685
For as it is the bronze walls of an urn close in
the ashes of a man who has been deeply mourned."

So much I know, no more. But whether I now talk
with those who have authority and concern in this
I do not know. I think his father should be told.   690

Clytaemestra

Ah me. You tell us how we are stormed from head to heel.
Oh curse upon our house, bitter antagonist,
how far your eyes range. What was clean out of your way
your archery brings down with a distant deadly shot
to strip unhappy me of all I ever loved.   695
Even Orestes now! He was so well advised
to keep his foot clear of this swamp of death. But now
set down as traitor the hope that was our healer once
and made us look for a bright revel in our house.

Orestes

I could have wished, with hosts so prosperous as you,   700
to have made myself known by some more gracious news
and so been entertained by you. For what is there
more kindly than the feeling between host and guest?
Yet it had been abuse of duty in my heart

had I not given so great a matter to his friends,   705
being so bound by promise and the stranger's rights.

Clytaemestra

You shall not find that your reception falls below
your worth, nor be any the less our friend for this.
Some other would have brought the news in any case.
But it is the hour for travelers who all day have trudged   710
the long road, to be given the rest that they deserve.
Escort this gentleman with his companion and
his men, to where our masculine friends are made at home.
Look after them, in manner worthy of a house
like ours; you are responsible for their good care.   715
Meanwhile, we shall communicate these matters to
the masters of the house, and with our numerous friends
deliberate the issues of this fatal news.

(Exeunt all but the Chorus.)

Chorus

Handmaidens of this house, who help our cause,
how can our lips frame   720
some force that will show for Orestes?
O Lady Earth, Earth Queen, who now
ride mounded over the lord of ships
where the King's corpse lies buried,
hear us, help us.   725
Now the time breaks for Persuasion in stealth
to go down to the pit, with Hermes of death
and the dark, to direct
trial by the sword's fierce edge.

I think our newcomer is at his deadly work;   730
I see Orestes' old nurse coming forth, in tears.

(Enter Cilissa.)

Now where away, Cilissa, through the castle gates,
with sorrow as your hireless fellow-wayfarer?

Cilissa

The woman who is our mistress told me to make haste
and summon Aegisthus for the strangers, "so that he   735
can come and hear, as man to man, in more detail
this news that they have brought." She put a sad face on
before the servants, to hide the smile inside her eyes
over this work that has been done so happily
for her—though on this house the curse is now complete   740
from the plain story that the stranger men have brought.
But as for that Aegisthus, oh, he will be pleased
enough to hear the story. Poor unhappy me,
all my long-standing mixture of misfortunes, hard
burden enough, here in this house of Atreus,   745
when it befell me made the heart ache in my breast.
But never yet did I have to bear a hurt like this.
I took the other troubles bravely as they came:
but now, darling Orestes! I wore out my life
for him. I took him from his mother, brought him up.   750
There were times when he screamed at night and woke me from
my rest; I had to do many hard tasks, and now
useless; a baby is like a beast, it does not think
but you have to nurse it, do you not, the way it wants.
For the child still in swaddling clothes can not tell us   755
if he is hungry or thirsty, if he needs to make
water. Children's young insides are a law to themselves.
I needed second sight for this, and many a time
I think I missed, and had to wash the baby's clothes.
The nurse and laundrywoman had a combined duty   760
and that was I. I was skilled in both handicrafts,
and so Orestes' father gave him to my charge.
And now, unhappy, I am told that he is dead
and go to take the story to that man who has
defiled our house; he will be glad to hear such news.   765

Chorus

Did she say he should come back armed in any way?

Cilissa

How, armed? Say it again. I do not understand.

Chorus

Was he to come with bodyguards, or by himself?

Cilissa

She said to bring his followers, the men-at-arms.

Chorus

Now, if you hate our master, do not tell him that,   770
but simply bid him come as quickly as he can
and cheerfully. In that way he will not take fright.
It is the messenger who makes the bent word straight.

Cilissa

But are you happy over what I have told you?

Chorus

Perhaps: if Zeus might turn our evil wind to good.   775

Cilissa

How so? Orestes, once hope of the house, is gone.

Chorus

Not yet. It would be a poor seer who saw it thus.

Cilissa

What is this? Have you some news that has not been told?

Chorus

Go on and take your message, do as you were bid.
The gods' concerns are what concern only the gods.   780

Cilissa

I will go then and do all this as you have told
me to. May all be for the best. So grant us god.

(Exit Cilissa.)

Chorus

Now to my supplication, Zeus,
father of Olympian gods,

grant that those who struggle hard to see   785
temperate things done in the house win their aim
in full. All that I spoke
was spoken in right. Yours, Zeus, to protect.

Zeus, Zeus, make him who is now
in the house stand above those who   790
hate. If you rear him to greatness,
double and three times
and blithely he will repay you.

See the colt of this man whom you loved
harnessed to the chariot   795
of suffering. Set upon the race he runs
sure control. Make us not see him break
stride, but clean down the course
hold the strain of his striding speed.

You that, deep in the house   800
sway their secret pride of wealth,
hear us, gods of sympathy.
For things done in time past
wash out the blood in fair-spoken verdict.
Let the old murder in   805
the house breed no more.

And you, who keep, magnificent, the hallowed and huge
cavern, o grant that the man's house lift up its head
and look on the shining of daylight
and liberty with eyes made
glad with gazing out from the helm of darkness.   810

And with right may the son
of Maia lend his hand, strong to send
wind fair for action, if he will.
Much else lies secret he may show at need.   815
He speaks the markless word, by
night hoods darkness on the eyes
nor shows more plainly when the day is there.

Then at last we shall sing
for deliverance of the house   820
the woman's song that sets the wind
fair, no thin drawn and grief
struck wail, but this: "The ship sails fair."
My way, mine, the advantage piles here, with wreck
and ruin far from those I love.   825

Be not fear struck when your turn comes in the action
but with a great cry *Father*
when she cries *Child* to you
go on through with the innocent murder.   830

Yours to raise high within
your body the heart of Perseus
and for those under the ground you loved
and those yet above, exact
what their bitter passion may desire; make   835
disaster a thing of blood inside the house;
wipe out the man stained with murder.

(Enter Aegisthus.)

Aegisthus

It is not without summons that I come, but called
by messenger, with news that there are strangers here
arrived, telling a story that brings no delight: 840
the death of Orestes. For our house, already bitten
and poisoned, to take this new load upon itself
would be a thing of dripping fear and blood. Yet how
shall I pass upon these rumors? As the living truth?
For messages made out of women's terror leap   845
high in the upward air and empty die. Do *you*
know anything of this by which to clear my mind?

Chorus

We heard, yes. But go on inside and hear it from
the strangers. Messengers are never quite so sure
as a man's questions answered by the men themselves.   850

Aegisthus

    I wish to question, carefully, this messenger
    and learn if he himself was by when the man died
    or if he heard but some blind rumor and so speaks.
    The mind has eyes, not to be easily deceived.

                           (Exit Aegisthus.)

Chorus

    Zeus, Zeus, what shall I say, where make   855
    a beginning of prayer for the gods' aid?
    My will is good
    but how shall I speak to match my need?
    The bloody edges of the knives that rip
    man-flesh are moving to work. It will mean   860
    utter and final ruin imposed
    on Agamemnon's
    house: or our man will kindle a flame
    and light of liberty, win the domain
    and huge treasure again of his fathers.   865
    Forlorn challenger, though blessed by god,
    Orestes must come to grips with two,
    so wrestle. Yet may he throw them.

                (A cry is heard from inside the house.)

    Listen, it goes   870
    but how? What has been done in the house?
    Stand we aside until the work is done, for so
    we shall not seem to be accountable in this
    foul business. For the fight is done, the issue drawn.

                (Enter a follower of Aegisthus.)

Follower

    O sorrow, all is sorrow for our stricken lord.   875
    Raise up again a triple cry of sorrow, for
    Aegisthus lives no longer. Open there, open
    quick as you may, and slide back the doorbars on the women's
    gates. It will take the strength of a young arm, but not
    to fight for one who is dead and done for. What use there?   880

Ahoy!
My cry is to the deaf and I babble in vain
at sleepers to no purpose. Clytaemestra, where
is she, does what? Her neck is on the razor's edge
and ripe for lopping, as she did to others before.

(*Enter Clytaemestra.*)

Clytaemestra

What is this, and why are you shouting in the house?　　　885

Follower

I tell you, he is alive and killing the dead.

Clytaemestra

Ah, so. You speak in riddles, but I read the rhyme.
We have been won with the treachery by which we slew.
Bring me quick, somebody, an ax to kill a man

(*Exit follower.*)

and we shall see if we can beat him before we　　　890
go down—so far gone are we in this wretched fight.

(*Enter Orestes and Pylades with swords drawn.*)

Orestes

I want you also: the other one has had enough.

Clytaemestra

Beloved, strong Aegisthus, are you dead indeed?

Orestes

You love your man, then? You shall lie in the same grave
with him, and never be unfaithful even in death.　　　895

Clytaemestra

Hold, my son. Oh take pity, child, before this breast
where many a time, a drowsing baby, you would feed
and with soft gums sucked in the milk that made you strong.

Orestes

What shall I do, Pylades? Be shamed to kill my mother?

Pylades

What then becomes thereafter of the oracles   900
declared by Loxias at Pytho? What of sworn oaths?
Count all men hateful to you rather than the gods.

Orestes

I judge that you win. Your advice is good.

(To Clytaemestra.)

Come here.
My purpose is to kill you over his body.
You thought him bigger than my father while he lived.   905
Die then and sleep beside him, since he is the man
you love, and he you should have loved got only your hate.

Clytaemestra

I raised you when you were little. May I grow old with you?

Orestes

You killed my father. Would you make your home with me?

Clytaemestra

Destiny had some part in that, my child.

Orestes

Why then   910
destiny has so wrought that this shall be your death.

Clytaemestra

A mother has her curse, child. Are you not afraid?

Orestes

No. You bore me and threw me away, to a hard life.

Clytaemestra

I sent you to a friend's house. This was no throwing away.

Orestes

I was born of a free father. You sold me.   915

Clytaemestra

So? Where then is the price that I received for you?

Orestes

I could say. It would be indecent to tell you.

Clytaemestra

Or if you do, tell also your father's vanities.

Orestes

Blame him not. He suffered while you were sitting here at home.

Clytaemestra

It hurts women to be kept from their men, my child.   920

Orestes

The man's hard work supports the women who sit at home.

Clytaemestra

I think, child, that you mean to kill your mother.

Orestes

                                                  No.

It will be you who kill yourself. It will not be I.

Clytaemestra

Take care. Your mother's curse, like dogs, will drag you down.

Orestes

How shall I escape my father's curse, if I fail here?   925

Clytaemestra

I feel like one who wastes live tears upon a tomb.

Orestes

Yes, this is death, your wages for my father's fate.

Clytaemestra

You are the snake I gave birth to, and gave the breast.

Orestes

Indeed, the terror of your dreams saw things to come
clearly. You killed, and it was wrong. Now suffer wrong.   930

(Orestes and Pylades take Clytaemestra inside the house.)

Chorus

I have sorrow even for this pair in their twofold
downfall. But since Orestes had the hardiness
to end this chain of bloodlettings, here lies our choice,
that the eyes' light in this house shall not utterly die.

Justice came at the last to Priam and all his sons   935
and it was heavy and hard,
but into the house of Agamemnon returned
the double lion, the double assault,
and the Pythian-steered exile
drove home to the hilt   940
vengeance, moving strongly in guidance sent by the god.

Raise up the high cry o over our lordships' house
won free of distress, free of its fortunes wasted
by two stained with murder,
free of its mournful luck.   945

He came back; his work lay in the secret attack
and it was stealthy and hard
but in the fighting his hand was steered by the very daughter
of Zeus: Right we call her,
mortals who speak of her and name her well. Her wind   950
is fury and death visited upon those she hates.

All that Loxias, who on Parnassus holds
the huge, the deep cleft in the ground, shrilled aloud,
by guile that is no guile   955
returns now to assault the wrong done and grown old.
Divinity keeps, we know not how, strength to resist
surrender to the wicked.
The power that holds the sky's majesty wins our worship.   960

Light is here to behold.
The big bit that held our house is taken away.
Rise up, you halls, arise; for time grown too long
you lay tumbled along the ground.

Time brings all things to pass. Presently time shall cross   965
the outgates of the house after the stain is driven
entire from the hearth
by ceremonies that wash clean and cast out the furies.
The dice of fortune shall be thrown once more, and lie
in a fair fall smiling   970
up at the new indwellers come to live in the house.

(The doors of the house open, to show Orestes standing over the
bodies of Clytaemestra and Aegisthus. His attendants display
the robe in which Clytaemestra had entangled Agamem-
non and which she displayed after his murder.)

Orestes

Behold the twin tyrannies of our land, these two
who killed my father and who sacked my house. For a time
they sat upon their thrones and kept their pride of state,   975
and they are lovers still. So may you judge by what
befell them, for as they were pledged their oath abides.
They swore together death for my unhappy sire
and swore to die together. Now they keep their oath.

Behold again, o audience of these evil things,   980
the engine against my wretched father they devised,
the hands' entanglement, the hobbles for his feet.
Spread it out. Stand around me in a circle and
display this net that caught a man. So shall, not my
father, but that great father who sees all, the Sun,   985
look on my mother's sacrilegious handiwork
and be a witness for me in my day of trial
how it was in all right that I achieved this death,
my mother's: for of Aegisthus' death I take no count:
he has his seducer's punishment, no more than law.   990

But she, who plotted this foul death against the man
by whom she carried the weight of children underneath
her zone, burden once loved, shown hard and hateful now,
what does she seem to be? Some water snake, some viper

whose touch is rot even to him who felt no fang   995
strike, by that brutal and wrong daring in her heart.

And this thing: what shall I call it and be right, in all
eloquence? Trap for an animal or winding sheet
for dead man? Or bath curtain? Since it is a net,
robe you could call it, to entangle a man's feet.   1000
Some highwayman might own a thing like this, to catch
the wayfarer and rob him of his money and
so make a living. With a treacherous thing like this
he could take many victims and go warm within.

May no such wife as she was come to live with me.   1005
Sooner, let God destroy me, with no children born.

Chorus

Ah, but the pitiful work.
Dismal the death that was your ending.
He is left alive; pain flowers for him.

Orestes

Did she do it or did she not? My witness is   1010
this great robe. It was thus she stained Aegisthus' sword.
Dip it and dip it again, the smear of blood conspires
with time to spoil the beauty of this precious thing.
Now I can praise him, now I can stand by to mourn
and speak before this web that killed my father; yet   1015
I grieve for the thing done, the death, and all our race.
I have won; but my victory is soiled, and has no pride.

Chorus

There is no mortal man who shall turn
unhurt his life's course to an end not marred.
There is trouble here. There is more to come.   1020

Orestes

I would have you know, I see not how this thing will end.
I am a charioteer whose course is wrenched outside
the track, for I am beaten, my rebellious senses

bolt with me headlong and the fear against my heart
is ready for the singing and dance of wrath. But while   1025
I hold some grip still on my wits, I say publicly
to my friends: I killed my mother not without some right.
My father's murder stained her, and the gods' disgust.
As for the spells that charmed me to such daring, I
give you in chief the seer of Pytho, Loxias. He   1030
declared I could do this and not be charged with wrong.
Of my evasion's punishment I will not speak:
no archery could hit such height of agony.
And look upon me now, how I go armored in
leafed branch and garland on my way to the centrestone   1035
and sanctuary, and Apollo's level place,
the shining of the fabulous fire that never dies,
to escape this blood that is my own. Loxias ordained
that I should turn me to no other shrine than this.
To all men of Argos in time to come I say   1040
they shall be witness, how these evil things were done.
I go, an outcast wanderer from this land, and leave
behind, in life, in death, the name of what I did.

Chorus

No, what you did was well done. Do not therefore bind
your mouth to foul speech. Keep no evil on your lips.   1045
You liberated all the Argive city when
you lopped the heads of these two snakes with one clean stroke.

Orestes

No!
Women who serve this house, they come like gorgons, they
wear robes of black, and they are wreathed in a tangle
of snakes. I can no longer stay.   1050

Chorus

Orestes, dearest to your father of all men
what fancies whirl you? Hold, do not give way to fear.

Orestes

These are no fancies of affliction. They are clear,
and real, and here; the bloodhounds of my mother's hate.

Chorus

It is the blood still wet upon your hands, that makes   1055
this shaken turbulence be thrown upon your sense.

Orestes

Ah, Lord Apollo, how they grow and multiply,
repulsive for the blood drops of their dripping eyes.

Chorus

There is one way to make you clean: let Loxias
touch you, and set you free from these disturbances.   1060

Orestes

You can not see them, but I see them. I am driven
from this place. I can stay here no longer.

                                                    (*Exit.*)

Chorus

May all come right for you then, and may the god look on
you with favor and guard you in kind circumstance.

Here on this house of the kings the third   1065
storm has broken, with wind
from the inward race, and gone its course.
The children were eaten: there was the first
affliction, the curse of Thyestes.
Next came the royal death, when a man   1070
and lord of Achaean armies went down
killed in the bath. Third
is for the savior. He came. Shall I call
it that, or death? Where
is the end? Where shall the fury of fate   1075
be stilled to sleep, be done with?

                                            (*Exeunt.*)

THE

EUMENIDES

Translated by

RICHMOND LATTIMORE

CHARACTERS

Priestess of Apollo, the Pythia

Apollo

Hermes (silent)

Ghost of Clytaemestra

Orestes

Athene

Chorus of Eumenides (Furies)

Second Chorus; women of Athens

Jurymen, herald, citizens of Athens (all silent parts)

THE EUMENIDES

SCENE: *For the first part of the play [1–234) the scene is Delphi, before the*
sanctuary of Pythian Apollo. The action of the rest of the play
(235 to the end) takes place at Athens, on the Acropolis before the
temple of Athene. A simple change in the backdrop will indicate
the shift.

(Enter, alone, the Pythia.)

Pythia

I give first place of honor in my prayer to her
who of the gods first prophesied, the Earth; and next
.to Themis, who succeeded to her mother's place
of prophecy; so runs the legend; and in third
succession, given by free consent, not won by force,   5
another Titan daughter of Earth was seated here.
This was Phoebe. She gave it as a birthday gift
to Phoebus, who is called still after Phoebe's name.
And he, leaving the pond of Delos and the reef,
grounded his ship at the roadstead of Pallas, then   10
made his way to this land and a Parnassian home.
Deep in respect for his degree Hephaestus' sons
conveyed him here, for these are builders of roads, and changed
the wilderness to a land that was no wilderness.
He came so, and the people highly honored him,   15
with Delphus, lord and helmsman of the country. Zeus
made his mind full with godship and prophetic craft
and placed him, fourth in a line of seers, upon this throne.
So, Loxias is the spokesman of his father, Zeus.
    These are the gods I set in the proem of my prayer.   20
But Pallas-before-the-temple has her right in all
I say. I worship the nymphs where the Corycian rock
is hollowed inward, haunt of birds and paced by gods.
Bromius, whom I forget not, sways this place. From here
in divine form he led his Bacchanals in arms   25

to hunt down Pentheus like a hare in the deathtrap.
I call upon the springs of Pleistus, on the power
of Poseidon, and on final loftiest Zeus,
then go to sit in prophecy on the throne. May all
grant me that this of all my entrances shall be   30
the best by far. If there are any Hellenes here
let them draw lots, so enter, as the custom is.
My prophecy is only as the god may guide.

(*She enters the temple and almost immediately comes out again.*)

Things terrible to tell and for the eyes to see
terrible drove me out again from Loxias' house   35
so that I have no strength and cannot stand on springing
feet, but run with hands' help and my legs have no speed.
An old woman afraid is nothing: a child, no more.
   See, I am on my way to the wreath-hung recess
and on the centrestone I see a man with god's   40
defilement on him postured in the suppliant's seat
with blood dripping from his hands and from a new-drawn
   sword,
holding too a branch that had grown high on an olive
tree, decorously wrapped in a great tuft of wool,
and the fleece shone. So far, at least, I can speak clear.   45
   In front of this man slept a startling company
of women lying all upon the chairs. Or not
women, I think I call them rather gorgons, only
not gorgons either, since their shape is not the same.
I saw some creatures painted in a picture once,   50
who tore the food from Phineus, only these had no
wings, that could be seen; they are black and utterly
repulsive, and they snore with breath that drives one back.
From their eyes drips the foul ooze, and their dress is such
as is not right to wear in the presence of the gods'   55
statues, nor even into any human house.
I have never seen the tribe that owns this company
nor know what piece of earth can claim with pride it bore

such brood, and without hurt and tears for labor given.

Now after this the master of the house must take 60
his own measures: Apollo Loxias, who is very strong
and heals by divination; reads portentous signs,
and so clears out the houses others hold as well.

(Exit. The doors of the temple open and show Orestes sur-
rounded by the sleeping Furies, Apollo and
Hermes beside him.)

Apollo

I will not give you up. Through to the end standing
your guardian, whether by your side or far away, 65
I shall not weaken toward your enemies. See now
how I have caught and overpowered these lewd creatures.
The repulsive maidens have been stilled to sleep, those gray
and aged children, they with whom no mortal man,
no god, nor even any beast, will have to do. 70
It was because of evil they were born, because
they hold the evil darkness of the Pit below
Earth, loathed alike by men and by the heavenly gods.
Nevertheless, run from them, never weaken. They
will track you down as you stride on across the long 75
land, and your driven feet forever pound the earth,
on across the main water and the circle-washed
cities. Be herdsman to this hard march. Never fail
until you come at last to Pallas' citadel.
Kneel there, and clasp the ancient idol in your arms, 80
and there we shall find those who will judge this case, and words
to say that will have magic in their figures. Thus
you will be rid of your afflictions, once for all.
For it was I who made you strike your mother down.

Orestes

My lord Apollo, you understand what it means to do 85
no wrong. Learn also what it is not to neglect.
None can mistrust your power to do good, if you will.

« 137 »

Apollo

Remember: the fear must not give you a beaten heart.
Hermes, you are my brother from a single sire.
Look after him, and as you are named the god who guides,   90
be such in strong fact. He is my suppliant. Shepherd him
with fortunate escort on his journeys among men.
The wanderer has rights which Zeus acknowledges.

(*Exit Apollo, then Orestes guided by Hermes. Enter the
ghost of Clytaemestra.*)

Clytaemestra

You would sleep, then? And what use are you, if you sleep?
It is because of you I go dishonored thus   95
among the rest of the dead. Because of those I killed
my bad name among the perished suffers no eclipse
but I am driven in disgrace. I say to you
that I am charged with guilt most grave by these. And yet
I suffered too, horribly, and from those most dear,   100
yet none among the powers is angered for my sake
that I was slaughtered, and by matricidal hands.
Look at these gashes in my heart, think where they came
from. Eyes illuminate the sleeping brain,
but in the daylight man's future cannot be seen.   105
    Yet I have given you much to lap up, outpourings
without wine, sober propitiations, sacrificed
in secrecy of night and on a hearth of fire
for you, at an hour given to no other god.
Now I watch all these honors trampled into the ground,   110
and he is out and gone away like any fawn
so lightly, from the very middle of your nets,
sprung clear, and laughing merrily at you. Hear me.
It is my life depends upon this spoken plea.
Think then, o goddesses beneath the ground. For I,   115
the dream of Clytaemestra, call upon your name.

(*The Furies stir in their sleep and whimper.*)

Clytaemestra

Oh, whimper, then, but your man has got away and gone
far. He has friends to help him, who are not like mine.

(They whimper again.)   120

Clytaemestra

Too much sleep and no pity for my plight. I stand,
his mother, here, killed by Orestes. He is gone.

(They moan in their sleep.)

Clytaemestra

You moan, you sleep. Get on your feet quickly, will you?
What have you yet got done, except to do evil?   125

(They moan again.)

Clytaemestra

Sleep and fatigue, two masterful conspirators,
have dimmed the deadly anger of the mother-snake.

(The Chorus start violently, then speak in their sleep.)

Chorus

Get him, get him, get him, get him. Make sure.   130

Clytaemestra

The beast you are after is a dream, but like the hound
whose thought of hunting has no lapse, you bay him on.
What are you about? Up, let not work's weariness
beat you, nor slacken with sleep so you forget my pain.
Scold your own heart and hurt it, as it well deserves,   135
for this is discipline's spur upon her own. Let go
upon this man the stormblasts of your bloodshot breath,
wither him in your wind, after him, hunt him down
once more, and shrivel him in your vitals' heat and flame.

(The ghost disappears, and the Chorus waken and, as they
waken, speak severally.)

Chorus

Waken. You are awake, wake her, as I did you.   140
You dream still? On your feet and kick your sleep aside.
Let us see whether this morning-song means vanity.

                        (*Here they begin to howl.*)

Sisters, we have had wrong done us.
When I have undergone so much and all in vain.
Suffering, suffering, bitter, oh shame shame,   145
unendurable wrong.
The hunted beast has slipped clean from our nets and gone.
Sleep won me, and I lost my capture.

Shame, son of Zeus! Robber is all you are.
A young god, you have ridden down powers gray with age,   150
taken the suppliant, though a godless man, who hurt
the mother who gave him birth.
Yourself a god, you stole the matricide away.
Where in this act shall any man say there is right?

The accusation came upon me from my dreams,   155
and hit me, as with goad in the mid-grip of his fist
the charioteer strikes,
but deep, beneath lobe and heart.
The executioner's cutting whip is mine to feel   160
and the weight of pain is big, heavy to bear.

Such are the actions of the younger gods. These hold
by unconditional force, beyond all right, a throne
that runs reeking blood,
blood at the feet, blood at the head.
The very stone centre of earth here in our eyes horrible   165
with blood and curse stands plain to see.

Himself divine, he has spoiled his secret shrine's
hearth with the stain, driven and hallooed the action on.   170
He made man's way cross the place of the ways of god
and blighted age-old distributions of power.

He has wounded me, but he shall not get this man away.
Let him hide under the ground, he shall never go free.   175
Cursed suppliant, he shall feel against his head
another murderer rising out of the same seed.

(Apollo enters again from his sanctuary.)

Apollo

Get out, I tell you, go and leave this house. Away
in haste, from your presence set the mantic chamber free,   180
else you may feel the flash and bite of a flying snake
launched from the twisted thong of gold that spans my bow
to make you in your pain spew out the black and foaming
blood of men, vomit the clots sucked from their veins.
This house is no right place for such as you to cling   185
upon; but where, by judgment given, heads are lopped
and eyes gouged out, throats cut, and by the spoil of sex
the glory of young boys is defeated, where mutilation
lives, and stoning, and the long moan of tortured men
spiked underneath the spine and stuck on pales. Listen   190
to how the gods spit out the manner of that feast
your loves lean to. The whole cast of your shape is guide
to what you are, the like of whom should hole in the cave
of the blood-reeking lion, not in oracular
interiors, like mine nearby, wipe off your filth.   195
Out then, you flock of goats without a herdsman, since
no god has such affection as to tend this brood.

Chorus

My lord Apollo, it is your turn to listen now.
Your own part in this is more than accessory.
You are the one who did it; all the guilt is yours.   200

Apollo

So? How? Continue speaking, until I understand.

Chorus

You gave this outlander the word to kill his mother.

Apollo

The word to exact price for his father. What of that?

Chorus

You then dared take him in, fresh from his bloodletting.

Apollo

Yes, and I told him to take refuge in this house.   205

Chorus

You are abusive then to those who sped him here?

Apollo

Yes. It was not for you to come near this house;

Chorus

                                                                            and yet

we have our duty. It was to do what we have done.

Apollo

An office? You? Sound forth your glorious privilege.

Chorus

This: to drive matricides out of their houses.   210

Apollo

                                                                            Then

what if it be the woman and she kills her man?

Chorus

Such murder would not be the shedding of kindred blood.

Apollo

You have made into a thing of no account, no place,
the sworn faith of Zeus and of Hera, lady
of consummations, and Cypris by such argument   215
is thrown away, outlawed, and yet the sweetest things
in man's life come from her, for married love between
man and woman is bigger than oaths, guarded by right
of nature. If when such kill each other you relent
so as not to take vengeance nor eye them in wrath,   220

then I deny your manhunt of Orestes goes
with right. I see that one cause moves you to strong rage
but on the other clearly you are unmoved to act.
Pallas divine shall review the pleadings of this case.

Chorus

Nothing will ever make me let that man go free.   225

Apollo

Keep after him then, and make more trouble for yourselves.

Chorus

Do not try to dock my privilege by argument.

Apollo

I would not take your privilege if you gave it me.

Chorus

No, for you are called great beside the throne of Zeus
already, but the motherblood drives me, and I go   230
to win my right upon this man and hunt him down.

Apollo

But I shall give the suppliant help and rescue, for
if I willingly fail him who turns to me for aid,
his wrath, before gods and men, is a fearful thing.

> (They go out, separately. The scene is now Athens, on the
> Acropolis before the temple and statue of Athene.
> Orestes enters and takes suppliant posture
> at the feet of the statue.)

Orestes

My lady Athene, it is at Loxias' behest   235
I come. Then take in of your grace the wanderer
who comes, no suppliant, not unwashed of hand, but one
blunted at last, and worn and battered on the outland
habitations and the beaten ways of men.
Crossing the dry land and the sea alike, keeping   240
the ordinances of Apollo's oracle

I come, goddess, before your statue and your house
to keep watch here and wait the issue of my trial.

(The Chorus enter severally, looking for Orestes.)

Chorus

So. Here the man has left a clear trail behind; keep on,   245
keep on, as the unspeaking accuser tells us, by
whose sense, like hounds after a bleeding fawn, we trail
our quarry by the splash and drip of blood. And now
my lungs are blown with abundant and with wearisome
work, mankilling. My range has been the entire extent
of land, and, flown unwinged across the open water,   250
I am here, and give way to no ship in my pursuit.
Our man has gone to cover somewhere in this place.
The welcome smell of human blood has told me so.

Look again, look again,
search everywhere, let   255
not the matricide
steal away and escape.

(They see Orestes.)

See there! He clings to defence
again, his arms winding the immortal goddess'
image, so tries to be quit out of our hands.   260
It shall not be. His mother's blood spilled on the ground
can not come back again.
It is all soaked and drained into the ground and gone.

You must give back for her blood from the living man
red blood of your body to suck, and from your own   265
I could feed, with bitter-swallowed drench,
turn your strength limp while yet you live and drag you down
where you must pay for the pain of the murdered mother,
and watch the rest of the mortals stained with violence
against god or guest   270
or hurt parents who were close and dear,
each with the pain upon him that his crime deserves.
Hades is great, Hades calls men to reckoning

there under the ground,
sees all, and cuts it deep in his recording mind.   275

Orestes

I have been beaten and been taught, I understand
the many rules of absolution, where it is right
to speak and where be silent. In this action now
speech has been ordered by my teacher, who is wise.
The stain of blood dulls now and fades upon my hand.   280
My blot of matricide is being washed away.
When it was fresh still, at the hearth of the god, Phoebus,
this was absolved and driven out by sacrifice
of swine, and the list were long if I went back to tell
of all I met who were not hurt by being with me.   285
Time in his aging overtakes all things alike.
Now it is from pure mouth and with good auspices
I call upon Athene, queen of this land, to come
and rescue me. She, without work of her spear, shall win
myself and all my land and all the Argive host   290
to stand her staunch companion for the rest of time.
Whether now ranging somewhere in the Libyan land
beside her father's crossing and by Triton's run
of waters she sets upright or enshrouded foot
rescuing there her friends, or on the Phlegraean flat   295
like some bold man of armies sweeps with eyes the scene,
let her come! She is a god and hears me far away.
So may she set me free from what is at my back.

Chorus

Neither Apollo nor Athene's strength must win
you free, save you from going down forgotten, without   300
knowing where joy lies anywhere inside your heart,
blood drained, chewed dry by the powers of death, a wraith, a
    shell.
You will not speak to answer, spew my challenge away?
You are consecrate to me and fattened for my feast,

and you shall feed me while you live, not cut down first 305
at the altar. Hear the spell I sing to bind you in.

Come then, link we our choral. Ours
to show forth the power
and terror of our music, declare
our rights of office, how we conspire 310
to steer men's lives.
We hold we are straight and just. If a man
can spread his hands and show they are clean,
no wrath of ours shall lurk for him.
Unscathed he walks through his life time. 315
But one like this man before us, with stained
hidden hands, and the guilt upon him,
shall find us beside him, as witnesses
of the truth, and we show clear in the end
to avenge the blood of the murdered. 320

Mother, o my mother night, who gave me
birth, to be a vengeance on the seeing
and the blind, hear me. For Leto's
youngling takes my right away,
stealing from my clutch the prey 325
that crouches, whose blood would wipe
at last the motherblood away.

Over the beast doomed to the fire
this is the chant, scatter of wits,
frenzy and fear, hurting the heart, 330
song of the Furies
binding brain and blighting blood
in its stringless melody.

This the purpose that the all-involving
destiny spun, to be ours and to be shaken 335
never: when mortals assume outrage
of own hand in violence,
these we dog, till one goes

under earth. Nor does death
set them altogether free.   340

Over the beast doomed to the fire
this is the chant, scatter of wits,
frenzy and fear, hurting the heart,
song of the Furies
binding brain and blighting blood   345
in its stringless melody.

When we were born such lots were assigned for our keeping.
So the immortals must hold hands off, nor is there   350
one who shall sit at our feasting.
For sheer white robes I have no right and no portion.

I have chosen overthrow
of houses, where the Battlegod   355
grown within strikes near and dear
down. So we swoop upon this man
here. He is strong, but we wear him down
for the blood that is still wet on him.

Here we stand in our haste to wrench from all others   360
these devisings, make the gods clear of our counsels
so that even appeal comes
not to them, since Zeus has ruled our blood dripping company 365
outcast, nor will deal with us.

I have chosen overthrow
of houses, where the Battlegod
grown within strikes near and dear
down. So we swoop upon this man
here. He is strong, but we wear him down
for the blood that is still wet on him.

Men's illusions in their pride under the sky melt
down, and are diminished into the ground, gone
before the onset of our black robes, pulsing   370
of our vindictive feet against them.

For with a long leap from high
above and dead drop of weight
I bring foot's force crashing down
to cut the legs from under even   375
the runner, and spill him to ruin.

He falls, and does not know in the daze of his folly.
Such in the dark of man is the mist of infection
that hovers, and moaning rumor tells how his house lies
under fog that glooms above.   380

For with a long leap from high
above, and dead drop of weight,
I bring foot's force crashing down
to cut the legs from under even
the runner, and spill him to ruin.

All holds. For we are strong and skilled;
we have authority; we hold
memory of evil; we are stern
nor can men's pleadings bend us. We
drive through our duties, spurned, outcast   385
from gods, driven apart to stand in light
not of the sun. So sheer with rock are ways
for those who see, as upon those whose eyes are lost.

Is there a man who does not fear
this, does not shrink to hear   390
how my place has been ordained,
granted and given by destiny
and god, absolute? Privilege
primeval yet is mine, nor am I without place
though it be underneath the ground   395
and in no sunlight and in gloom that I must stand.

                        (Athene enters, in full armor.)
Athene

From far away I heard the outcry of your call.
It was beside Scamandrus. I was taking seisin
of land, for there the Achaean lords of war and first

fighters gave me large portion of all their spears 400
had won, the land root and stock to be mine for all
eternity, for the sons of Theseus a choice gift.
From there, sped on my weariless feet, I came, wingless
but in the rush and speed of the aegis fold. And now
I see upon this land a novel company 405
which, though it brings no terror to my eyes, brings still
wonder. Who are you? I address you all alike,
both you, the stranger kneeling at my image here,
and you, who are like no seed ever begotten, not 410
seen ever by the gods as goddesses, nor yet
stamped in the likenesses of any human form.
But no. This is the place of the just. Its rights forbid
even the innocent to speak evil of his mates.

Chorus

Daughter of Zeus, you shall hear all compressed to brief 415
measure. We are the gloomy children of the night.
Curses they call us in our homes beneath the ground.

Athene

I know your race, then, and the names by which you are called.

Chorus

You shall be told of our position presently.

Athene

I can know that, if one will give me a clear account. 420

Chorus

We drive from home those who have shed the blood of men.

Athene

Where is the place, then, where the killer's flight shall end?

Chorus

A place where happiness is nevermore allowed.

Athene

Is he one? Do you blast him to this kind of flight?

Chorus

Yes. He murdered his mother by deliberate choice.   425

Athene

By random force, or was it fear of someone's wrath?

Chorus

Where is the spur to justify man's matricide?

Athene

Here are two sides, and only half the argument.

Chorus

He is unwilling to give or to accept an oath.

Athene

You wish to be called righteous rather than act right.   430

Chorus

No. How so? Out of the riches of your wit, explain.

Athene

I say, wrong must not win by technicalities.

Chorus

Examine him then yourself. Decide it, and be fair.

Athene

You would turn over authority in this case to me?

Chorus

By all means. Your father's degree, and yours, deserve as much.   435

Athene

Your turn, stranger. What will you say in answer? Speak,
tell me your country and your birth, what has befallen
you, then defend yourself against the anger of these;
if it was confidence in the right that made you sit
to keep this image near my hearth, a supplicant   440
in the tradition of Ixion, sacrosanct.
Give me an answer which is plain to understand.

Orestes

Lady Athene, first I will take the difficult thought
away that lies in these last words you spoke. I am
no supplicant, nor was it because I had a stain   445
upon my hand that I sat at your image. I
will give you a strong proof that what I say is true.
It is the law that the man of the bloody hand must speak
no word until, by action of one who can cleanse,
blood from a young victim has washed his blood away.   450
Long since, at the homes of others, I have been absolved
thus, both by running waters and by victims slain.

I count this scruple now out of the way. Learn next
with no delay where I am from. I am of Argos
and it is to my honor that you ask the name   455
of my father, Agamemnon, lord of seafarers,
and your companion when you made the Trojan city
of Ilium no city any more. He died
without honor when he came home. It was my mother
of the dark heart, who entangled him in subtle gyves   460
and cut him down. The bath is witness to his death.
I was an exile in the time before this. I came back
and killed the woman who gave me birth. I plead guilty.
My father was dear, and this was vengeance for his blood.
Apollo shares responsibility for this.   465
He counterspurred my heart and told me of pains to come
if I should fail to act against the guilty ones.
This is my case. Decide if it be right or wrong.
I am in your hands. Where my fate falls, I shall accept.

Athene

The matter is too big for any mortal man   470
who thinks he can judge it. Even I have not the right
to analyse cases of murder where wrath's edge
is sharp, and all the more since you have come, and clung
a clean and innocent supplicant, against my doors.
You bring no harm to my city. I respect your rights.   475

Yet these, too, have their work. We cannot brush them aside,
and if this action so runs that they fail to win,
the venom of their resolution will return
to infect the soil, and sicken all my land to death.
Here is dilemma. Whether I let them stay or drive   480
them off, it is a hard course and will hurt. Then, since
the burden of the case is here, and rests on me,
I shall select judges of manslaughter, and swear
them in, establish a court into all time to come.

Litigants, call your witnesses, have ready your proofs   485
as evidence under bond to keep this case secure.
I will pick the finest of my citizens, and come
back. They shall swear to make no judgment that is not
just, and make clear where in this action the truth lies.

                                                          (*Exit.*)

Chorus

Here is overthrow of all   490
the young laws, if the claim
of this matricide shall stand
good, his crime be sustained.
Should this be, every man will find a way
to act at his own caprice;   495
over and over again in time
to come, parents shall await
the deathstroke at their children's hands.

We are the Angry Ones. But we
shall watch no more over works   500
of men, and so act. We shall
let loose indiscriminate death.
Man shall learn from man's lot, forejudge
the evils of his neighbor's case,
see respite and windfall in storm:
pathetic prophet who consoles   505
with strengthless cures, in vain.

Nevermore let one who feels
the stroke of accident, uplift
his voice and make outcry, thus: 510
"Oh Justice!
Throned powers of the Furies, help!"
Such might be the pitiful cry
of some father, of the stricken
mother, their appeal. Now   515
the House of Justice has collapsed.

There are times when fear is good.
It must keep its watchful place
at the heart's controls. There is
advantage   520
in the wisdom won from pain.
Should the city, should the man
rear a heart that nowhere goes
in fear, how shall such a one
any more respect the right?   525

Refuse the life of anarchy;
refuse the life devoted to
one master.
The in-between has the power
by God's grant always, though   530
his ordinances vary.
I will speak in defence
of reason: for the very child
of vanity is violence;
but out of health   535
in the heart issues the beloved
and the longed-for, prosperity.

All for all I say to you:
bow before the altar of right.
You shall not   540
eye advantage, and heel
it over with foot of force.

Vengeance will be upon you.
The all is bigger than you.
Let man see this and take   545
care, to mother and father,
and to the guest
in the gates welcomed, give all rights
that befall their position.

The man who does right, free-willed, without constraint   550
shall not lose happiness
nor be wiped out with all his generation.
But the transgressor, I tell you, the bold man
who brings in confusion of goods unrightly won,
at long last and perforce, when ship toils   555
under tempest must strike his sail
in the wreck of his rigging.

He calls on those who hear not, caught inside
the hard wrestle of water.
The spirit laughs at the hot hearted man,   560
the man who said "never to me," watches him
pinned in distress, unable to run free of the crests.
He had good luck in his life. Now
he smashes it on the reef of Right
and drowns, unwept and forgotten.   565

(Athene re-enters, guiding twelve citizens chosen as jurors
and attended by a herald. Other citizens follow.)

Athene

Herald, make proclamation and hold in the host
assembled. Let the stabbing voice of the Etruscan
trumpet, blown to the full with mortal wind, crash out
its high call to all the assembled populace
For in the filling of this senatorial ground   570
it is best for all the city to be silent and learn
the measures I have laid down into the rest of time.
So too these litigants, that their case be fairly tried.

(Trumpet call. All take their places. Enter Apollo.)

Chorus

  My lord Apollo, rule within your own domain.
  What in this matter has to do with you? Declare.   575

Apollo

  I come to testify. This man, by observed law,
  came to me as suppliant, took his place by hearth and hall,
  and it was I who cleaned him of the stain of blood.
  I have also come to help him win his case. I bear
  responsibility for his mother's murder.

                                        (*To Athene.*)
                                        You   580
  who know the rules, initiate the trial. Preside.

Athene (*to the Furies*)

  I declare the trial opened. Yours is the first word.
  For it must justly be the pursuer who speaks first
  and opens the case, and makes plain what the action is.

Chorus

  We are many, but we shall cut it short. You, then,   585
  word against word answer our charges one by one.
  Say first, did you kill your mother or did you not?

Orestes

  Yes, I killed her. There shall be no denial of that.

Chorus

  There are three falls in the match and one has gone to us.

Orestes

  So you say. But you have not even thrown your man.   590

Chorus

  So. Then how did you kill her? You are bound to say.

Orestes

  I do. With drawn sword in my hand I cut her throat.

Chorus

  By whose persuasion and advice did you do this?

Orestes

By order of this god, here. So he testifies.

Chorus

The Prophet guided you into this matricide?   595

Orestes

Yes. I have never complained of this. I do not now.

Chorus

When sentence seizes you, you will talk a different way.

Orestes

I have no fear. My father will aid me from the grave.

Chorus

Kill your mother, then put trust in a corpse! Trust on.

Orestes

Yes. She was dirtied twice over with disgrace.   600

Chorus

Tell me how, and explain it to the judges here.

Orestes

She murdered her husband, and thereby my father too.

Chorus

Of this stain, death has set her free. But you still live.

Orestes

When she lived, why did you not descend and drive her out?

Chorus

The man she killed was not of blood congenital.   605

Orestes

But am I then involved with my mother by blood-bond?

Chorus

Murderer, yes. How else could she have nursed you beneath
her heart? Do you forswear your mother's intimate blood?

Orestes

Yours to bear witness now, Apollo, and expound
the case for me, if I was right to cut her down.   610
I will not deny I did this thing, because I did
do it. But was the bloodshed right or not? Decide
and answer. As you answer, I shall state my case.

Apollo

To you, established by Athene in your power,
I shall speak justly. I am a prophet, I shall not   615
lie. Never, for man, woman, nor city, from my throne
of prophecy have I spoken a word, except
that which Zeus, father of Olympians, might command.
This is justice. Recognize then how great its strength.
I tell you, follow our father's will. For not even   620
the oath that binds you is more strong than Zeus is strong.

Chorus

Then Zeus, as you say, authorized the oracle
to this Orestes, stating he could wreak the death
of his father on his mother, and it would have no force?

Apollo

It is not the same thing for a man of blood to die   625
honored with the king's staff given by the hand of god,
and that by means of a woman, not with the far cast
of fierce arrows, as an Amazon might have done,
but in a way that you shall hear, o Pallas and you
who sit in state to judge this action by your vote.   630

He had come home from his campaigning. He had done
better than worse, in the eyes of a fair judge. She lay
in wait for him. It was the bath. When he was at
its edge, she hooded the robe on him, and in the blind
and complex toils tangled her man, and chopped him down.   635

There is the story of the death of a great man,
solemn in all men's sight, lord of the host of ships.

I have called the woman what she was, so that the people
whose duty it is to try this case may be inflamed.

Chorus

Zeus, by your story, gives first place to the father's death.   640
Yet Zeus himself shackled elder Cronus, his own
father. Is this not contradiction? I testify,
judges, that this is being said in your hearing.

Apollo

You foul animals, from whom the gods turn in disgust,
Zeus could undo shackles, such hurt can be made good,   645
and there is every kind of way to get out. But once
the dust has drained down all a man's blood, once the man
has died, there is no raising of him up again.
This is a thing for which my father never made
curative spells. All other states, without effort   650
of hard breath, he can completely rearrange.

Chorus

See what it means to force acquittal of this man.
He has spilled his mother's blood upon the ground. Shall he
then be at home in Argos in his father's house?
What altars of the community shall he use? Is there   655
a brotherhood's lustration that will let him in?

Apollo

I will tell you, and I will answer correctly. Watch.
The mother is no parent of that which is called
her child, but only nurse of the new-planted seed
that grows. The parent is he who mounts. A stranger she   660
preserves a stranger's seed, if no god interfere.
I will show you proof of what I have explained. There can
be a father without any mother. There she stands,
the living witness, daughter of Olympian Zeus,
she who was never fostered in the dark of the womb   665
yet such a child as no goddess could bring to birth.
In all else, Pallas, as I best may understand,

I shall make great your city and its populace.
So I have brought this man to sit beside the hearth
of your house, to be your true friend for the rest of time,   670
so you shall win him, goddess, to fight by your side,
and among men to come this shall stand a strong bond
that his and your own people's children shall be friends.

Athene

Shall I assume that enough has now been said, and tell
the judges to render what they believe a true verdict?   675

Chorus

Every arrow we had has been shot now. We wait
on their decision, to see how the case has gone.

Athene

So then. How shall I act correctly in your eyes?

Apollo

You have heard what you have heard, and as you cast your votes,
good friends, respect in your hearts the oath that you have sworn.   680

Athene

If it please you, men of Attica, hear my decree
now, on this first case of bloodletting I have judged.
For Aegeus' population, this forevermore
shall be the ground where justices deliberate.
Here is the Hill of Ares, here the Amazons   685
encamped and built their shelters when they came in arms
for spite of Theseus, here they piled their rival towers
to rise, new city, and dare his city long ago,
and slew their beasts for Ares. So this rock is named
from then the Hill of Ares. Here the reverence   690
of citizens, their fear and kindred do-no-wrong
shall hold by day and in the blessing of night alike
all while the people do not muddy their own laws
with foul infusions. But if bright water you stain
with mud, you nevermore will find it fit to drink.   695

No anarchy, no rule of a single master. Thus
I advise my citizens to govern and to grace,
and not to cast fear utterly from your city. What
man who fears nothing at all is ever righteous? Such
be your just terrors, and you may deserve and have   700
salvation for your citadel, your land's defence,
such as is nowhere else found among men, neither
among the Scythians, nor the land that Pelops held.
I establish this tribunal. It shall be untouched
by money-making, grave but quick to wrath, watchful   705
to protect those who sleep, a sentry on the land.

These words I have unreeled are for my citizens,
advice into the future. All must stand upright
now, take each man his ballot in his hand, think on
his oath, and make his judgment. For my word is said.   710

Chorus

I give you counsel by no means to disregard
this company. We can be a weight to crush your land.

Apollo

I speak too. I command you to fear, and not
make void the yield of oracles from Zeus and me.

Chorus

You honor bloody actions where you have no right.   715
The oracles you give shall be no longer clean.

Apollo

My father's purposes are twisted then. For he
was appealed to by Ixion, the first murderer.

Chorus

Talk! But for my part, if I do not win the case,
I shall come back to this land and it will feel my weight.   720

Apollo

Neither among the elder nor the younger gods
have you consideration. I shall win this suit.

Chorus

Such was your action in the house of Pheres. Then
you beguiled the Fates to let mortals go free from death.

Apollo

Is it not right to do well by the man who shows   725
you worship, and above all when he stands in need?

Chorus

You won the ancient goddesses over with wine
and so destroyed the orders of an elder time.

Apollo

You shall not win the issue of this suit, but shall
be made to void your poison to no enemy's hurt.   730

Chorus

Since you, a young god, would ride down my elder age,
I must stay here and listen to how the trial goes,
being yet uncertain to loose my anger on the state.

Athene

It is my task to render final judgment here.
This is a ballot for Orestes I shall cast.   735
There is no mother anywhere who gave me birth,
and, but for marriage, I am always for the male
with all my heart, and strongly on my father's side.
So, in a case where the wife has killed her husband, lord
of the house, her death shall not mean most to me. And if   740
the other votes are even, then Orestes wins.
You of the jurymen who have this duty assigned,
shake out the ballots from the vessels, with all speed.

Orestes

Phoebus Apollo, what will the decision be?

Chorus

Darkness of night, our mother, are you here to watch?   745

Orestes

This is the end for me. The noose, or else the light.

Chorus

Here our destruction, or our high duties confirmed.

Apollo

Shake out the votes accurately, Athenian friends.
Be careful as you pick them up. Make no mistake.
In the lapse of judgment great disaster comes. The cast   750
of a single ballot has restored a house entire.

Athene

The man before us has escaped the charge of blood.
The ballots are in equal number for each side.

Orestes

Pallas Athene, you have kept my house alive.
When I had lost the land of my fathers you gave me   755
a place to live. Among the Hellenes they shall say:
"A man of Argos lives again in the estates
of his father, all by grace of Pallas Athene, and
Apollo, and with them the all-ordaining god
the Savior"—who remembers my father's death, who looked   760
upon my mother's advocates, and rescues me.
I shall go home now, but before I go I swear
to this your country and to this your multitude
of people into all the bigness of time to be,
that never man who holds the helm of my state shall come   765
against your country in the ordered strength of spears,
but though I lie then in my grave, I still shall wreak
helpless bad luck and misadventure upon all
who stride across the oath that I have sworn: their ways
disconsolate make, their crossings full of evil   770
augury, so they shall be sorry that they moved.
But while they keep the upright way, and hold in high
regard the city of Pallas, and align their spears
to fight beside her, I shall be their gracious spirit.

And so farewell, you and your city's populace.   775
May you outwrestle and overthrow all those who come
against you, to your safety and your spears' success.

(Exit. Exit also Apollo.)

Chorus

Gods of the younger generation, you have ridden down
the laws of the elder time, torn them out of my hands.
I, disinherited, suffering, heavy with anger   780
shall let loose on the land
the vindictive poison
dripping deadly out of my heart upon the ground;
this from itself shall breed
cancer, the leafless, the barren   785
to strike, for the right, their low lands
and drag its smear of mortal infection on the ground.
What shall I do? Afflicted
I am mocked by these people.
I have borne what can not   790
be borne. Great the sorrows and the dishonor upon
the sad daughters of night.

Athene

Listen to me. I would not have you be so grieved.
For you have not been beaten. This was the result   795
of a fair ballot which was even. You were not
dishonored, but the luminous evidence of Zeus
was there, and he who spoke the oracle was he
who ordered Orestes so to act and not be hurt.
Do not be angry any longer with this land   800
nor bring the bulk of your hatred down on it, do not
render it barren of fruit, nor spill the dripping rain
of death in fierce and jagged lines to eat the seeds.
In complete honesty I promise you a place
of your own, deep hidden under ground that is yours by right   805
where you shall sit on shining chairs beside the hearth
to accept devotions offered by your citizens.

Chorus

Gods of the younger generation, you have ridden down
the laws of the elder time, torn them out of my hands.
I, disinherited, suffering, heavy with anger   810
shall let loose on the land
the vindictive poison
dripping deadly out of my heart upon the ground;
this from itself shall breed
cancer, the leafless, the barren   815
to strike, for the right, their low lands
and drag its smear of mortal infection on the ground.
What shall I do? Afflicted
I am mocked by these people.
I have borne what can not   820
be borne. Great the sorrow and the dishonor upon
the sad daughters of night.

Athene

No, not dishonored. You are goddesses. Do not
in too much anger make this place of mortal men   825
uninhabitable. I have Zeus behind me. Do
we need to speak of that? I am the only god
who know the keys to where his thunderbolts are locked.
We do not need such, do we? Be reasonable
and do not from a reckless mouth cast on the land   830
spells that will ruin every thing which might bear fruit.
No. Put to sleep the bitter strength in the black wave
and live with me and share my pride of worship. Here
is a big land, and from it you shall win first fruits
in offerings for children and the marriage rite   835
for always. Then you will say my argument was good.

Chorus

That they could treat me so!
I, the mind of the past, to be driven under the ground
out cast, like dirt!
The wind I breathe is fury and utter hate.   840

Earth, ah, earth
what is this agony that crawls under my ribs?
Night, hear me, o Night,
mother. They have wiped me out   845
and the hard hands of the gods
and their treacheries have taken my old rights away.

Athene

  I will bear your angers. You are elder born than I
  and in that you are wiser far than I. Yet still
  Zeus gave me too intelligence not to be despised.   850
  If you go away into some land of foreigners,
  I warn you, you will come to love this country. Time
  in his forward flood shall ever grow more dignified
  for the people of this city. And you, in your place
  of eminence beside Erechtheus in his house   855
  shall win from female and from male processionals
  more than all lands of men beside could ever give.
  Only in this place that I haunt do not inflict
  your bloody stimulus to twist the inward hearts
  of young men, raging in a fury not of wine,   860
  nor, as if plucking the heart from fighting cocks,
  engraft among my citizens that spirit of war
  that turns their battle fury inward on themselves.
  No, let our wars range outward hard against the man
  who has fallen horribly in love with high renown.   865
  No true fighter I call the bird that fights at home.
  Such life I offer you, and it is yours to take.
  Do good, receive good, and be honored as the good
  are honored. Share our country, the beloved of god.

Chorus

  That they could treat me so!   870
  I, the mind of the past, to be driven under the ground
  out cast, like dirt!
  The wind I breathe is fury and utter hate.
  Earth, ah, earth

what is this agony that crawls under my ribs? 875
Night, hear me, o Night,
mother. They have wiped me out
and the hard hands of the gods
and their treacheries have taken my old rights away. 880

Athene

I will not weary of telling you all the good things
I offer, so that you can never say that you,
an elder god, were driven unfriended from the land
by me in my youth, and by my mortal citizens.
But if you hold Persuasion has her sacred place 885
of worship, in the sweet beguilement of my voice,
then you might stay with us. But if you wish to stay
then it would not be justice to inflict your rage
upon this city, your resentment or bad luck
to armies. Yours the baron's portion in this land 890
if you will, in all justice, with full privilege.

Chorus

Lady Athene, what is this place you say is mine?

Athene

A place free of all grief and pain. Take it for yours.

Chorus

If I do take it, shall I have some definite powers?

Athene

No household shall be prosperous without your will. 895

Chorus

You will do this? You will really let me be so strong?

Athene

So we shall straighten the lives of all who worship us.

Chorus

You guarantee such honor for the rest of time?

Athene

I have no need to promise what I can not do.

Chorus

I think you will have your way with me. My hate is going.   900

Athene

Stay here, then. You will win the hearts of others, too.

Chorus

I will put a spell upon the land. What shall it be?

Athene

Something that has no traffic with evil success.
Let it come out of the ground, out of the sea's water,
and from the high air make the waft of gentle gales   905
wash over the country in full sunlight, and the seed
and stream of the soil's yield and of the grazing beasts
be strong and never fail our people as time goes,
and make the human seed be kept alive. Make more
the issue of those who worship more your ways, for as   910
the gardener works in love, so love I best of all
the unblighted generation of these upright men.
All such is yours for granting. In the speech and show
and pride of battle, I myself shall not endure
this city's eclipse in the estimation of mankind.   915

Chorus

I accept this home at Athene's side.
I shall not forget the cause
of this city, which Zeus all powerful and Ares
rule, stronghold of divinities,
glory of Hellene gods, their guarded altar.   920
So with forecast of good
I speak this prayer for them
that the sun's bright magnificence shall break out wave
on wave of all the happiness   925
life can give, across their land

Athene

Here are my actions. In all good will
toward these citizens I establish in power
spirits who are large, difficult to soften.
To them is given the handling entire   930
of men's lives. That man
who has not felt the weight of their hands
takes the strokes of life, knows not whence, not why,
for crimes wreaked in past generations
drag him before these powers. Loud his voice   935
but the silent doom
hates hard, and breaks him to dust.

Chorus

Let there blow no wind that wrecks the trees.
I pronounce words of grace.
Nor blaze of heat blind the blossoms of grown plants, nor   940
cross the circles of its right
place. Let no barren deadly sickness creep and kill.
Flocks fatten. Earth be kind
to them, with double fold of fruit   945
in time appointed for its yielding. Secret child
of earth, her hidden wealth, bestow
blessing and surprise of gods.

Athene

Strong guard of our city, hear you these
and what they portend? Fury is a high queen   950
of strength even among the immortal gods
and the undergods, and for humankind
their work is accomplished, absolute, clear:
for some, singing; for some, life dimmed
in tears; theirs the disposition.   955

Chorus

Death of manhood cut down
before its prime I forbid:

girls' grace and glory find
men to live life with them.
Grant, you who have the power. 960
And o, steering spirits of law,
goddesses of destiny,
sisters from my mother, hear;
in all houses implicate,
in all time heavy of hand 965
on whom your just arrest befalls,
august among goddesses, bestow.

Athene

It is my glory to hear how these
generosities
are given my land. I admire the eyes 970
of Persuasion, who guided the speech of my mouth
toward these, when they were reluctant and wild.
Zeus, who guides men's speech in councils, was too
strong; and my ambition
for good wins out in the whole issue. 975

Chorus

This my prayer: Civil War
fattening on men's ruin shall
not thunder in our city. Let
not the dry dust that drinks
the black blood of citizens 980
through passion for revenge
and bloodshed for bloodshed
be given our state to prey upon.
Let them render grace for grace.
Let love be their common will; 985
let them hate with single heart.
Much wrong in the world thereby is healed.

Athene

Are they taking thought to discover that road
where speech goes straight?

In the terror upon the faces of these   990
I see great good for our citizens.
While with good will you hold in high honor
these spirits, their will shall be good, as you steer
your city, your land
on an upright course clear through to the end.   995

Chorus

Farewell, farewell. High destiny shall be yours
by right. Farewell, citizens
seated near the throne of Zeus,
beloved by the maiden he loves,
civilized as years go by,   1000
sheltered under Athene's wings,
grand even in her father's sight.

Athene

Goddesses, farewell. Mine to lead, as these
attend us, to where
by the sacred light new chambers are given.   1005
Go then. Sped by majestic sacrifice
from these, plunge beneath the ground. There hold
off what might hurt the land; pour in
the city's advantage, success in the end.
You, children of Cranaus, you who keep   1010
the citadel, guide these guests of the state.
For good things given,
your hearts' desire be for good to return.

Chorus

Farewell and again farewell, words spoken twice over,
all who by this citadel,   1015
mortal men, spirits divine,
hold the city of Pallas, grace
this my guestship in your land.
Life will give you no regrets.   1020

Athene

Well said. I assent to all the burden of your prayers,
and by the light of flaring torches now attend
your passage to the deep and subterranean hold,
as by us walk those women whose high privilege
it is to guard my image. Flower of all the land   1025
of Theseus, let them issue now, grave companies,
maidens, wives, elder women, in processional.
In the investiture of purple stained robes
dignify them, and let the torchlight go before
so that the kindly company of these within   1030
our ground may shine in the future of strong men to come.

Chorus (by the women who have been forming for processional)

Home, home, o high, o aspiring
Daughters of Night, aged children, in blithe processional.
Bless them, all here, with silence.   1035

In the primeval dark of earth-hollows
held in high veneration with rights sacrificial
bless them, all people, with silence.

Gracious be, wish what the land wishes,   1040
follow, grave goddesses, flushed in the flamesprung
torchlight gay on your journey.
Singing all follow our footsteps.

There shall be peace forever between these people
of Pallas and their guests. Zeus the all seeing   1045
met with Destiny to confirm it.
Singing all follow our footsteps.

                                        (Exeunt omnes, in procession.)

THE
SUPPLIANT
MAIDENS

Translated and with an Introduction by

SETH G. BENARDETE

INTRODUCTION TO
THE SUPPLIANT MAIDENS

IT HAD always been thought by modern scholars that *The Suppliant Maidens* was the earliest Greek play still preserved, and the date of its production was given as *circa* 490 B.C. This opinion was based on stylistic considerations as well as on the fact that the protagonist of the play is the chorus itself, which Aristotle tells us to have been the early condition of the drama. A papyrus recently published, however, would seem to suggest that the trilogy, of which *The Suppliant Maidens* is the first part, was first produced after 470 B.C. Should this prove to be the case, it will be a real puzzle why Aeschylus kept the play in his drawer for twenty years; for it is hardly likely that he should have reverted to the archaism of *The Suppliant Maidens* after having written *The Persians*.

The plot of the play is simple. The fifty daughters of Danaus, descendants of the Argive Io, flee from Egypt to Argos because their Egyptian cousins wish, without their consent, to marry them. They come to a sacred grove near Argos, where the rest of the action takes place. Pelasgus, the King of Argos, is unwilling to grant them sanctuary unless the populace seconds his request; and the populace, convinced by the king and their own father, does grant it. But it is not a moment too soon; for after the maidens hear they are saved, their father informs them that the Egyptian cousins are just landing, and while he goes to bring aid, a herald of their cousins comes to take them away. Pelasgus, however, returns with an armed force, and the herald, threatening war, is forced to withdraw. Then Danaus returns again, counseling them to behave decently, and the play ends with a song of deliverance. Since the second and third parts of the trilogy are lost, and only a few scattered notices of the plot remain, we cannot be certain what Aeschylus' purpose was. In the second play the maidens were somehow forced to marry their cousins (per-

haps because Pelasgus dies), but they swear to their father to kill
them on their wedding night. All except Hypermnestra fulfil their
oath, while she—"splendide mendax," Horace calls her—out of love
for her husband saves him. In the last play Hypermnestra is forced
to stand trial because she violated her oath; and in a scene reminiscent
of that in the *Eumenides*, Aphrodite herself appears and defends her.
Part of her speech survives:

> As the sacred heaven longs to pierce the earth,
> So love takes hold of earth to join in marriage,
> And showers, fallen from heaven brought to bed,
> Make the earth pregnant; and she in turn gives birth
> To flocks of sheep and Ceres' nourishment—
> A marriage that drenches the springtime of the woods—
> For all this I am in part responsible.

The Suppliant Maidens is an international play. The Danaids are
refugees, Greeks by descent, Egyptians in appearance (ll. 234-37,
277-90, 496 ff.), and according to Egyptian law they have no legal
right to refuse to marry their cousins. For when Pelasgus wishes to
know what right they have, the maidens in reply only declare their
hatred of their cousins, implying by their evasion of the question
the absence of any legal claim to his protection (ll. 387-91). Thus
both by nature and by law they are defenseless. If they really looked
like Greeks, as well as were Greeks by an obscure genealogy, and if
they had some legal justification, Pelasgus might have been willing
to take up their defense without the consent of the people; but once
it becomes a case of pure or natural justice independent of all legality, with the maidens' arbitrary dislike of their cousins their only
motive, Pelasgus must defer to the will of the people. Since the
maidens insist upon the rights of the will alone, Pelasgus allows in
turn the people's will to sanction it and make it law. In the second
play the oath of the Danaids becomes law, and Hypermnestra, in
violating it, repeats her sisters' original defiance of Egyptian law;
but as on this occasion it is not a human law that she has betrayed,
a goddess must justify her conduct. Aphrodite insists upon the pre-
rogatives of love, a force that transcends even the sacredness of

oaths. Thus the trilogy is complete. At first the Egyptians embodied law, though strangely enough lust also supported them, while the Danaids represented a freedom that was not bound by any positive enactments. But once this freedom has been approved by law, Hypermnestra alone remains outside it; and as she cannot be defended merely by a democratic procedure, a universal divine law, more authoritative than even the people's will, must rescue her. Having only the first part of the trilogy, we cannot be confident that Aeschylus' purpose was exactly this; but the claims of the city as opposed to claims still more powerful would seem to underlie the play, claims that at each stage become more contrary to one another and more difficult to resolve.

The Suppliant Maidens as a play is not very exciting, and we can easily see why the chorus was later abandoned as the protagonist. A chorus can convey only a lyrical mood; it can hardly support any genuine passion. The Danaids, for example, say they are frightened when the Egyptians are coming, but we do not believe them: their songs, divided into strophe and antistrophe,* betray their detachment, and they always talk more like commentators on their actions than like the actors themselves. Although the choruses of *The Suppliant Maidens* are some of the most beautiful Aeschylus ever wrote, the dialogue seems extremely artificial and forced, with the air of set speeches directed more to the audience than to the other actors. *The Persians*, on the other hand, suffers from the opposite fault: the speeches, even though long, are dramatic, while the choral songs are far inferior to those of *The Suppliants*. Only in the *Oresteia* did Aeschylus achieve a perfect balance between them.

* Throughout this play and *The Persians*, strophes and antistrophes are marked by the symbols — and = respectively.

THE SUPPLIANT MAIDENS

CHARACTERS

Chorus of maidens, daughters of Danaus

Danaus, their father

Pelasgus, King of Argos

Herald of Egyptians, cousins to the Danaans

THE SUPPLIANT MAIDENS

SCENE: *A sacred grove near Argos, adorned with statues of Greek gods.*

Chorus

Zeus Protector, protect us with care.
From the subtle sand of the Nile delta
Our ship set sail. And we deserted:
From a holy precinct bordering Syria
We fled into exile, condemned
Not for murder by a city's decree,
But by self-imposèd banishment abhorring
Impious marriage with Egyptus' sons.   10

Danaus, father, adviser and lord,
Setting the counters of hope,
Picked the smallest pawn of grief,
Quickly to fly through the sea,
And find anchor at Argos,
Whence we boast to descend,
By the breathing caress of Zeus
On a cow driven wild.

With suppliant olive branch,
To what kinder land could we turn?   20

Whose city, whose earth and bright water,
Olympian gods, ancient gods below
Possessing the tomb, and Zeus Savior,
Keeper of pious men, receive
(Respectful the air of this land)
These suppliant maidens well.

But that thick swarm of insolent men,   30
Before ever landing in this swamp waste,
Return them and their ship to the sea;

And by the winter sting of hurricane,
Facing the wild sea, by thunder and lightning,
By rain-winds may they die;
Before appropriating what law forbids,
Cousins to lie on unwilling beds.   40

Now I invoke
The calf of Zeus Avenger
Beyond the sea:
A child from grazing
Cow, genetrix,
Held by the breath of Zeus,
Born with a fateful name:
Epaphus, Caress.—

Him I invoke:
In pastures here our mother
Suffered before: 50
I'll show a witness
Faithful but unex-
pected to natives here.
They shall know the truth
At last and at length.=

And if some neighbor here knows bird cries,
Hearing our bitter passion he will think
He hears the hawk-chased, sad bird Metis,   60
The wife of Tereus,—
                        Who weeps with passion
Barred from rivers and the countryside;
Who sang a child's death-dirge, whom she killed,
Perverse her wrath.=

Thus melancholy I
With Ionian songs
Eat my Nile-soft cheek,
My heart unused to tears.   70
We gather blooms of sorrow,

Anxious if a friend,
Someone, will protect us,
Exiles from a misty land.—

But gods ancestral, hear!
Behold justice kindly.
Truly hating pride
Grant nothing undecreed: 80
So just you'd be to marriage.
Even war has havens,
Bulwark for the weary
Exile, a respect of gods.=

May his will, if it's Zeus's, be well,
His will not easily traced.
Everywhere it gleams, even in blackness,
With black fortune to man.—

And so certain it falls without slips,   90
By sign of Zeus fulfilled.
Dark are the devices of his counsel,
His ways blind to our sight.=

From towered hopes
He casts men destructive,
No violence
He armors.
All providence
Is effortless: throned,
Holy and motionless,
His will is accomplished.—   100

On mortal pride
Look down, how it waxes
And flourishes
By marriage
Remorselessly:
Intent in its frenzy,

Spur inescapable,
Deceived to destruction. =   110

I sing suffering, shrieking,
Shrill and sad am weeping,
My life is dirges
And rich in lamentations,
Mine honor weeping.
   I invoke your Apian land,
    You know my foreign tongue.
    Often I tear my Sidonian veils. —   120

We grant gods oblations
Where all is splendid
And death is absent.
O toils undecipherable!
Where lead these billows?
   I invoke your Apian land.
    You know my foreign tongue.
    Often I tear my Sidonian veils. =   130

Linen-bound ship, secure from the sea,
With fair winds brought me;
Nor do I blame.
May Father, timely omniscient,
Perfect a gracious end, that   140
   Seeds mighty of solemn mother
    Escape, O woe,
    Unwed, virgin to the bed of man. —

Daughter of Zeus pure, may she behold,
Who guards walls sacred,
Willing my will.
May virgin, rescuing virgins,
In all her power come, that   150
   Seeds mighty of solemn mother
    Escape, alas,
    Unwed, virgin to the bed of man. =

But if not,
A sunburnt race
Shall go beseeching
To Zeus of the dead
(Gracious to strangers),
Hanging ourselves,
If Gods Olympian heed not.   160
   O Zeus! Sought out by the gods,
   By snake-hate of Io:
   I know Hera's madness
   Conquering all.
   Winter comes by sharp winds.—

Then Zeus in
Injustice hates
His son begotten,
And that is unjust: 170
Face now averted
Away from my prayers.
But would that Zeus hearken!
   O Zeus! Sought out by the gods,
   By snake-hate of Io:
   I know Hera's madness
   Conquering all.
   Winter comes by sharp winds.=

Danaus
   Prudence, my daughters; prudently you came
   With an agèd father as your trusted pilot.
   And now, with foresight, I advise your taking
   Care to seal my words within your mind.
   I see dust, the silent clarion of arms,   180
   But not in silence are the axles turned;
   Crowds I see, armed with shield and spear,
   Followed by horses and curved chariots.
   Perhaps the princes of this land have come

To meet us, informed by messenger;
But whether kindly purposed or provoked
To savageness they speed their armament,
Here it is best to act the suppliant,
This rock, this altar of assembled gods,
Stronger than ramparts, a shield impenetrable.   190
Now quickly prepare white suppliant wreaths,
Sign of Zeus sacred, held in the left hand;
Mournful, respectful, answer needfully
The strangers; tell distinctly of an exile
Unstained by murder. Let nothing bold
Attend your voice, and nothing vain come forth
In glance but modesty and reverence.   200
Not talkative nor a laggard be in speech:
Either would offend them. Remember to yield:
You are an exile, a needy stranger,
And rashness never suits the weaker.

Chorus

With prudence, father, you speak to the prudent.
I shall keep a watch on your discreet commands.
May Zeus, my ancestor, look on us.

Danaus

May he look then with propitious eye.

Chorus

Now would I wish to be near your side.

Danaus

Delay not.

Chorus   210

        O Zeus, compassion ere we die.

Danaus

If Zeus is willing, this will end well.
And now that bird of Zeus invoke.

Chorus

Preserving rays of the sun we call.

Danaus

Call on Apollo, the god, who from heaven once fled.

Chorus

So knowing this fate, may he have compassion.

Danaus

Let him be compassionate, defend us with care.

Chorus

What other gods must I invoke?

Danaus

                                    I see

This trident, a god's symbol.

Chorus

                                    Who brought us

Here well: may he receive us now well.

Danaus

And that is another Hermes, a Greek custom.   220

Chorus

May he be a good herald to those who are free.

Danaus

All gods here at a common altar worship.
Settle on the sacred ground like doves
Clustering together, fearing the winged hawks,
Who hatefully pollute their very blood.
Bird consumes bird, how could it be pure?
How, unwilling brides, myself unwilling,
Could they be pure? Who not even in hell,
Where another Zeus among the dead (they say)   230
Works out their final punishment, can flee
Their guilt of lust. Fix your eye on that
In answer, that victory be with you well.
                    (*Enter the King of Argos and company.*)

King

Whence come these barbarians?
What shall we call you? So outlandishly

Arrayed in the barbaric luxury
Of robes and crowns, and not in Argive fashion
Nor in Greek? But at this I wonder: how   240
Without a herald, without a guide, without patron,
You have yet dared to come, without trembling.
The suppliant olive branch before these gods
You've placed (it is custom); but Greece no more
Than that will guess: in other things I could
Conjecture only, unless your voice will guide.

Chorus

You did not lie about our dress. But to whom
Do I speak? an Argive citizen, or a herald
With his sacred staff, or the city's head?

King

Answer me with trust: I am Pelasgus,
Founder of this land, and son of Palaechthon   250
Earth-born. Pelasgians bear my royal name,
And reap the fruits of this earth. I rule the lands
In which the pure Strymon turns, where the sun
Sinks in the west, and limits the Perrhaebi,
Beyond the Pindus, near the Paeoni
And the mountain Dodona: oceans bound my rule:
I lord it over all within that frame.
It is called Apia, after a surgeon   260
Of ancient times, the prophet Apis, son
To Apollo, who from Naupactus once did come,
And cleansed this land of deadly, monstrous
Serpents, that the earth, soaked in old
Curses of blood, had sprung and smeared in wrath.
His remedies and herbs did work a cure
For Argos, where his pay's remembrance found
In litanies. There are my testaments.   270
And now you must tell your own ancestry.
The city, though,'s impatient with long speeches.

Chorus
> Brief and clear is my tale: by race we claim
> Argos, the offspring of a fruitful cow.
> I'll tell how close truth clings to it.

King
> You speak beyond my credence, strangers, claiming
> Argive birth: more like Libyans you seem
> Than like to women native here; or the Nile may foster   280
> Such a likeness; or the images
> Of Cyprus, carved by native craftsmen;
> And of the camel-backed nomads I've heard,
> Neighbors to the Ethiopian;
> I should have thought you were the unwed
> Barbarous Amazons, were you armed with bows.
> But, once instructed, I should more fully know
> How your birth and ancestry is Argive.   290

Chorus
> Wasn't Io once in Argos charged
> With Hera's temple?

King
>   Io was, the tale
> Is prevalent.

Chorus
>   And wasn't Zeus to a mortal
> Joined?

King
>   Which was from Hera unconcealed.

Chorus
> How end these royal jealousies?

King
>   A goddess
> Changed a woman to a cow.

Chorus
>   And Zeus,   300
> Did he approach the hornèd cow?

King

　　　　　　　　　　　Zeus

　　Became a bull, they say.

Chorus

　　　　　　　　　　　How then did Hera answer?

King

　　She placed on her a guard, all-seeing.

Chorus

　　　　　　　　　　　Who?

King

　　Argos, a son of Earth, whom Hermes slew.

Chorus

　　But what did Hera appoint for ill-omened Io?

King

　　A gnatlike goad it was, or driving sting.

Chorus

　　That the Nile-dwellers call the gadfly.

King

　　That drove her from Argos.

Chorus

　　　　　　　　　　　It confirms my tale.　　　　　　　310

King

　　And so to Canobus and to Memphis she came.

Chorus

　　Where Zeus by touch begot a son.

King

　　Who claims to be the calf of Zeus?

Chorus

　　　　　　　　　　　Epaphus,

　　Truly named Caress.

King

　　　　　　　　And who from him?

Chorus

　　Libya, reaping the greatest name.

King
> And then?

Chorus
> Belus of two sons, my father's father.

King
> Tell me his name.

Chorus
> Danaus, whose brother   320
> Fathered fifty sons.

King
> Disclose his name
> Ungrudgingly.

Chorus
> Egyptus. Now knowing my ancient
> Lineage, might you succor an Argive band.

King
> You seem to share of old this land: but how
> Did you bring yourself to leave your father's
> Home? What fortune did swoop upon you?

Chorus
> Lord Pelasgus, shifting are the ills of men.
> Nowhere is trouble seen of the same wing.
> Who wished for this unexpected flight,
> To land at Argos, formerly natives here,   330
> Cowering in hate of the marriage bed?

King
> Why have you come to these assembled gods?
> Why do you hold the fresh white olive branch?

Chorus
> To be no household-slave to Egyptus' sons.

King
> By hatred or by law? . . . (*Some verses are missing.*)

Chorus

Who buys a master

From kin? . . . *(Some verses are missing.)*

King

So greater grows the strength of mortals.

Chorus

To desert those distressed is easy.

King

How

With piety could I act?

Chorus

Deny the demand   340

Of Egyptus' sons.

King

But hard's *your* demand to wage

A new war.

Chorus

But justice protects her allies.

King

If only she shared from the start.

Chorus

Respect the ship of state thus crowned.

King

I shudder before these shaded altars.

Chorus

Yet hard is the wrath of Zeus the protector.
Son of Palaechthon,
Listen to me with a caring heart,
Lord of Pelasgians.
Protector, behold an exile surrounded:
A calf, wolf-pursued, on steep rocks,   350
Confides in the herdsman's strength,
And bleats her pains.—

King
    I see this crowd of gods assenting, each
    Shadowed by the fresh-cut olive branch.
    Yet may this friendship conceal no doom,
    Nor strife for us arise in unexpected
    And unpremeditated ways.

Chorus
    Daughter of Zeus,
    Master of lots, may behold a flight   360
    Innocent, Themis!
    And thou from the younger, ancient in wisdom,
    Learn, . . .
    Respecting the suppliant,
    A holy man. =

King
    You are not suppliants at my own hearth.
    If the city stains the commonweal,
    In common let the people work a cure.
    But I would make no promises until
    I share with all the citizens.

Chorus
    You are, yes, the city, the people,   370
    A prince is not judged.
    The land, the hearth, the altar you rule
    With the single vote and scepter;
    Enthroned you command,
    And fill every need.
    Of pollution be watchful. —

King
    Pollution on my enemies! Without
    Harm I cannot aid you; nor is it sensible
    To despise these your earnest prayers.
    I am at a loss, and fearful is my heart,
    To act or not to act and choose success.   380

Chorus

    Regard him, above, the protector,
    A watchdog of men
    Distressed who sit at neighboring hearths,
    But obtain no lawful justice.
    Yet anger of Zeus
    The Suppliant remains,
    Who is charmed by no pity. =

King

    If Egyptus' sons rule you by customs
    Native to your city, claiming nearest
    Of kin, who would wish in that to oppose them?
    According to laws at home you must plead,   390
    How over you they lack authority.

Chorus

    Yet subject to men would I never be!
    I plot my course under the stars,
    An escape from a heartless marriage.
    Take as an ally justice.
    Choose the side of the gods. —

King

    The choice is not easy: choose me not as judge.
    I said before that never would I act
    Alone, apart from the people, though I am ruler;
    So never may people say, if evil comes,   400
    "Respecting aliens the city you destroyed."

Chorus

    Both sides he surveys, of related blood
    Zeus is, impartial his scales,
    To the evil and lawful weighs out
    The holy and unjust fairly.
    Why fear to act justly? =

King

    We need profound, preserving care, that plunges

Like a diver deep in troubled seas,
Keen and unblurred his eye, to make the end
Without disaster for us and for the city;   410
That neither strife may bring reprisals, nor,
If we should give you back, seated thus
On seats of gods, we settle the god, destructive
Alastor, in this land, who even in Hades
Never frees the dead. Seem we not
To need preserving counsel?

Chorus
    Take care and be,
    Justly, the pious protector,
    Exile betray not,   420
    Exile pursued by,
    Cast out by, the godless. —

    See me not seized,
    From seat of gods to be seized,
    O lord with full power.
    Know the pride of men,
    Beware of god's anger. =

    Bear not to see
    A supplicant by force   430
    Led from these statues,
    Seized by my garments,
    Like a horse by the bridle. —

    Do what you will,
    Thy house remains to pay,
    Fined in thy children:
    Justice is equal.
    Mark the justice of Zeus. =

King
    I have pondered, and here I'm run aground:
    'Gainst you or them necessity is strained   440

For mighty war, as fastly drawn as ships
Held by the windlass: yet anchorage is never
Free from pain. When wealth is sacked and homes
Are pillaged, Zeus yet another fortune may bestow;
Or when the tongue has failed, a healing word
May spread a counter-balm: but if consanguine
Blood is to stay unshed, we must sacrifice
To slaughter many kine to many gods,   450
A cure of grief. I am spent by this dispute:
I wish an ignorance more than art of ill:
Against my judgment may it turn out well.

Chorus
But hear the end of my reverent prayers.

King
Well?

Chorus
Clasps and belts and bands I have.

King
They are doubtless proper for women.

Chorus
Here, you know,
Are fine devices.

King
Tell me.   460

Chorus
Unless you promise—

King
What would your bands accomplish?

Chorus
Statues with new tablets to adorn.

King
Speak simply.

Chorus
From these gods to hang.

King

A whip to the heart.

Chorus

Now you understand, for eyes I gave you.

King

Alas! everywhere I'm gripped in strangle holds,
And like a swollen river evils flood:
Embarked on a sea of doom, uncrossed, abysmal,   470
Nowhere is anchorage. If I leave
This debt unpaid, you've warned of pollution
That shall strike unerringly; but if
I stand before these walls, and bring the battle
To the very end against Egyptus'
Sons, wouldn't that become a bitter waste—
Men to bleed the earth for women's sake?
But yet the wrath of Zeus the Suppliant—
The height of mortal fear—must be respected.
Now then, agèd father of these maidens,   480
Gather those wreaths in your arms; and at other
Altars of the native gods replace them:
Then no one of the native people, who delight
In blame, by seeing proof of your arrival,
Could reproach me; and pity they may feel
For you, and hate those men's arrogance.
May the people be gracious! Everyone,
To those weaker than themselves, is kind.

Danaus

To have found a stranger, reverent and kind,   490
We highly prize. And now, let native guides,
To grant me safety as I go, escort me
To the temple altars: nature made
My shape unlike to yours, even as the Nile
And the Inachus bear no resemblance
In their nurture. Beware lest rashness burgeon
Into fear: ignorance has often killed
A friend.

King

              Attend: the stranger speaks well.   500
Guide him to the civil altars, the seats
Of gods; and say no more than this to whom
You meet: "To the gods' hearth we bring a sailor."

                          (*Exit Danaus, attended.*)

Chorus

Him you instructed, and he is gone; but I,
How shall I act? What sign of confidence
Is yours to give me?

King

                    Leave your wreaths here,
A sign of grief.

Chorus

                And here I leave them by your
Command.

King

              Toward that grove now turn.

Chorus

                        But how
Would a public grove protect me?

King

                      Never   510
To rape of birds shall we expose you.

Chorus

But to them more hateful than heartless snakes?

King

Propitiated, speak auspiciously.

Chorus

You know how fear does fret impatiently?

King

Excessive fear is always powerless.

Chorus

Soothe then my heart in word and deed.

King
 Your father will not long desert you; and I,
 Assembling all the native people, shall
 Make the commons well disposed, and teach
 Your father all that he must say.
 Now remain here, and beseech the native   520
 Gods with your prayers to bring what you desire.
 I shall go arranging all: may Persuasion
 And Fortune attend me!

             (Exit King.)

Chorus
 Lord of Lords most bless'd,
 Most perfect strength of bless'd,
 Happy Zeus obey
 And let it be:
 Remove the pride of men,
 Pride well hated;
 And cast in a purpled sea
 The black-benched doom.—   530

 Look upon our race
 Ancient of ancestor loved,
 Change to a happy tale
 Favoring us:
 Remember many things,
 You touched Io.
 We claim a descent from Zeus,
 And birth from this land. =

 To my mother's ancient track I turned,
 In a rich pasture eating flowers
 She was seen, whence Io   540
 By gadfly raged
 Distraught escaped;
 Passing many races,
 Cutting in two the land,
 The raging strait defined;—

Through lands of Asia fast she went,
And across Phrygia grazing sheep;
And the city of Teuthras passing,
And Lydian vales,   550
Cilician hills,
Race Pamphylian hurried
Through ever-flowing streams,
And land of Aphrodite. =

She came by dart distressed
Of a cowherd winged
To rich groves of Zeus,
A pasture fed by snow and attacked
By Typhon's rage,   560
The Nile-waters by disease untouched;
Herself crazed,
With grief, stinging pains,
Bacchant of Hera. —

And men who then lived there
At her strangeness trembled,
With pale fear at heart,
Beheld a creature vexed, half-breed,
In part a cow,
And woman in turn, a monster marveled at.   570
Who then charmed
The wretch wandering-far
Furious Io? =

Of endless sovereignty
Lord Zeus charmed,
By strength gentle of Zeus
And divine breaths
Was she cured, weeping
Her grievous shame,
Bearing the burden of Zeus,   580
Told without falsehood,
She bore a blameless child, —

Through great time bless'd;
All earth shouts,
"Of Zeus fruitful in truth
This race: who else
Would cure her of sly
Diseases of Hera?"
There is the working of Zeus,
Here is Epaphus' race:
Of both the truth is spoken. =

Whom beside him   590
More justly would I call?
Father our gardener, worker, and lord,
A craftsman aged in wisdom,
Propitious the wind is of Zeus. —

Stronger none rule,
Beneath no one enthroned,
Seated above he respects none below.
His deeds are quick as words,
He hastens what counsel decrees. =

(*Enter Danaus.*)

Danaus
  Take heart, my children, well are cast the people's   600
  Final vote.

Chorus
        O hail, my envoy, my dearest
  Herald. Tell us what end's been authorized?
  And where the populace, by show of hands,
  Has thrown its weight.

Danaus
          The Argives have decreed
  Not doubtfully, so as to change my aging
  Heart to youth again; so bristled thick
  The air with hands, resolving thus the law:
  Free we are to settle here, subject

Neither to seizure nor reprisal, claimed   610
Neither by citizen nor foreigner.
But if they turn to force, whoever rich
In lands refuses succor, shall be stripped
Of offices and banished publicly.
The king persuaded, prophesying Zeus
The Suppliant would fatten rich his wrath
To feed insatiate suffering,
And show itself as twin defilements,   620
In and outside the city. Hearing this,
The Argives, not even summoned, voted all.
They heard, and easily were convinced by supple
Rhetoric; but Zeus still crowned the end.

Chorus

Come then, let us offer
For the Argives good prayers,
A return for good things.
And may Zeus Stranger behold
From the mouth of a stranger
Offerings in true frankness,
A perfect end for all things.

And now Zeus-born gods   630
Might you hear our prayers,
When libations we pour:
Never slain by fire
This Pelasgian land,
Never wanton War
Found a danceless cry,
Harvesting mortals
In a changed harvest;
    For compassion they showed us,
    And voted with kindness,   640
    Respecting Zeus's suppliants,
    This wretched flock of sheep. —

Nor cast they their votes
On the side of men
By dishonoring us;
Watching Zeus Avenger
(Like a spy he sees)
Who is hard to fight:
Who desires his home
Stained in its rafters?   650
For he heavily presses.
   The suppliants of Zeus sacred,
   Related blood, they respected.
   Then to gods shall they be pleasing
   With altars scoured clean. =

So out of shadowed lips let fly
Honorable prayers:
Never a plague
Empty the city,   660
Strife never bleed
With native dead the land.
   Flower of youth may it ripen unplucked,
   And partner of Aphrodite, War,
   May he cut not their bloom. —

And laden altars, welcoming,
Set them ablaze.
Well would be ruled
Cities respecting   670
Zeus above all,
Who guides by ancient law.
   Other protectors we pray to be born
   For always, and Hecate-Artemis
   Birth by women protect. =

Let no murderous plague
Come upon the city destroying,   680
Without the dance, without lute

Father of tears Ares arming,
And the intestine war's shout.
   May the bitter swarms of ill
   Far from the people sit;
   May the Lycian Apollo
   To all the youth be kind. —

And may Zeus to perfection
Bring the fruit of each season;   690
And many young in the fields
Pasturing cattle beget:
May they obtain from gods all.
   May the pious songs be sung
   At altars by minstrels;
   May the lyre-loving voices
   From holy lips arise. =

May the people who strengthen the city
Protect its dignity well;
Whose rule's providential in common counsel;   700
And before arming Ares,
To strangers without grief
May they grant justice. —

May the gods who possess the city
Be honored by citizens well
With sacrificial laurel, ancestral.
For respect of one's parents
Is third among laws
Written by Justice. =

Danaus
   Thank you, dear children, for these modest prayers;   710
   But from your father tremble not to hear
   New intelligence. From this outpost,
   Protector of suppliants, I spy that ship;
   Clearly it shows; nor do I fail to mark
   How its sails are trimmed and sides made fast,

And how her bow does seek the way with painted
Eye; and the ship, obedient, hears all too well
Her tiller's governance. And the men on board
I see, black in limb, their clothes white linen.
All the other ships and allied force   720
I see; but under land the lead, its sail
Now furling, rows with timèd beat. And you
Must, quietly and temperately facing
The event, ignore none of these gods.
And I, with advocates, shall come. Perhaps
An envoy or a herald comes, desiring
To lead you away as reprisals.
But nothing shall happen. Never fear him.
Still it is better, if we are slow,   730
That refuge to remember. Take heart.
Surely in time the day shall come when all
Who had dishonored the gods shall pay.

Chorus

Father, I fear, as swift ships come;
No length of time does stand between us.
    Terror holds me, excessive fear,
    If flights of wandering profit not.
    Father, I am spent by fear.—

Danaus

As final was the Argive vote, my daughters,
Take heart: they shall fight for you, I know.   740

Chorus

Mad is the race Egyptian, cursed,
In war unsated: I speak what you know.
    Dark ships they have, and strongly built;
    They sailed and so succeed in anger
    With an army large and dark. =

Danaus

But here many shall they find, whose limbs
The sun's made lean in noonday heat.

Chorus

Leave us not behind, alone, father! I pray.
Women are nothing alone; no Ares is in them.
   Deadly purposed and crafty minds   750
   With impure hearts, just as ravens,
   They heed no altar.—

Danaus

Well that would aid us, my daughters,
If to the gods, as to you, they are hateful.

Chorus

They feared not these tridents, no awe of gods;
Their hands they shall not keep from me, father.
   Arrogant with unholy rage,
   Gluttonous, dog-hearted, obeying
   In nothing the gods.=

Danaus

A fable tells that wolves possess more strength   760
Than dogs, and reeds cannot conquer wheat.

Chorus

We must guard ourselves against the rage
Of wanton men, monstrous and profane.

Danaus

The reefing of a sail is never swift,
Nor is the anchoring, with ropes to be secured;
And even safe at anchorage the helmsman
Lacks courage, and mostly when come to harborless
Shores, and the sun has sneaked away to night,
It breeds in prudent pilots pain as sharp   770
As birth itself; nor would a host find landing
Easy, before each ship takes courage in
Her moorings. But you, fearful at heart, take heed
Of the gods, while I, bringing aid, shall return
To defend you: an agèd messenger the city
Cannot blame, youthful in eloquence.

                             (*Exit Danaus.*)

Chorus

O mountainous land, justly respected,
What shall befall us? Where shall we flee,
If in Apian lands some dark abyss somewhere?
Black smoke might I be
Bordering clouds of Zeus;   780
Invisible completely
As unseen dust might I die.—

My heart without fright would no longer be;
Darkness flutters in my heart.
I am seized by his warnings: I am spent by fear.
And willing would I be
Fated to die hanging,
Before that man should touch me: 790
May Hades rule me before!=

Where might there be a throne of air?
Against it wet clouds become snow?
Or smooth, steep, lonely,
Overhanging, distant,
Vulture-haunted rocks,
Witnessing my fall,
Before by force meet
A heart-rending marriage?—

Prey then for dogs and native birds,   800
A feast I shall not refuse them.
For death grants freedom
From lámentable ills.
Let that fate before
My marriage-bed come.
But where is still means
To free us from marriage?=

Shriek and shout a cry to heaven,
Perfect prayers to the gods,
To me relief and fulfilment;   810

And Father, seeing the battle,
Behold with just eyes
Violence unkindly.
Respect your suppliants,
Protector, omnipotent Zeus!—

Proud and heartless Egyptians—
Men pursuing an exile,
Intent on capturing me,
With shouts many and wanton.   820
But you completely,
Zeus, hold the beam of
The balance. What without you
Is brought to completion for men?=

　　　　　　　　(Enter Herald Of Egyptians, attended.)*

Cry! O woe! Alas!
Here, this ravisher from the ship!
Before that, ravisher, would you die!
I see this beginning of my woes.   830
Alas! O woe! Escape!
Stern-hearted in insolence,
Hard to bear on land, at sea,
Lord of the land, protect us!

Herald
　　Hurry!
　　Hasten to the boats
　　Fast as you are able.
　　Lest torn and pricked,
　　Pricked and scratched you'll be,
　　Bloody and bloodstained,   840
　　Your heads cut off!
　　Hurry, hasten, curses! curses! to the boats!

Chorus
　　On the flowing salt-path
　　With your masterful pride

« 206 »

*The Herald sometimes speaks in "broken Greek."

With your bolted ship
Would you had died!

Herald

Cease your cries. Leave your seats.   850
Go to the ships. You without honor,
You without city, I cannot respect.—

Chorus

Never fruitful water
Might I see again, whence
Grows the living root—
Murder!—and blooms.

Herald

I shall lead—I am brave—
Down to the ship, up on the ladder.   860
Willing, unwilling, you shall go.=

Chorus

Oh, alas, woe.
Oh, would that you had helpless died
By the sea-washed grove
Wandering at Sarpedon's tomb,
Piled up with sand   870
Among wet breezes.

Herald

Shriek and shout and call the gods.
You shall not jump the Egyptian ship.
Bewail and shout and mourn with sorrow.—

Chorus

Oh, alas, woe.
Outrage! when you howl off-shore,
With your boasts overflow;
Whom the great Nile might behold
Raging in your pride,   880
And drown your violence.

Herald

    Board the swift boat at once!
    Let no one falter: I'll have no awe
    Of precious curls when I shall drag you. =

Chorus

    Alas, father, to the sea he leads me;
    Like a spider, step by step,
    A dream, a black dream,
    Cry, O woe, cry!
    Earth, Mother Earth,   890
    Avert his fearful cry.
    O son, son of Earth, O Zeus.

Herald

    I do not fear these gods before me: they
    Did not nurse me, their nursing did not age me. —

Chorus

    A two-footed serpent quivers near,
    Like a viper, bites my foot,
    A poisonous thing.
    Cry, O woe, cry!
    Earth, Mother Earth,
    Avert his fearful cry.   900
    O son, son of Earth, O Zeus.

Herald

    Your finery I shall not pity, if
    None will go to the ship resignedly. =

Chorus

    We perish, lord, we suffer pain!

Herald

    O many lords, Egyptus' sons, you soon
    Will see—take heart!— and blame no anarchy!

Chorus

    O first commanders, undone am I!

Herald

　　As you're not hasty to heed my words,
　　It seems I'll have to drag you by the hair.　　　　　　910

　　　　　　　　　　(*Enter the King, attended.*)

King

　　You there! What is done? By what insolence
　　Dare you insult this land of Pelasgian men?
　　Think you you have come to a woman's land? You are
　　Barbarians, and you trifle insolently
　　With Greeks, and, off the mark in everything,
　　In nothing upright stand.

Herald

　　　　　　　　　　How did I err?
　　What do I do without justice?

King

　　　　　　　　　　　　You know
　　Not how to be a stranger.

Herald

　　　　　　　　　　Though finding what I lost?

King

　　To what patron did you speak?

Herald

　　　　　　　　　　　　To Hermes the Searcher,　　920
　　The greatest patron.

King

　　　　　　　　　　You speak of gods but have
　　No reverence.

Herald

　　　　　　　　The Nile deities I revere.

King

　　And these gods are nothing?

Herald

　　　　　　　　　　　　I'll lead them away,
　　If no one robs me.

King
> You shall regret it,

If you touch them.

Herald
> You speak unkindly to strangers.

King

The thieves of gods I shall not befriend.

Herald

I shall tell Egyptus' sons.

King

What's that to me that I should yield my flock?

Herald

But if I knew, more clearly could I tell— 930
A herald should report exactly each
Particular. What shall I say? Who's he
That robs me of these cousins? Yet Ares gives
His verdict without witnesses, nor in the grip
Of silver quits his suit, but first many
Are thrown and kick off life.

King
> Why must you tell a name?

You and your shipmates will know soon enough;
Though, were these willing, with good will of heart,
You could lead them away, if pious speech 940
Persuaded them: thus unanimous the vote
Decreed, never to surrender them to force.
Joined, doweled, and bolted stays this law,
That neither scratched on tablets, nor book-sealed,
You hear announced by the tongue of freedom's voice.
Now get out of my sight!

Herald
> We seem to wage new wars. 950

May victory and conquest fall to men!

King

    And men is what you'll find here, who don't
    Guzzle a brew of barley-beer!

                                (Exit Herald.)

    Now all of you, attended by your maids,
    Take heart and go to the well-protected city,
    Locked by towers in dense array. And many
    Homes there are of public property, and I
    Am also housed with a lavish hand; there you may
    With many others live; or if it pleases   960
    More, you may live alone. Of these the best
    And most agreeable choose. Myself and all
    The citizens protect you, whose voted will
    Is now fulfilled. Why wait for those with more
    Authority?

Chorus

    In return for good things,
    May good things teem,
    Best of Pelasgians!
    Kindly escort my father here,
    Danaus, prudent, brave and wise.   970
    His is the counsel where to dwell,
    Kindly disposed the place with good
    Fame and repute among the people:
    Everyone's quick to blame the alien.
    May it be for the best!

                (Exit King. Enter Danaus, attended.)

Danaus

    My children, to Argives it is meet to pour   980
    Libations, pray and sacrifice as to gods
    Olympian, who unhesitant preserved us.
    What had been done, for native friends kindly,
    Bitterly against your cousins, they heard;
    And gave these armed attendants as a meed
    Of honor, that no spear-wielded fate be mine

In dying, lest I burden on the land
An ever-living grief. You must be grateful
Even more than I for what I have obtained.   990
Above my other counsels cut this wisdom:
Time becomes the touchstone of the alien,
Who bears the brunt of every evil tongue,
The easy targe of calumny. I beg
You not to bring me shame, you who have
That bloom which draws men's eyes: there is no simple
Guard for fruit most delicate, that beasts
And men, both winged and footed, ravage: 1000
So Venus heralds harvests lush with love;
And all, at the sleek comeliness of maidens,
Do shoot enchanted arrows from their eyes,
Overcome by desire. Let no shame for us,
But pleasure for our enemies, be done,
For which, in great toil, great seas were ploughed.
We have the choice (mere luck) of living either
With Pelasgus, or at the city's cost.   1010
Only regard this command of your father:
Honor modesty more than your life.

Chorus
All else may gods Olympian bless; but, father,
Be not anxious for our summer's blush,
For, lest the gods deliberate anew,
We'll hold to the course our past intent has set.

Chorus A (of maidens)
Come now to the city,
Praising blessèd lord gods,
Who shelter the city
And about the Erasinus dwell.   1020
Take up and accompany,
Servants, the song, and praise
For the city, no longer the Nile,
Respect with your psalms,—

But streams, that with quiet
Through the land fulness pour,
And gladden this earth with
Waters brilliant and rich.   1030
May Artemis sacred see,
Pitying us: by force
Of Aphrodite no marriage come,
A prize for the hated. =

Chorus B (of servants)
But careless not of Cypris this gracious song:
With power equal to Hera nearest to Zeus,
Honored the goddess sly-intent
In rites sacred and solemn;
Which share with a fond mother
Desire and, to whom no denial,   1040
Persuasion; and Aphrodite
A province to Concord bestowed,
And Eros whispering wanton. —

But bitter winds, and harsh and evil grief,
And battles bloody and deadly I fear before.
How did they sail so easily
In swift-winged pursuit?
Whatever is doomed becomes.
Infinite the mind is of Zeus,
Who cannot be bypassed.   1050
To many a woman before
Has marriage come as an ending. =

Chorus A
May great Zeus ward oft
An Egyptian marriage for me.
Chorus B
That would be best.
Chorus A
Would you charm the intractable?

Chorus B
> But the future you know not.—

Chorus A
> But Zeus's mind profound,
> How am I to plumb?

Chorus B
> Pray for the mean.   1060

Chorus A
> What limit do you teach me now?

Chorus B
> Ask the gods nothing excessive.=

Chorus
> Lord Zeus may he deprive us
> Of an ill marriage
> And a bad husband,
> As Io was released from ill,
> Protected by a healing hand,
> Kind might did cure her.—

> And strength may he assign us.
> I am content if ill   1070
> Is one-third my lot,
> And justly, with my prayers,
> Beside the saving arts of god,
> To follow justice.=

(Exeunt omnes.)

THE
PERSIANS

Translated and with an Introduction by

SETH G. BENARDETE

INTRODUCTION TO *THE PERSIANS*

The Persians was produced at Athens in 472 B.C., eight years after the naval battle at Salamis, which the play celebrates. We learn from its Argument that it was modeled on a lost play, *The Phoenissae* of Phrynichus, but that Phrynichus had announced at once the defeat of Xerxes, whereas Aeschylus presents a chorus of old men who voice their hopes and fears, by themselves and with Xerxes' mother, before the news of the defeat comes. This delay of course makes the Persians' defeat so much the greater, as it heightens the magnificence of their doom. The Queen then invokes her dead husband Darius (at whose tomb the scene is laid), who had led an unsuccessful expedition against Greece ten years before. He consoles the Queen and Chorus but predicts another disaster at Plataea (479 B.C.). Soon afterward, Xerxes, his garments torn, returns alone, and he and the Chorus conclude the play with a lament.

The Persians is unique in several ways. It is the only extant Greek tragedy that is not mythical but based on a contemporary event. The daring of such a presentation is easy to imagine. To show sympathetically, *sine ira et studio*, on the stage at Athens the defeat of her deadliest enemy testifies to the humanity of Aeschylus and the Athenians. No other tragedian we know of, of any country at any time, has ever dared to go so far in sympathizing with his country's foe. It is the more remarkable when we consider that Aeschylus himself and almost all of his audience fought at Salamis or Plataea and that the war, moreover, was between freedom and slavery. Here are the Persians, having started an unjust war and suffering a deserved defeat, presented not as criminals but rather as great and noble, dying deaths that are to be as much pitied as the deaths of Athenians. To praise the Athenians at Athens, Socrates remarks, or the Spartans at Sparta is not very difficult; but to praise the Athenians at Sparta or the Spartans at Athens demands great rhetorical skill; and for Aeschylus to praise before their conquerors the Persians, the enemies of all Greece, is without precedent and without imitation.

Although *The Persians* is historical in substance, Aeschylus deliberately introduced what the entire audience must have known to be false. He makes up Persian names, very few of which correspond to the generals we know to have been at the battle; his figures for the size of Xerxes' fleet at Salamis are greatly exaggerated; the Persians call upon Greek gods, though everyone knew that their gods were different; the Queen performs a Greek sacrifice at the tomb of Darius; neither the Chorus (except once) nor Darius mention the Persians' defeat at Marathon only ten years before; and perhaps what is most striking, Aeschylus invokes from the past Darius, so that his presence, being both ghostly and real, might transform an ugly reality into a poetic past. By thus changing many details of the real story, Aeschylus removes the Persian War to the realm of myth, where the memory of his audience is prevented from confirming or denying at every point the truth of what he says.

The contemporary is almost perforce untragic, for excessive attention to detail (and the contemporary must be shown accurately) stifles poetry and does not allow the poet to alter his subject; whereas tragedy, being abstracted from the present, is given a free rein, unhampered by what the audience knows to be so, to mold the story to its own demands. Just as verse is an abstraction from prose, reducing it to order, so tragedy abstracts from history and brings necessity out of chance.

If Aeschylus addressed his play specifically to his Athenian countrymen, how can he also speak to us, who are not Athenians, across the reach of time? This certainly must be said. The Persian War was not merely one parochial war among others, in which the issues of right and wrong are ambiguous, as was the case in the Peloponnesian War. The Persian War was a war of liberty versus despotism, and all free men of all times in reading *The Persians* will identify their cause with the cause of the Greeks. In this sense, then, we are

Athenians ourselves, and thus our sympathies and understanding become sufficiently enlarged to comprehend the merits of our foes.

Since the doom of the Persians is impressed upon us by the regular meters of the chorus, which convey even to our ears the effect of marching or lament, I have tried, so far as English would allow, to reproduce them in such a way that the reader can "hear" the mood of each song. I hope that, after a little practice on his part, the rhythm will become clear.

THE PERSIANS

CHARACTERS

Chorus of Persian elders

*Queen of Persia, wife of Darius,
mother of Xerxes*

Persian Herald

Ghost of Darius

Xerxes

THE PERSIANS

SCENE: *In the background the palace of Xerxes at Sousa, in the center foreground the tomb of Darius.*

Chorus
   Of the Persians gone
   To the land of Greece
   Here are the trusted:
   As protectors of treasure
   And of golden thrones
   We were chosen by Xerxes—
   Emperor and king,
   Son of Darius—
   In accord with age
   Guards of the country.

   For the king's return
   With his troops of gold
   Doom is the omen   10
   In my heart convulsed,
   As it whines for its master;
   For all Asia is gone:
   To the city of Persians
   Neither a herald nor horseman returns.

   And some Agbatana
   And some Sousa and
   Ancient Kissa leaving,
   Both on horse and on ship
   And on foot displayed
   Legions of battle: 20
   Artaphrenes, Megabates,
   Astaspes, Amistres,

Leaders of Persians, kings,
Who are slaves of the greatest of kings,
Guarding the legions they rush,
And as bowman and knight,
With their temper resolved,
Fearful in aspect,
Dreadful in battle.

And exultant in horses
Artembares, Masistres,   30
The brave archer Imaeus,
And Pharandakas,
And the driver of horses
Sousthenes.

And others were sent
By the flourishing Nile:
Egyptian-born Sousiscanes,
Pegastagon, great Arsames
Ruler of sacred Memphis;
And Ariomardus
Governing ancient Thebes;
And who dwelling by marshes
Are rowers of ships,
Skilful and countless.   40

And the Lydians soft
Who inhabit the coast
Follow commanders and kings:
Metrogathes and brave Arkteus,
And golden Sardis send
Many charioteers,
Horses by threes and by fours,
Fearful the sight to behold.

And the neighbors of Tmolus—
They threaten to yoke

In servitude Hellas;   50
And the Mysian lancers,
Tharybis, Mardon,
Anvils of battle.
And golden Babylon
Pours forth her crowds—
Borne by their ships—
Who in drawing the bow
Rely on their boldness.
And the tribes from all Asia
Who carry the sword
Follow beneath the
Awesome parade of their king.

Thus of the Persian land
Of her men the flower is gone,
Nursed by the earth, and all Asia   60
Laments, consumed by desire;
And parents and wives
Counting the days
Tremble at lengthening time.

The destroyer of cities now,
That kingly army, has gone
Over the strait to the land
On linen-bound pontoons—
Tightly was clamped the way—
Helle of Athamas crossing,   70
Yoking the neck of the sea. —

And the furious leader the herd
Of populous Asia he drives,
Wonderful over the earth,
And admirals stern and rough
Marshals of men he trusts:
Gold his descent from Perseus,
He is the equal of god. =   80

In his eyes lazuli flashing
Like a snake's murderous glances,
With his mariners, warriors, many,
And his Syrian chariot driving,
Hard on the glorious spearmen
The archer Ares he leads.—

To the great torrent of heroes
There is none worthily equal,
Who resist, by defenses securèd,
The unconquerable billows of ocean: 90
Persians are never defeated,
The people tempered and brave.=

For divine fate has prevailed since   102
It enjoined Persians to wage wars,
Which destroy towers and ramparts,
And the glad tumult of horsemen,
And cities overthrown.—

When the vast ocean was foaming,
By the winds boisterous whitened,
Then they learned, trusting to cables
And to pontoons which convey men,
To scan the sacred sea.=   113

  Deceitful deception of god—   93
  What mortal man shall avoid it?
  With nimbleness, deftness, and speed,
  Whose leaping foot shall escape it?
  Benign and coaxing at first
  It leads us astray into nets which
  No mortal is able to slip,
  Whose doom we never can flee.   101

Thus sable-clad my heart is torn,
Fearful for those Persian arms,

Lest the city hear, alas!
That reft of men is Sousa;—

And lest the city Kissa shall,
When the crowds of women cry,
Sing antiphonal, alas!   120
And rend their garb of mourning. =

All the horse and infantry
Like a swarm of bees have gone
With the captain of the host,
Who joined the headlands of either land,
Crossing the yoke of the sea.—   130

Beds with longing fill with tears,
Persian wives in softness weep;
Each her armèd furious lord
Dismissed with gentle love and grief,
Left all alone in the yoke. =

But come, Persians,   140
Let us in this ancient palace sit,
And deep and wisely found our thoughts:
How does King Xerxes fare, Darius' son,
How fare his people? Has arrows' hail
Or strength of spear conquered?   150
But lo! she comes,
A light whose splendor equals eyes of gods,
The mother of our king, I kneel.
Now all must address and salute her.

                                        (*Enter Queen.*)

O most majestic Queen of Persians
In ample folds adorned,
Hail, agèd Xerxes' mother,
Consort of Darius, hail!
Mistress of the god of Persians,
Mother of a god thou art,

Unless the fortune of their arms
Now at last has altered.

Queen

Leaving my gold-clad palace, marriage-
Chamber of Darius, and my own,   160
His queen I'm come. Care quite grates my heart;
I fear, my friends, though not fearful for myself,
Lest great wealth's gallop trip prosperity—
Exalted by Darius and some god—
In its own dust. But, unexpectedly,
That dread has doubled: sums of cowardly
Wealth do court contempt, and indigence
Quenches ambition's flame, even if there's strength.
Though wealth we have unstinted; yet fear
Is for mine eye, Xerxes, whose presence here
I count the palace-eye. So things stand thus.   170
Advise my reason, Persians, old sureties:
All my gains with your counsel lie.

Chorus

O Queen of Persia, be assured that never
Twice hast thou to tell us word or deed,
Which our willing strength can guide; for we
Are loyal, whom thou dost call thy counselors.

Queen

With frequent, constant, and nocturnal dreams
I have lived, as soon as my son, gathering
His host had gone, his will to pillage Greece;
But never a more vivid presence came
Than yesternight's.   180
Two women as an apparition came,
One in Persian robes instructed well,
The other Doric, both in splendor dressed,
Who grand and most magnificent excelled
Us now, their beauty unreproached, spotless;

Sisters they, who casting for their father's land,
She Greece received, she Asia, where to dwell.
Then strife arose between them, or so I dreamed;
And my son, observing this, tries to check   190
And soothe them; he yokes them to a chariot,
Bridles their necks: and one, so arrayed, towers
Proud, her mouth obedient to reins;
But the other stamps, annoyed, and rends apart
Her trappings in her hands; unbridled, seizes
The car and snaps its yoke in two;
My son falls, and his father, pitying,
Stands by his side, but at whose sight Xerxes
Tears his robes. Thus in the night these visions
Dreamed: but when, arisen, I touched the springs'   200
Fair-flowing waters, approached the altar, wishing
To offer sacrifice religiously
To guardian deities, whose rites these are,
Then to Phoebus' hearth I saw an eagle fleeing:
Dumb in dread I stood: a falcon swooped
Upon him, its wings in flight, its claws plucked
At his head: he did no more than cower, hare-like.
Those were my terrors to see, and yours to hear.   210
My son, should he succeed, would be admired;
But if he fails, Persia cannot hold him
To account. Whichever comes, safe returned, sovereign
He shall rule.

Chorus
                    Queen mother, excessive fear
Or confidence we do not wish to give thee.
If thy dreams were ominous, approach
The gods with supplications; pray that these
Be unfulfilled, and blessings be fulfilled
For thee, thy son, thy city, and thy friends.
Next thou must libations pour to Earth

And dead; and beg Darius, of whom thou didst dream,   220
Send thee those blessings from the nether world
To light, for thee and for thy son; and hide
In darkness evils contrary, retained
Within the earth. Propitious be thy prayers.
We, prophetic in our spirit, kindly
Counsel thee: all will prosper.

Queen
    Ah, loyally have answered the first expounders
    Of my dreams. May these blessings ripen!
    And all, as you enjoin, I'll sacrifice
    To nether gods and friends, as soon as I
    Return. But one thing more I wish to know: 230
    My friends, where is Athens said to be?

Chorus
    Far toward the dying flames of sun.

Queen
    Yet still my son lusts to track it down?

Chorus
    Then all Hellas would be subject to the king.

Queen
    So rich in numbers are they?

Chorus
                            So great a host
    As dealt to Persians many woes.

Queen
    Are bow-plucked shafts their armament?

Chorus
    Pikes wielded-close and shielded panoplies.

Queen
    What else besides? Have they sufficing wealth?   240

Chorus
    Their earth is veined with silver treasuries.

Queen

Who commands them? Who is shepherd of their host?

Chorus

They are slaves to none, nor are they subject.

Queen

But how could they withstand a foreign foe?

Chorus

Enough to vanquish Darius' noble host.

Queen

We mothers dread to calculate—

Chorus

But soon thou'lt know all: a Persian runner comes,
Bearing some fresh report of weal or woe.

(*Enter Herald.*)

Herald

O cities of Asia, O Persian land,
And wealth's great anchorage!
How at a single stroke prosperity's   250
Corrupted, and the flower of Persia falls,
And is gone. Alas! the first herald of woe,
He must disclose entire what befell:
Persians, all the barbarian host is gone.

Chorus

O woe! woeful evil,
Novel and hostile.
Alas! Persians weep
Hearing this woe,—

Herald

How all has been destroyed, and I behold   260
The unexpected light of my return.

Chorus

Oh long seems our aged
Life to us elders,

Alas! hearing woe
Unexpected. =

Herald

And since I was witness, deaf to rumor's tales,
I can indicate what sorrows came.

Chorus

Woe upon woe, in vain
The crowd of arrows, massed,   270
Came on the hostile land. —

Herald

The lifeless rotting corpses glut the shore,
And adjacent fields of Salamis.

Chorus

Woe upon woe, of friends
The sea-dyed corpses whirl
Vagrant on craggèd shores. =

Herald

The bow protected none, but all the host,
Defeated in the naval charge, was lost.

Chorus

Raise a mournful, doleful cry   280
For Persians wretched:
All they made all woe.
Alas! the host destroyed. —

Herald

O most hateful name of Salamis!
O woe! how I mourn recalling Athens.

Chorus

Athens hateful to her foes.
Recall how many
Persians widowed vain,
And mothers losing sons. =

Queen

    Long am I silent, alas! struck down
    By disasters exceeding speech and question.   290
    Yet men perforce god-sent misfortunes must
    Endure. Speak, disclose entire what
    Befell, quietly, though you grieve.
    Who did not die? For whom of the captains
    Shall we lament? Whose sceptered death drained his ranks
    Manless?

Herald

              Xerxes lives to behold the light, but—

Queen

    O for my palace a greater light,   300
    And after blackest night a whiter day.

Herald

    Artembares, captain of ten thousand
    Horse, was dashed against Silenia's
    Rugged shore; and satrap Dadakes,
    Spear-struck, did lightly tumble from his ship;
    And native-born Tenagon, the bravest
    Bactrian, still haunts sea-buffeted
    Ajax' isle; and Lilaeus, Arsames,
    And Argestes, conquered near the island
    Where doves do thrive, beat a stubborn coast;   310
    And neighbors of Egyptian Nile-waters,
    Adeues, Arkteus, and, third, shielded
    Pharnouchus, from a single ship
    Were drowned; and Matallus, satrap of Chrysa,
    Dying, leader of a thousand horse,
    Changed to richest red his thickset flowing
    Beard, and dipped his skin in crimson dyes;
    And Magian Arabus and Bactrian
    Artabes, all aliens in a savage
    Country, perished; Amphistreus, who wielded

The much-belaboring spear, and Amistris,   320
Brave Ariomardus, all made Sardis weep;
And Mysian Seisames, Tharybis,
Commander of five times fifty ships,
His race Lyrnaean, fair to look upon
(His fortune was not), dead he lies;
And the leader of Cilicians single-handed
Taxed the enemy with toil, and nobly
Died. So many of the rulers I
Recall, but of the many woes, report
But few.   330

Queen

   Alas! I hear the greatest
Of misfortunes, shame of Persians, and shrill
Lament. But tell me, returning to your tale,
What was the number of the Grecian ships,
That thought themselves a match for Persian
Arms in naval combat?

Herald

    Had numbers counted,
The barbarian warships surely would have won;
The Greeks but numbered thirty tens, and ten   340
Apart from these a chosen squadron formed;
But Xerxes, and this I know full well, a thousand
Led; and seven and two hundred ranked
As queens in swiftness. The count stood so.
Seemed we unequal? Some deity destroyed
Our host, who weighing down the balance swung
The beam of fortune. The gods saved the city
Of the goddess.

Queen

   What? Athens still
Stands unsacked?

Herald

              As long as there are men
The city stands.

Queen

              What was the beginning   350
Of disaster? Tell me. Who began?
The Greeks? My son—exultant in his numbers?

Herald

Either an avenger or a wicked
God, my Lady (whence it came I know not),
Began the whole disaster. From Athenian
Ranks a Greek approached, addressing Xerxes
Thus: "When the gloom of blackest night
Will fall, the Greeks will not remain, but leap
To rowing-bench, and each by secret course
Will save his life." And he your son, upon   360
His hearing this, in ignorance of Greek
Guile and the jealousy of gods,
Harangued his captains publicly: "As soon
As sunlit rays no longer burn the earth,
And darkness sweeps the quarters of the sky,
Rank the swarm of ships in three flotillas,
Guard they the entrances, the straits sea-pound,
And girdle others round Ajax' isle;
But if the Greeks escape their evil doom,   370
Contriving secret flight, all your heads
Will roll. I warrant it." So he spoke
In humored pride: of the god-given future
Nothing he knew. And, having supped, they set
Themselves in order, each heart obedient;
And sailors bound a thong about each oar.
When the glare of sunlight died, and night
Came on, every man was at his oar,
Every man at arms who knew them.

Rank encouraged rank, and long-boats sailed   380
To stations each had been assigned.
All night the captains kept the fleet awake;
And night ran on. No Grecian army set
Secret sail: but when the steeds of day,
White and luminous, began to cross
The sky, a song-like, happy tumult sounded
From the Greeks, and island rocks returned   390
The high-pitched echo. Fear fell among us,
Deceived in hope; for they (and not as if to flee)
A solemn paean chanted, and to battle
Rushed with fervent boldness: trumpets flared,
Putting every Greek aflame. At once
Concordant strokes of oars in dissonance
Slapped the waters' depths: soon we saw
Them all: first the right wing led in order,
Next advanced the whole armada;   400
A great concerted cry we heard: "O Greek
Sons, advance! Free your fathers' land,
Free your sons, your wives, the sanctuaries
Of paternal gods, the sepulchers
Of ancestors. Now the contest's drawn:
All is at stake!" And babel Persian tongues
Rose to meet it: no longer would the action
Loiter. Warships struck their brazen beaks
Together: a Grecian man-of-war began
The charge, a Phoenician ornamented stern   410
Was smashed; another drove against another.
First the floods of Persians held the line,
But when the narrows choked them, and rescue hopeless,
Smitten by prows, their bronze jaws gaping,
Shattered entire was our fleet of oars.
The Grecian warships, calculating, dashed
Round, and encircled us; ships showed their belly:
No longer could we see the water, charged

With ships' wrecks and men's blood.   420
Corpses glutted beaches and the rocks.
Every warship urged its own anarchic
Rout; and all who survived that expedition,
Like mackerel or some catch of fish,
Were stunned and slaughtered, boned with broken oars
And splintered wrecks: lamentations, cries
Possessed the open sea, until the black
Eye of evening, closing, hushed them. The sum
Of troubles, even if I should rehearse them
For ten days, I could not exhaust. Rest   430
Content: never in a single day
So great a number died.

Queen
    Alas! a sea of troubles breaks in waves
    On the Persians and barbarian tribes.

Herald
    But what we've told would scarcely balance woes
    Untold: misfortune came upon them, which
    Swung the beam to weigh them double these.

Queen
    But what greater hatred could fortune show?
    What misfortune came upon the soldiers,
    Swinging the beam of troubles to greater woes?   440

Herald
    All the Persians, who were in nature's prime,
    Excellent in soul, and nobly bred to grandeur,
    Always first in trust, met their death
    In infamy, dishonor, and in ugliness.

Queen
    Oh, wretched am I, alas! What doom
    Destroyed them?

Herald
    There is an island fronting Salamis,

Small, scarce an anchorage for ships,
Where the dancer Pan rejoices on the shore;
Whither Xerxes sent those men to kill   450
The shipwrecked enemies who sought the island
As a refuge (easily, he thought,
The Grecian arms would be subdued);
He also bid them rescue friends. He conned
The future ill. For when a god gave Greeks
The glory, that very day, fenced in bronze,
They leaped ashore, and drew the circle tight
At every point: mewed up, we could not turn.
Many rattled to the ground, whom stones
Had felled, and arrows, shot by bowstring,   460
Others killed; and in a final rush,
The end: they hacked, mangled their wretched limbs,
Until the life of all was gone.
Xerxes mourned, beholding the lowest depths
Of woe; who, seated on a height that near
The sea commanded all his host, his robes
Destroying (and his lamentations shrill),
Dispatched his regiments on land: they fled   470
Orderless. Now you may lament their fate,
Added to the others' summed before.

Queen
O hateful deity! how the Persians
You deceived! Bitter was the vengeance
Which my son at famous Athens found:
She could not sate her appetite with those
Whom Marathon had made the Persians lose.
For these my son, exacting as requital
Punishment (or so he thought)
Called on himself so numerous
A train of woes. Tell me, what ships escaped?
Where are they now? Can you clearly tell?

Herald

  Who captained the remaining ships set sail   480
  Before the wind, fleeing in disorder;
  But the army perished in Boeotia: some,
  In want of precious water, were racked with thirst,
  And some, gasping emptily on air,
  Crossed to Phocis, Locria, the Malian
  Gulf, where Spercheian waters kindly drench
  The plain; and thence Achaea and Thessaly
  Received us, wanting: there most died   490
  In hunger and in thirst: both we felt.
  To Magnesia and Macedonia we came,
  The River Axius, the reedy marsh
  Of Bolba, the mountain Pangaeon,
  And Thrace. There in the night a god
  Roused winter out of season: all, who had
  Believed the gods were naught, sang their chants,
  To earth and sky obeisance made.
  When we ceased invoking gods, we tried   500
  Waters that had turned to ice:
  Whoever started before Apollo's rays
  Spread and scattered in the sky, he
  Was saved. Soon the brilliant orb of sun,
  Its rays aflame, melts the river's midst:
  One falls upon the next: happy he whose life
  Was first cut short! The rest did make their way   510
  But painfully through Thrace: not many fled
  To hearth and home. Thus the city of Persians
  May lament, regretting the loss of youth.
  Truthful I have been, but omit many
  Of the woes a god has hurled against
  The Persians.

                                (*Exit Herald.*)

Chorus

     O toilsome deity! how heavily
 You leaped upon all Persia!

Queen

 Alas! woe is me, the host destroyed.
 O bright night's spectacle of dreams,
 How clearly you foresaw my woe,
 And you, my counselors, how poorly judged.   520
 But yet, as you counseled thus,
 First to the gods I'll offer prayer; and then
 To Earth and dead I'll come to offer gifts,
 A sacrificial cake. I know I pray
 For what is done and gone, but a brighter
 Fortune, in time to come, may there be.
 And you, worthy of trust, exchange worthy counsel;
 My son, should he return before my own
 Return, comfort and escort him home:
 I fear to woes he'll add more woe.   530

             (*Exit Queen.*)

Chorus

 O! royal Zeus destroyed
 The multitudinous, proud
 Host of the Persian men,
 And the cities of Sousa
 And of Agbatana
 Concealed in the darkness of grief.

 Many with delicate hands
 Rending their veils,
 Drenching their breasts,
 Swollen with tears,   540
 Sharing their woe,
 Ladies of Persia
 Softly are weeping,
 Desiring each

Him to behold
Wedded but lately,
Couches forsaking,
Soft as their coverlets
(Youth was voluptuous),
Their sorrows, insatiate woe.
And I the paean's song recite,
Doom of the gone,
Woe upon woe.

Now all Asia
Desolate, void,
Sighs lament:
Xerxes led,   550
Alas,
Xerxes lost,
O woe,
Xerxes heedless all discharged
With ocean argosies.
Why was Darius so long without harm,
Archery's captain of citizens,
Loved Sousa's lord?—

Armies, navies
Lazuli-eyed,
Linen-winged   560
Warships led,
O woe,
Warships rammed destructively
By Grecian arms.
Scarcely escaped was the leader alone
(So we have heard) in the Thracian
Plains, bitter ways. =

They of the first death,
Alas,

Left by necessity,
Woe,
Round by Kychraean shores,   570
Oh,
Moan in your anguish,
Cry to the heavens your grief,
Oh,
Wail long-weeping
Mournful cries.—

Torn in the sea-swirl,
Alas,
Mangled by voiceless,
Woe,
Fish of the unstained sea.
Oh,
Houses deprived grieve,
Sonless, to heavens their grief,   580
Oh,
Elders mourning,
Hear all woe. =

They throughout the Asian land
No longer Persian laws obey,
No longer lordly tribute yield,
Exacted by necessity;
Nor suffer rule as suppliants,
To earth obeisance never make:
Lost is the kingly power.—   590

Nay, no longer is the tongue
Imprisoned kept, but loose are men,
When loose the yoke of power's bound,
To bawl their liberty.
But Ajax' isle, spilled with blood
Its earth, and washed round by sea,
Holds the remains of Persia. =

(Enter Queen.)

Queen
    My friends, whoever's wise in ways of evil
    Knows how, when a flood of evil comes,
    Everything we grow to fear; but when   600
    A god our voyage gladdens, we believe
    Always that fortune's never-changing wind
    Will blow. As my eyes behold all things
    As fearful visitations of the gods,
    So my ears already ring with cureless songs:
    Thus consternation terrifies my sense.
    Therefore I departed from the palaces,
    Alone returning, unaccompanied
    By chariots, by pomp and ceremony.
    To the father of my son I bring
    Propitious offerings, libations   610
    For the dead: a milk-sweet draught of sacred kine
    Unblemished; and resplendent liquors of the honey-
    Working bee, with liquid droplets of a maiden
    Stream are mingled; and this elixir
    Of an antique vine, whose mother is
    The wild fields; and golden-green the fruit
    Of fragrant olive trees, always flourishing
    Their leafy age; and plaited flowers, children
    Of the fecund earth. My friends, recite
    Your chants and threnodies; recall
    Darius, daemon over these libations   620
    To the dead, sepulchral honors, which
    I lavish on the nether gods.

Chorus
    O Queen of the Persians,
    To the dark chambers
    Libations pour;
    While, kindness imploring
    Of the gods, the conductors,

We offer prayer:
Ye sacred divinities,
Earth and King Hermes, 630
Conduct him to light
Up from the dead,
Who alone of all mortals,
A remedy knowing,
May show us the end.

Hearest thou, blessèd king
Equal to god,
As I proclaim now
Chantings unpleasant
Barbarous mournful
Clear and diverse?
Miserable sorrows
I shall cry out.
Below dost thou hearken?—

Earth and the other gods 640
Leaders of dead,
Glorious demon
Him let arise thence,
God of the Persians
Sousa his mother;
Send up the man whom
Never surpassed
The Persian land buried. =

Loved is the man, loved his tomb
Hiding his loving ways.
Aedoneus conductor,
Would that Aedoneus send 650
Lord Darius alone:—

Never by war wasted his men,
Never infatuate,

Called a god in wisdom,
God in wisdom he was,
Ruled his people well. =

Padshah, ancient Padshah,
Appear on the height of thy tomb,
Raise thy slipper saffron-dyed,   660
Flash the lappets of thy crown:
Father Darius, Oh hither come, woe. —

Hear the recent sorrows,
O master of masters appear.
Stygian gloom doth flit about;
All the youth hath perished now.   670
Father Darius, Oh hither come, woe. =

Oh, alas, Oh!
O much-lamented by his friends in death:
The ships with triple banks of oars are gone.   680

(The Ghost of Darius rises.)

Darius

O faithful followers, companions
Of my youth! O Persian counselors!
What burden's burdening the city, which
In lamentation moans, and makes the plains
Tremble? And terrified I saw my wife
Beside my tomb, and graciously received
Her offerings; and you lamented, standing
Near my tomb, with cries of resurrection
Calling piteously. Ascent is not easy.
The chthonic deities more readily
Receive than give; but I, a potentate   690
Among them, came: be quick, that I be un-
Reproached for being late. What recent woe
Upon the Persians weighs?

Chorus

>I'm shamed to behold thee,
>I'm shamed to address thee,
>Who was anciently feared.—

Darius

>Since I have risen obeying
>Lamentations, lengthen not
>Your tale, but speak succinctly,
>Recounting all. Lay aside your
>Reverence toward me.

Chorus

>I tremble to please thee,
>I tremble to tell thee
>What is loth to be told.=

700

Darius

>As an ancient fear obstructs your sense,
>You, agèd consort of my marriage,
>Noble Queen, cease your weeping; tell me
>Clearly: many woes arise by sea, many
>Come by land, the longer life is racked.

Queen

>O King, exceeding mortal happiness
>By happy fate! How, as long as you beheld
>The eyes of sun, you spent, how envied! a blessed
>Life like god's; and now I envy you
>Your dying, ere you saw this depth of woe.
>Everything, Darius, you will hear
>Succinctly: Persia is destroyed.

710

Darius

>How? A lightning-bolt of hunger? Civil
>Strife within the city?

Queen

>   No, but all
>The host's destroyed at Athens.

Darius

                       Who among
  My sons was general? Tell me.

Queen

  Furious Xerxes, who drained the plain manless.

Darius

  By foot or warship was his vain attempt?

Queen

  By both: a double front of doubled hosts.   720

Darius

  But how did so great an army cross the strait?

Queen

  Devices, yoking Helle's strait, a path
  Afforded.

Darius

            He accomplished this? To close
  Great Bosphorus?

Queen

               So it was; some god
  Contrived it.

Darius

            Alas! a great divinity
  Deceived his sense.

Queen

              The evil end he made
  Is present to the eye.

Darius

              What befell them
  That you thus lament?

Queen

              The naval host,
  Destroyed, destroyed the landed host.

Darius

  Thus all the people spears destroyed.

Queen

Thus Sousa groans desolate. 730

Darius

Alas! the goodly host! Alas! defenders!

Queen

All the Bactrians destroyed, no youth remains.

Darius

O woe! the youth of allies gone.

Queen

Xerxes

Alone with few they say.

Darius

Perished how?

Perished where?

Queen

To the joyous bridge
They came, the yoke of continents.

Darius

He was saved? Can this be true?

Queen

Yes, a clear report without dispute.

Darius

Alas! that prophecy was quick to act!
Zeus hurled against my son its lightning-end, 740
While I expected after many years
The gods would make an end; but when a man's
Willing and eager, god joins in. The spring
Of evil's found: my son in ignorance
Discovered it, by youthful pride; who hoped
To check the sacred waters of the Hellespont
By chains, just as if it were a slave. He smoothed
His way, yoking Neptune's flowing Bosphorus
With hammered shackles. Mortal though he was,

By folly thought to conquer all the gods
And Neptune. Had not my son diseased his sense?   750
I fear my labored wealth will fall the prey
Of conquerors.

Queen

              Wicked men counseled this, furious
Xerxes learned; saying you acquired wealth
By spear, while he, in cowardice, played
The warrior at home, and multiplied
By nothing his ancestral wealth. So often
These wicked men reproached him, until he
Did plot his martial way toward Greece.

Darius

So their great, eternal deed is done!
Never had anyone before made this   760
Sousa so empty and so desolate,
Since Zeus, our Lord, bestowed that honor:
One man to wield his rod's authority
Over all of Asia, rich in flocks.
First was Medus leader of the host;
Next his son fulfilled the office well,
Whose reason was the helmsman to his spirit;
Third was Cyrus, fortunate, whose rule
Brought peace to all: the Lydian people
And the Phrygian he acquired,   770
And marched his might against Ionia:
No god resented him, for he was wise;
And fourth was Cyrus' son, who shamed his country
And ancestral throne; but Artaphrenes
(Aided by his guile) and his friends,
Whose task this was, slew him in his palace.
After him, I, willing, drew the lot
To rule, and often led a mighty host;   780
But never did I cast so great a woe

Upon my city. Xerxes, my son, as young
In age as sense, ignored my wisdom. Know
This well, my comrades old as I, all of us
Who held these powers, never wrought so many
Woes.

Chorus

      To what end, my Lord Darius, dost thou
Harp on this? How could we, the Persian
People, fare the best?

Darius

              If you lead
No expedition to the land of Greece,   790
Not even if the Median host be more;
For Grecian soil is their own ally.

Chorus

What dost thou intend by that, "their own ally"?

Darius

It starves to death excessive numbers.

Chorus

But, be sure, we'll raise a well-equipped
And chosen host.

Darius

           But even they, who now
Remain in Greece, shall find no safe return.

Chorus

What? Shall not all the host return
Across the strait of Helle?

Darius

           Few of many,
If the oracles of gods are credited: 800
As we gaze at what has passed, no half
Prophecy succeeds, but either all
Or none. If we credit them, he leaves

Behind, his empty hopes persuading, chosen
Numbers of his host, who now are stationed
Where Asopus floods the plain, its rich sap
Kind to Boeotia; here await them
The lowest depths of woe to suffer, payment
For his pride and godless arrogance.
They, invading Greece, felt no awe,
They did not hesitate to plunder images
Of gods, and put temples to the torch;   810
Altars were no more, and statues, like trees,
Were uprooted, torn from their bases
In all confusion. Thus their wickedness
Shall no less make them suffer:
Other woes the future holds in store,
And still the fount of evils is not quenched,
It wells up, and overflows: so great will be
The sacrificial cake of clotted gore
Made at Plataea by Dorian spear.
And corpses, piled up like sand, shall witness,
Mute, even to the century to come,
Before the eyes of men, that never, being
Mortal, ought we cast our thoughts too high.   820
Insolence, once blossoming, bears
Its fruit, a tasseled field of doom, from which
A weeping harvest's reaped, all tears.
Behold the punishment of these! remember
Greece and Athens! lest you disdain
Your present fortune, and lust after more,
Squandering great prosperity.
Zeus is the chastener of overboastful
Minds, a grievous corrector. Therefore advise
Him, admonished by reason, to be wise,   830
And cease his overboastful temper from
Sinning against the gods. And you, aged
Mother of Xerxes, go to the palace;

Gather up rich and brilliant cloths, and go
To meet your son; for he, in grief, has rent
His embroidered robes to shreds. Gently soothe
Him with your words: to yours alone he'll listen.
Now shall I descend to nether gloom.
Elder counselors, farewell, and though
In time of troubles, give daily pleasures   840
To your soul, as wealth cannot benefit
The dead.

(The Ghost of Darius descends.)

Chorus

Alas! the woes upon us and the woes
To come have grieved me hearing them.

Queen

O god! how many sorrows move against me!
But one torment has the deepest fang,
Hearing that dishonor folds about my son
Its robes. But I shall go to gather up
Adornments, and try to meet my son.   850
When evils come on those we dearly love,
Never shall we betray them.

(Exit Queen.)

Chorus

Oh! alas, Oh! what a great and a good life was ours,
Civilly ordered, as long as the agèd
Ruler of all,
Mild, unconquerable king,
Equal to god,
Darius ruled the land.—

Glorious arms we displayed, and the bulwarks of custom
All they did guide. And returning from battle   860
Grief had we none,
Victors, unburdened of all,
Happy and glad,
To home again we came.=

For many the cities he sacked never crossing the Halys,
Nor leaving his hearth in a rush:
At the mouth of the River Strymon,
Near Thracian places,
The islands of Achelous; —

Both cities beyond the Aegean, surrounded by towers,   870
Obeyed him our lord, and who round
The broad strait of Helle boasting,
And recessed Propontis,
And gateway of Pontus, Bosphor; =

And the isles along the headland washed by sea   880
Lying close to shore:
Samos and Chios and Lesbos the olive-planted,
Paros and Naxos and Mykonos,
And Tenos the neighbor of Andros. —

And the islands in the midst of sea he ruled:
Ikaros and Lemnos,   890
Rhodus and Knidos and cities of Aphrodite,
Paphos and Solus and Salamis,
Whose founder's the cause of these sorrows. =

Thus the wealthy and populous lands,
The Ionian province, he ruled;   900
And the strength of his helmeted men
Was unwearied, innumerable allies.
But now we bear god-routed fortunes,
Overcome by the blows of the sea.

                                          (*Enter Xerxes alone.*)

Xerxes
   Oh, hateful this doom, woe is me,
   Wretched alas, without augury.   910
   How savagely swooped the deity.
   What will befall me? I swoon
   Beholding these citizens agèd.

Zeus! would that fate had covered me
With the Persians gone!

Chorus

Oh alas, King, for a brave host,
For the great honor of Persian rule,
For the ranks of men whom a god has slain.   920

Nations wail their native sons,
Who by Xerxes stuffed up hell;
Many heroes, Persia's bloom,
Archers, thick array of men,
Myriads have perished.
Woe, O King of noble strength.
Cruel! Cruel! Asia kneels.   930

Xerxes

Here am I, alas, O woe:
To my native and ancestral land
Woe is the evil I've become.

Chorus

Loudly shall I send, for your return,
An evil-omened shout, an evil-practiced cry:
A weeping wail of Persian mourners shall I sing.—

Xerxes

Send a wail of evil sound
Lamenting and grievous: now
Fortune again has changed for me.   940

Chorus

Mourning wail all-weeping shall I send,
In honor of your woes and sea-struck grief:
Again a wailing filled with tears I'll cry.=

Xerxes

Ionian Ares spoiled,
Protected by their ships,   950
Their partisan in war,

Reaping gloomy flats of sea
  and demon-haunted shores.

Chorus
  Oh alas!

Xerxes
          Lament and ask for all.

Chorus
  But where are the others?
  Where is thy retinue,
  Like Pharandakas,
  Sousas, Pelagon, and Agabatas,
  Dotamas, Psammis, Sousiscanes   960
  Leaving Agbatana?—

Xerxes
  The lost I deserted there,
  Who from the ships of Tyre
  To Salaminian shore
  Vanished and were gone, their corpses
      pounding stubborn shores.

Chorus
  Oh alas! but where is Pharnouchus
  And brave Ariomardus?
  Where is Seualkes lord,
  Or Lilaeus grand,
  Memphis, Tharybis, and Masistres,   970
  Artembares and Hystaechmes?
  These I ask you about. =

Xerxes
  Oh alas, woe,
  Who all, beholding ancient, hateful Athens, gasp on shore,
  Woe upon woe, wretched in a single sweep of oar.

Chorus
  Did you leave that Persian there,
  Your trusted universal eye,   980

Who made his count by myriads,
Batanochus' son Alpistus?
. . . .
Of Sesames, of Megabates,
Great Parthus and Oebares you left behind?
O woe, O woe, O miseries.
You tell of woes on woes.—

Xerxes

Oh alas, woe,
The magic wheel of longing for my friends you turn, you tell
Me hateful sorrows. Within my frame my heart resounds,
    resounds.

Chorus

And for the others still we long:
The leader of ten thousand men
Of Mardia, Xanthes, Angchares,
And Diaexis and Arsamas,
Masters of horsemen,
And Dadakas and Lythimnas,
And Tolmus who never slaked his spear.
I see about the mo ving tents,
I see no followers. =

Xerxes

Gone are the hunters of the pack.

Chorus

Gone, alas, fameless.

Xerxes

Oh alas, woe.

Chorus

Woe, O gods
Who brought these unexpected woes!
How baleful gleams the eye of doom.—

Xerxes

Struck by woes perpetual.

990

1000

Chorus
    Struck by recent—

Xerxes
    A recent woe.   1010

Chorus
    Woe, alas,
    They met the men-of-war without success:
    How luckless was the Persians' war. =

Xerxes
    Alas, in so vast an army I am struck.

Chorus
    What is not lost, thou curse of the Persians?

Xerxes
    Behold the remnants of my power.

Chorus
    I see, I see.

Xerxes
    And this receptacle.   1020

Chorus
    What is this that is saved?

Xerxes
    A treasure of arrows.

Chorus
    How few from so many!

Xerxes
    We are reft of protectors.

Chorus
    Greeks stand firm in combat. —

Xerxes
    Alas, too firm! I scan an unexpected woe.

Chorus
    You mean the host, routed and broken?

Xerxes

  My garments I rent at my woe.

Chorus

  Alas, O woe.   1030

Xerxes

  And even more than woe.

Chorus

  Double and triple the woe.

Xerxes

  Painful to us, but to enemies joy.

Chorus

  And docked was our power.

Xerxes

  I am stripped of escorters.

Chorus

  Sea-dooms stripped us of our friends. =

Xerxes

  Weep, weep, weep for the woe, and homeward depart.

Chorus

  Alas, O woe, misery.

Xerxes

  Shout antiphonal to me.   1040

Chorus

  To woebegone woeful gift of woes.

Xerxes

  Raising a cry, join together our songs.

Xerxes and Chorus

  Alas, O woe, woe, woe upon woe.

Chorus

  Hearing this calamity,
  Oh! I am pierced. —

Xerxes

  Sweep, sweep, sweep with the oar, and groan for my sake.

Chorus
   I weep, alas, woe is me.

Xerxes
   Shout antiphonal to me.

Chorus
   My duty is here, O master, lord.

Xerxes
   Lift up your voice in lamenting now.   1050

Xerxes and Chorus
   Alas, O woe, woe, woe upon woe.

Chorus
   Black again the blows are mixed,
   Oh, with the groans. =

Xerxes
   Beat your breast and cry Mysian songs.

Chorus
   Woe upon woe.

Xerxes
   Tear your whitened hair tightly clenched.

Chorus
   Tightly clenched, plaintive.

Xerxes
   Piercing cry.

Chorus
   And so I shall. —

Xerxes
   Full-fold garments with strength of hand rend.   1060

Chorus
   Woe upon woe.

Xerxes
   Pluck your hair and pity the host.

Chorus
   Tightly clenched, plaintive.

Xerxes
Drench your eyes.
Chorus
And so I weep. =
Xerxes
Shout antiphonal to me.
Chorus
Alas, O woe.
Xerxes
Wretched, homeward depart.
Chorus
O woe, alas.
Xerxes
Through the city lamentation.
Chorus
Lament indeed.
Xerxes
Softly stepping, moan.
Chorus
O Persian land in hardness stepped.
Xerxes
O woe, woe, in triple banks of oars,
O woe, woe, in argosies destroyed.
Chorus
We shall escort thee
With mournful lament.

1070

(*Exeunt omnes.*)

SEVEN

AGAINST

THEBES

Translated and with an Introduction by

DAVID GRENE

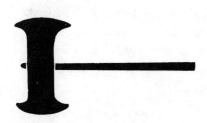

INTRODUCTION TO
SEVEN AGAINST THEBES

THIS strange, archaic play was produced in 467 B.C. It is probably
the last play of a trilogy written by Aeschylus on the theme of the
Oedipus cycle. It is at once undramatic and yet, in a paradoxical
way, very theatrical. Who can take seriously a play with almost no
action, in which the main event is the recital of the blazonry on the
shields of the Seven Champions? But a careful reading will reveal
the tremendous effect that the dancing accompaniments would have
made. The effect of the whole is, despite its disadvantages for a
modern reader, very powerful.

The play is extremely hard to translate. The style is heroic in the
good parts and bombastic in the bad. It is never simple and luminous.
Whereas the same quality of diction in the elevated parts of the
Prometheus is always suited to a majesty of theme comprehensible to
a modern reader, the matter of the *Seven* is remote from the interest
of a reader today, and it needs imagination to conceive of it in the
Greek theater, let alone on the stage as we now know it.

It is perhaps better understood by a modern reader in the mood in
which he would now attend a ritual ceremony, a church service, or a
pageant such as the coronation of an English monarch. The recital of
the devices on the shields, the matching of the champions, and, in
the last part of the play, the antiphonal keening of the sisters over
the dead bodies of their brothers are all properly traditional ritual.
They were probably filled for the Greek spectator with matter
pertinent to his own time. The political relation of Argos, Thebes,
and Athens was then much discussed, and Aeschylus has undoubted-
ly used the popular interest in these matters to render the old story
vital for his audience. It may be that the names of the champions had
many associations for the mid-fifth-century Greek. Aeschylus has

similarly used the general interest in the Areopagus in the years 462–459 B.C. for the pageant drama of the *Oresteia*. Though many of the clues to his employment of this method in the *Seven* are lost to us, we are almost certainly correct in assuming that this is again the course he adopted. The *Seven*, like the *Eumenides*, is the last play of the trilogy, and in both Aeschylus has managed to raise progressively a particular story to the level of a general process of history culminating in a particular historical occurrence known to his contemporaries.

CHARACTERS

Eteocles, son of Oedipus and
present ruler of Thebes

Antigone ⎫
⎬ *his sisters*
Ismene ⎭

Messenger

Chorus of Theban Women

SEVEN AGAINST THEBES

SCENE: *Thebes. The Prince Eteocles confronts a crowd of Thebans.*

Eteocles

You citizens of Cadmus, he must speak home
that in the ship's prow watches the event
and guides the rudder, his eye not drooped in sleep.
For if we win success, the God is the cause
but it—may it not chance so—there is disaster,
throughout the town, voiced by its citizens,
a multitudinous swelling prelude
cries on one name "Eteocles" with groans:
which Zeus defender keep from the city of Cadmus
even as his name implies.
You must help her now—you still something short   10
of your young manhood and you whose time of youth
is gone, your body grown to its full bigness—
each of you to such charge as fits you:
help the city, help the altars of your country's Gods;
save their honors from destruction:
help your children, help Earth your Mother.
She reared you, on her kindly surface, crawling
babies, welcomed all the trouble of your nurture,
reared you to live in her, to carry a shield
in her defense, loyally, against such needs as this.   20
Now to this God kindly inclines this day.
For those who have been held in siege so long
the Gods grant commonly a favorable fight.
So says the prophet now, bird shepherding
with skill unlying, ears and mind and fire
tending the oracular birds.
The master of these prophecies declares

enemy's night council framed a plot
for the greatest Achaean assault upon us.
All to the battlements, to the gates of the towers!　　　　30
Haste, in full armor, man the breastworks:
stand on the scaffolding and at the exit gates
be firm, abide, your hearts confident:
fear not that mighty mob of foreigners.
God will dispose all well:
I have sent scouts and spies upon their host:
they will not—well I know it—make the journey
vainly, and by their information
I shall be armed against enemy's stratagems.

Messenger

Eteocles, great prince of the Cadmaeans,
I come bringing a clear word from the army　　　　40
of matters there: I myself too
have seen the things I speak of.
There were seven men, fierce regiment commanders,
who cut bulls' throats into an iron-rimmed
shield, and with hands touched the bulls' blood,
taking their oaths by Ares and Enyo,
by the bloodthirsty God of Battle Rout
either to lay your city level
with the ground, sacked, or by their death to make
a bloody paste of this same soil of yours.
Remembrances of themselves for parents at home
their hands have hung upon Adrastus' chariot:　　　　50
their tears ran down,
but never a word of pity was in their mouths.
Their spirits were hard as iron and ablaze
breathed courage: war looked through their lion-eyes.
You will not wait long for confirmation
of this my news: I left them casting lots
how each should lead his regiment against your gates.
Wherefore the choicest men within your city

set at the entrance gates: set them quickly
for near already the armed host of Argives
comes in a cloud of dust, flecks of white,   60
panted from horses' lungs, staining the ground.
You, like the skilful captain of a ship
barricade your town before the blast of Ares
strikes it in storm: already bellows
the armed land wave. Take quickest opportunity
for all these things and I for the rest
will keep my eye, a trusty day watcher.
Thanks to my clear reports you shall know whatever
happens within the gates, and come to no harm.

Eteocles

O Zeus and Earth and Gods that guard the city
My father's Curse, mighty evil spirit,   70
do not root out this city of mine, do not
give her to ruin and destruction, do not
give her to capture nor her homes and hearths.
This is a town that speaks with a Greek tongue.
City and land of the Cadmaeans are free:
do not bind her in slavish yoke; be her protector.
I think I speak for everybody's good,
for a city prosperous honors the Gods.

Chorus

My sorrows are great and fearful: I cry aloud:
the army has left the camp and is gone.
Look at the forward rushing river, the great tide of horsemen!   80
I see a cloud of dust, sky high, and am convinced;
a messenger clear and unlying, though voiceless.

Treading feet on the earth of my country,
trampling hoofs, the sound of these draws near.

                                                        (*Shout is heard.*)

It floats, it rings
like a resistless mountain waterfall.

O gods, O goddesses, the trouble raised!
Turn it aside!

(Shouts.)

Over the walls they spring
the Horse of the White Shield
well equipped, hastening upon our city.   90

Who will protect us? Who will be our champion
of gods or goddesses?
Shall I kneel at the images of the Gods?
O Blessed Ones, throned in peace,
it is time to cling to your images.
We delay and wail too much.

Do you hear or do you not the rattle of shields?   100

When, if not now, shall we hang
robes and garlands on your statues, supplicating?

I see the sound!
No one spear rattled so.

What will you do? Will you betray,
ancient lord of our land Ares,
your own land?

O spirit of the golden helmet look down upon us,
look down upon a city
which once you dearly loved.

City guarding gods of our land, come, come all of you!
Look upon us a band of virgins,   110
suppliants against slavery!
Around our city the wave of warriors, with waving plumes,
roars; blasts of the War God stirred them.
Alas alas Zeus, Father Omnipotent! all fulfilling!
Let us not fall into the hands of the foeman!
For the Argives are around Cadmus' city.   120
Fear is stronger than arms.

There is murder in the ringing bits
between their horses' jaws.
Seven proud captains of the host,
with harness and spear,
having won their place by lot,
stand champions at seven gates.
O victory, battle-loving, Zeus begotten,
save our city!

O Pallas, and the Horseman, Prince of the Sea,   130
King of the Trident, Poseidon,
deliverance from fear,
deliverance grant.
You, Ares, protect the city of Cadmus, that bears your name.

Show your care for it, in manifest presence.
And Cypris, who are our ancestress   140
turn destruction away. We are sprung from your blood
we approach you and cry
with prayers for the ears of the Gods.

And you, Wolf God, be a very Wolf
in the enemy host. And you, daughter of Leto,
make ready your bow.

Ah, ah,   150
the rattle of chariots round the city: I hear it.
O Lady Hera,
the groaning axles of the loaded wheels.
Beloved Artemis!
The air is mad with the whirr of spears.
What will happen our city, what will become of it,
whereto shall the Gods bring an end upon us?

There comes a shower of stones on the top of the battlements!
O beloved Apollo!
There is the rattle of bronze-bound shields at our gates!   160

O Son of Zeus
from whom comes the war's fulfilment,
from whom comes the fight's holy consummation.

O Athene, Blessed Queen, Champion of the city,
deliver her from the assault of the Seven.
O Gods all sufficient,
O Gods and Goddesses, Perfecters,
Protectors of our country's forts,
do not betray this city, spear-won,
to a foreign-tongued enemy.   170
Hear O hear the prayers, hand outstretched,
of the virgins supplicating in justice.

O beloved Spirits,
that encompass our city to its deliverance,
show how much you love it:
Bethink you of the public sacrifices.
As we have thought of you, rescue us.
Remember, I pray you, the rites
with loving sacrifice offered.   180

Eteocles

You insupportable creatures, I ask you,
is this the best, is this for the city's safety,
is this enheartening for our beleaguered army,
to have you falling at the images
of the city's gods crying and howling,
an object of hatred for all temperate souls?
Neither in evils nor in fair good luck
may I share a dwelling with the tribe of women!
When she's triumphant, hers a confidence
past converse with another, when afraid
an evil greater both for home and city.   190
Here now running wild among the citizenry
you have roared them into spiritless cowardice.
So, outside of our gates, gains strength the enemy

while we are by ourselves, within, undone.
All this you may have, for living with women.
Now if there is anyone that will not hear
my orders, be he man or woman or in between,
sentence of death shall be decreed against him
and public stoning he shall not escape.
What is outside is a man's province: let no   200
woman debate it: within doors do no mischief!
Do you hear me or not? Or are you deaf?

Chorus

Dear son of Oedipus, the bumping rattle of the chariots,
rattle, rattle, I am afraid when I hear,
when the naves of the axles screech in their running
when the fire-forged bits speak ringingly,
rudder oars in horses' mouths.

Eteocles

What, shall the sailor, then, leave the stern
and run to the prow and find device for safety
when his vessel is foundering in the sea waves?   210

Chorus

But it was to the images of the Gods
the ancient images I ran, trusting in the Gods,
when the stony snowflakes crashed upon our gates:
nay, then I was lifted up with force and betook me to prayer
to the Blessed Ones, for our city,
that they may make their strength its protection.

Eteocles

For protection pray that our towers
hold off the enemy's spears.

Chorus

And shall not that be
as the Gods dispose?

Eteocles

The Gods, they say,
of a captured town desert her.

Chorus

> Never in my lifetime, never may this assembly
> of Gods desert us: never may I live to see
> this city overrun, an enemy soldiery
> putting the torch to it.

Eteocles

> Do not call upon the Gods
> and then be guided wrongly.
> Obedience is mother to success,
> and success is parent of rescue—
> so runs the proverb.

Chorus

> This is true: but the strength of God is still greater.
> Oftentimes when a man is hopelessly sunk
> in misfortune He raises him, yes from his greatest sorrow
> while the clouds still hang over him, high above our eyes.

Eteocles

> But it is man's part, the sacrifice, the consultation
> of the Gods, when the enemy assault us;
> it is yours to be silent and stay within doors.

Chorus

> It is thanks to the Gods that we have our city
> unconquered: it is thanks to them
> that our towers reject the mob of foemen.
> What should be resented in these words?

Eteocles

> I do not grudge your honoring the Gods.
> But lest you make our citizens cowards,
> be quiet and not overfearful.

Chorus

> It was but now that I heard the noise and the confusion
> and trembling in fear came to this citadel,
> sacred seat.

Eteocles

If you shall learn of men dying or wounded,
do not be eager to anticipate it with cries,
for murdered men are the War God's nourishment.

Chorus

The snorting of horses! There, I hear it.

Eteocles

Do not listen; do not hear too much.

Chorus

Our city groans from its foundation: we are surrounded.

Eteocles

I shall think of this: that is enough for you.

Chorus

I am afraid: the din at the gates grows louder.

Eteocles

Silence! Do not speak of this throughout the city.   250

Chorus

O Blessed Band, do not betray this fort.

Eteocles

Damnation! Can you not endure in silence?

Chorus

Fellow-citizen Gods, grant me not to be a slave.

Eteocles

It is you who enslave yourselves, and all the city.

Chorus

O Zeus, All Mighty, your bolt upon our foes!

Eteocles

O Zeus, what a tribe you have given us in women!

Chorus

Base is the tribe of men of a captured town.

Eteocles

Words of ill omen, your hands on the images!

Chorus

Fear captures my tongue, and my spirit is nought.

Eteocles

Grant me, I pray you, the small thing I ask.   260

Chorus

Speak it quickly, that I may know.

Eteocles

Silence, you wretches, don't frighten your friends.

Chorus

I am silent: with others I'll endure what is fated.

Eteocles

I like this word better than those before.
Furthermore, get you away from the statues,
and being so, utter a better prayer:
"May the Gods stand our allies." First hear my
prayer and then offer yours—
a holy gracious paean of thanksgiving,
the cry of sacrifice, our Grecian custom,
joy to our friends, dissolving fear of foes.   270

(*He approaches the images himself and prays.*)

Gods of the city, of this country Gods,
Lords of its fields, and its assembly places,
Springs of Dirce, waters of Ismenus—
to you my vow:
if all go well with us, if the city is saved,
my people shall dye your hearths with the blood
of sacrificed sheep, aye with the blood
of bulls slaughtered to honor the Gods.
I shall myself dedicate trophies,
spoils of my enemies, their garments fixed
on spear points, in your sanctuaries.

(*To the Chorus*)

These be your prayers, unlamenting   280
with no vain wild panting and moaning.
For all such you will not escape your doom.

I will take six men, myself to make a seventh
and go to post them at the city's gates,
opponents of the enemy, in gallant style,
before quick messengers are on us and
their words of haste burn us with urgency.

Chorus

I heed him but through fear
my spirit knows no sleep:
and neighbors to my heart,   290
anxieties, kindle terror
of the host that beleaguers us.
As the all-fearing dove
dreads for its nestlings' sake
the snakes that menace them.
For they against our forts
with all their host, with all their people,
come. What will become of me?
Jagged rocks they hurl
upon our citizens, on both sides pelted.   300
O children of Zeus, ye Gods,
I pray you—protect
the city and the army,
the Cadmus born.
What country will you take in exchange,
than this one better,
if you abandon this deep-soiled land
to her enemies,
and Dirce's water, fairest to drink
of all that come from Poseidon   310
the Earth Upholder, and Tethys' sons?
Therefore, you city-guarding Gods,
upon the men outside our forts
rain slaughtering destruction
and ruin, that will cast away their shields:
and for these citizens here

win glory and of the city
be the rescuers.
Then stand fair in your places   320
to receive our shrill prayers.

Pity it were that this city, so ancient,
should be cast to the House of Death,
a spear-booty, a slave,
in crumbling ashes, dishonorably,
sacked by an Achaean, with the Gods' consent;
that its women be haled away,
captives, young and old,
dragged by the hair, as horses by the mane,
and their raiment torn about them.
Emptied the city wails   330
as the captive spoil, with mingled cries,
is led to its doom.
This heavy fate is what I fear.
It is a woeful thing for maidens unripe,
before the marriage rites, to tread
this bitter journey from their homes.
I would say that the dead
are better off than this.
Alas, unlucky indeed the fate
of a city captured—   340
murder, fire, and rapine,
all the city polluted by smoke,
and the breath of Ares on it
maddened, desecrating piety, slaying the people.

There is tumult through the town.
Against her comes a towering net.
Man stands against man with the spear and is killed.
Young mothers, blood-boltered,
cry bitterly for the babes at their breast.   350
The roving bands of pillagers are all brothers;

he that has plunder meets with another;
he that is empty calls him that is empty,
wishing to have a partner, eager for a share
neither less nor yet equal.
From such things what shall one augur?

All sorts of grain fallen
strewn on the ground vex,
embitter the eye of the housewife.
The great, profuse gifts of the earth 360
in reckless streams of waste are poured out.
The girls, new servants, new to misery,
must endure a war captive's bed,
bed of a man successful.
Theirs the expectation of night's consummation
but for a triumphant enemy
to help their tearful sorrow.

Half-Chorus
Here, I think, friends, your scout comes bringing
some news of the enemy—hastily urging 370
the joints of his legs to carry him here.

Half-Chorus
And here is the king himself, the son
of Oedipus in the nick of time to hear
the messenger's story. He too is in haste
and nimbly steps along.

Messenger
                I can declare—
I know it well—the enemy's position:
how each at the gates has won by lot his station.
At the Proetid gate Tydeus now thunders
but dares not cross Ismenus' ford; the prophet
forbids. The sacrifices are unfavorable.
Tydeus, enraged and thirsting for the fight, 380
threatens, like serpents' hiss at noonday;

strikes with abuse the wise seer, Oecleides,
"battle and death make him cringe
through cowardice"—so he shouts aloud
and shakes his threefold shadowing plumes,
mane of his crested helm. Beneath his shield,
inside, ring brazen bells, a peal of terror,
and on the shield he bears this arrogant
device—a fashioned sky afire with stars.
In the shield's midst a glorious full moon,
night's eye, the eldest of the stars, stands out.   390
With such mad bragging and with overweening
trappings of war he roars along the banks
in love with battle, like the horse that chafes
against the bit, high mettled, impatient, hearing
the trumpet's sound. Against this champion
whom will you set?
When the bolts are shot back at the Proetid gates,
who will be champion fit to deserve our trust?

Eteocles
No equipment of a man will make me tremble
Devices on a shield deal no one wounds.
The plumes and bells bite not without the spear.
And for this night you speak of on his shield   400
glistening with all the stars of heaven—someone
may find his folly prophetic to himself.
For if in death night fall upon his eyes,
to him that bears this pompous blazonry
it shall be truly and most justly pregnant,
and he shall make his insolence prophesy
against himself.
        I nominate against him
as champion of these gates to challenge Tydeus,
the worthy son of Astacus—right noble,
one honoring the throne of Modesty
and hating insolent words.   410

Laggard in all things base he is wont to be
but not a coward. From those sown men
whom Ares spared his root springs—very native
is Melanippus to this land. His deeds
shall Ares with his dice determine;
but Justice, blood of his blood, sends him forth,
surely, to turn the enemy's spear away
from the mother that has borne him.

Chorus

May the Gods grant
good luck to our champion,
since justly he comes forward
a fighter for us.
But I fear for our friends   420
to look upon bloodshed
of those we love, dying.

Messenger

Yes, may the Gods grant him good luck.
At Electra's gates stands by lot Capaneus,
a giant this man, taller than the other,
and his threats breathe inhuman arrogance.
Our towers he menaces with terrors—Fortune
fulfil them not!—for he declares he'll sack
our city with the Gods' good will or ill.
Not even Zeus's wrath striking the earth
before him shall be obstacle to his purpose.
The lightnings and the thunderbolts he likened   430
to the sun's warm rays at noontide.
His device a naked man that carries fire,
in his hands, ablaze, a torch all ready. In gold
are letters that declare "I'll burn the city."
Against this man send—who will meet him?
Who will abide his threats and never tremble?

Eteocles

This man's boasts, too, beget us other gain.
For of the haughtiness of vain men, true
accuser proves their own tongue. Capaneus
threatens to do—and is prepared to do—   440
disdains the Gods, and giving exercise
to his mouth, in vain joy, up to heaven
mortal though he is, against Zeus sends his words,
shouted in swelling pride. I trust on him
will justly come the bolt that carries fire
in no way like the sun's warm rays at noontide.
Against him, be his lips never so insolent,
a man of fiery spirit shall be stationed,
strong Polyphontes, a guard trustworthy,
by favor of protecting Artemis
and of the other Gods. Tell me another   450
that has his place by lot at another gate.

Chorus

Destruction on him that against the city
vaunts huge threats;
may the thunderbolt's blast restrain him
before he burst into my house,
before he ravish me from my maiden room.

Messenger

Now I shall tell him that by lot won next
station at the gates. The third lot cast
jumped from the upturned brazen helmet
in favor of a third man, Eteoclus,
that he should lead his regiment in a charge   460
against the gates of Neïs. He wheels his mares
snorting in their nose bands, ready to charge the gate.
Pipes on the bridle bands filled with insolent
nostril breath whistle in a foreign note.
His shield, too, has its design—and that no lowly—

a man in armor mounts a ladder's steps
to the enemy's town to sack it. Loud
cries also this man in his written legend
"Ares himself shall not cast me from the tower."
Against him send some champion trustworthy   470
to turn the yoke of slavery from this city.

Eteocles

This man I'll send and may good luck go with him!

There, he is gone. His boast is in his hands
Megareus, Creon's son, and of the seed
and race of the sown men. He will not blench
at the furious neighing of horses nor yield the gates.
Either by death he'll pay his nurture's due
to his own land or he will capture two men
and city as depicted on the shield
and crown his father's house with the spoils of war.
On with another's boasts—don't grudge me the story.   480

Chorus

Good success to you, I pray,
Champion of my house,
and to the enemy ill success!
as with wild extravagance
they prate against the city
with maddened heart, so may Zeus
the Avenger look on them in wrath.

Messenger

Another, the fourth, holds the gate that neighbors
Onca Athena, and takes his station with a shout,
Hippomedon's vast frame and giant form.
He whirled a disc around—I mean the circle
of his shield—until I shuddered. I speak truth.   490
The armorer cannot have been a poor one
that put upon the shield this work of art—
a Typho hurling from his fiery mouth

black smoke, the flickering sister of fire.
The rim that ran around the hollow boss
of the shield is solid wrought with coiling snakes.
The man himself cried out his warcry, he,
inspired by Ares, revels in violence
like a Bacchanal with murder in his glance.
Take good heed how you deal with such a man;
he boasts even now at the gate he will raise panic.   500

Eteocles

First Onca Pallas, with her place beside
our city, neighbor to our gates, will hate
the fellow's violence and keep him off,
as it were a chill snake from her nestling brood.
And then Hyperbius, the stout son of Oenops,
has been chosen to match him man for man, right willing,
at fortune's need, to put his fate to question—
no man to be reproached either in form
or spirit or in bearing of his arms.
Hermes has matched the two with excellent reason,
for man with man they shall engage as foes
and on their shields shall carry enemy Gods.   510
The one has Typho breathing fire, the other,
Hyperbius, has father Zeus in station
sitting upon his shield, and in his hand
a burning bolt.
No one has yet seen Zeus defeated anywhere.
Such on each side are the favors of the Gods;
we are on the winning side, they with the vanquished
if Zeus than Typho mightier prove in battle.   520

Chorus

Sure am I that he who hath
Zeus's foe upon his shield
the unloved form of the earth-born God,
the likeness hated by men

and the long-living Gods,
shall lay his head before our gates.

Messenger

So may it prove. Now I shall take the fifth
that has his station at the fifth, the Northern gate,
right by Amphion's tomb that sprung from Zeus.
By his lance he swears—and with sure confidence
he holds it more in reverence than a god,   530
more precious than his eyes—he will sack the town
of Thebes in despite of Zeus. Such the loud vaunt
of this creature sprung of a mountain mother, handsome,
something between man and boy.
The beard is newly sprouting on his cheeks,
the thick, upspringing hair of youth in its bloom.
His spirit unlike his maiden name* is savage,
and with a grim regard he now advances.
He too boasts high as he draws near our gates.
For on his brazen shield, his body's rounded
defense, he swings an insult to our city,   540
the Sphinx that ate men raw, cunningly wrought,
burnished, embossed, secured with rivets there.
A man she bears beneath her, a Cadmaean,
so that at him most of our darts shall fly.
When he comes to the battle, so it seems,
he will not play the petty shopkeeper
nor shame the course of his long journey here—
Parthenopaeus of Arcadia.
He lives among our enemy presently
and pays to Argos a fair wage for his keep,
with threats against our forts—which God fulfil not.

Eteocles

Would that they might obtain what from the Gods   550
they pray against us—them, and their impious boasts.

* Parthenopaeus: Maiden One.

« 281 »

Then would they perish utterly and ill.
We have a man to encounter your Arcadian,
a man unboasting but his hand looks for
the thing that should be done—Actor, the brother
of him I spoke of earlier. He will not suffer
a heedless tongue to flow within our gates
and to breed mischief, nor to cross our walls,
one bearing on an enemy shield the likeness
of the most hateful Sphinx—or else the beast
borne outside shall have cause of blame against   560
him that would carry her in, for many a hammering
blow she will get beneath the city's walls.
With the God's will, I may indeed speak truth.

Chorus

The words go through my heart;
the hair stands upright on my head;
as I listen to mighty words
of impious boasting men.
May the Gods destroy them within our land!

Messenger

A sixth I'll tell you of—a most modest man
greatest in might of battle, yet a prophet,
strong Amphiaraus, at the Homoloian gates   570
stationed, shouts insults at strong Tydeus: "Murderer,
cause of confusion to the city, greatest
teacher of evil to Argos; of the Fury
a summoning herald; servant of bloodshed;
adviser to Adrastus of all these evils."
And then again with eyes uplifted calling
on your own brother, strong prince Polyneices,
he dwells twice on the latter part of his name.*
And this is the speech to which his lips give utterance:
"Is such a deed as this dear to the Gods,   580

* The latter half of the Greek word Polyneices means "strife."

and fair to hear and tell of, for posterity,
for one to sack his native city, destroy
the gods of his country, bringing in
an alien enemy host?
                        What justice
shall quench the spring of guilt of another murder?
Your fatherland destroyed by the spear
which your own zeal impelled—shall it be your ally?
But for myself I shall make fat this soil
a prophet buried under enemy ground.
Let us fight. The fate I look for is right honorable."
So spoke the prophet brandishing his round   590
brazen shield. No device is on its circle.
He is best not at seeming to be such
but being so. Deep indeed is the furrow
of his mind from which he gathers fruit, and good
the counsels that do spring from it. For him
send out, I recommend, wise and good challengers,
for he is dangerous who reveres the gods.

Eteocles
Alas, the luck which among human beings
conjoins an honest man with impious wretches!
In every enterprise is no greater evil
than bad companionship: there is no fruit   600
that can be gathered. The field of doom
bears death as its harvest.
Indeed, a pious man, going on board
as shipmate of a crew of rascal sailors
and of some mischief they have perpetrated,
has often died with the God-detested breed;
or a just man, with fellow citizens
themselves inhospitable, forgetful of the Gods,
has fallen into the same snare as the unrighteous,
and smitten by the common scourge of God
has yielded up his life.

Even so this seer,
this son of Oecles, wise, just, good, and holy,   610
a prophet mighty, mingling with the impious—
against his better reason—with loud-mouthed
men who pursue a road long to retrace,
with God's will shall be dragged to their general doom.
I think he will not even assault the gate—
not that he is a coward or faint of spirit—
but well he knows how he must die in the battle
if Loxias' prophecies shall bear fruit.
Loxias either says nothing or speaks seasonably.
Yet against him, the strong prince Lasthenes   620
we shall range in combat, an inhospitable
sentry, in mind an old man but a young one
in his body's vigor, in his swift-swooping charge,
in his hand, undelaying to snatch a spear
and hurl it against the unprotected shield side.
But success—that is for men the gift of God alone.

Chorus

Hear, O ye Gods, our lawful prayers
and bring them to fulfilment that
the city prosper, averting
the horrors of war upon our invaders.
May Zeus strike them and slay them
with his bolt outside of our walls.   630

Messenger

Lo, now, the seventh at the seventh gate
I shall unfold—your own, your very brother.
Hear how he curses the city and what fate
he invokes upon her. He prays that once his feet
are set upon her walls, once he is proclaimed
a conqueror of this land, once he has cried
paean of triumph in its overthrow,
he then may close in fight with you and killing
may find his death beside your corpse.

Or if you live, that he may banish you—
in the selfsame way as you dishonored him—
to exile. So he shouts and calls the Gods
of his race and of his fatherland to witness   640
his prayers—a very violent Polyneices.
He bears a new-made, rounded shield
and a twofold device contrived thereon:
a woman leading modestly a man
conducts him, pictured as a warrior,
wrought all in gold. She claims she is Justice,
and the inscription reads: I will bring him home
and he shall have his city and shall walk
in his ancestral house.
                Such are the signs.
But you yourself determine whom to send.   650
You shall not find a fault in my report:
but you determine how to steer the state.

Eteocles

Our race, our race, the race of Oedipus,
by the Gods maddened, by them greatly hated;
alas, my father's curses are now fulfilled!
But for me no crying and no lamentation
lest even sorer sorrow be begotten.
I tell you, Polyneices, so well named,
soon we shall know the pertinence of your sign,
whether your golden characters on the shield,   660
babbling, in wild distraction of the mind,
will indeed bring you home. This might have been,
if Justice, Zeus's virgin daughter had stood
by his actions and his mind. But in his flight
out of the darkness of his mother's womb,
in his growth as a child, in his young manhood,
in the first gathering of his chin's hair—no, never
did Justice look upon him nor regard him.
I do not think that now he comes to outrage

this fatherland of his she will stand his ally,
or else she is called falsely Justice, joining   670
with a man whose mind conceives no limit in villainy.
In this I trust and to the conflict with him
I'll go myself. What other has more right?
King against king, and brother against brother,
foe against foe we'll fight.
                      Bring me my greaves
to shield me from the lances and the stones.

Chorus

O dearest son of Oedipus, do not
be like in temper to this utterer
of dreadful sayings. There are enough Cadmaeans
to grapple with the Argives: such blood is expiable.   680
But for the blood of brothers mutually shed
there is no growing old of the pollution.

Eteocles

If a man suffer ill, let it be without shame;
this is the only gain when we are dead.
For deeds both evil and disgraceful never
will you say word of good.

Chorus

What do you long for, child?
Let not the frantic lust
for battle, filling the heart
carry you away. Expel
the evil passion at its birth.

Eteocles

It is the God that drives this matter on.
Since it is so—on, on with favoring wind   690
this wave of hell that has engulfed for its share
all kin of Laius, whom Phoebus has so hated.

Chorus

Bitter-biting indeed
is the passion that urges you

to accomplish manslaying,
bitter in fruit,
where the blood to be shed is unlawful.

Eteocles

Yes, for the hateful black
curse of my father loved
sits on my dry and tearless eyes
and tells me first of gain and then of death.

Chorus

Resist its urging: coward
you shall not be called
if you rule your life well.
Forth from your house the black-robed Fury   700
shall go, when from your hands
the Gods shall receive a sacrifice.

Eteocles

We are already past the care of Gods.
For them our death is the admirable offering.
Why then delay, fawning upon our doom?

Chorus

Not when the chance is yours—
for in the veering change
of spirit though late
perhaps the God may change
and come with kinder breath.
Now his blast is full.

Eteocles

The curse of Oedipus has fanned that blast.
Too true the vision of sleepy nightmares   710
showing division of my father's heritage.

Chorus

Listen to women though you like it not.

Eteocles

Speak then of what may be. Nor should it be long.

Chorus

Go not you, go not, to the seventh gate.

Eteocles

No words of yours will blunt my whetted purpose.

Chorus

Yet even bad victory the Gods hold in honor.

Eteocles

No soldier may endure to hear such words.

Chorus

Do you wish to reap as harvest a brother's blood?

Eteocles

If Gods give ill, no man may shun their giving.

Chorus

I shudder at the Goddess,   720
unlike all other Gods,
who compasses destruction of the house,
utterly unforgetting, prophet of ill,
the Fury invoked by a father's curse.
I dread that it bring to pass
the furious invocations
of Oedipus astray in his mind.
This strife, death to his sons, spurs it on.

A stranger grants them land-allotment,
a Chalyb, Scythian colonist,
a bitter divider of possessions—
iron-hearted Steel.   730
Yes, he has allotted them land to dwell in
as much as the dead may possess:
no share theirs of their broad acres.

When they die with mutual hand
mutually slaughtering
and earth's dust shall drink
black clotted murder-blood,

who shall then give purification,
who shall wash away the stain?
O new evils of the house,   740
new mingled with the old.

Old is the tale of sin I tell
but swift in retribution:
to the third generation it abides.
Thrice in Pythian prophecies
given at Navel-of-Earth
Apollo had directed
King Laius all issueless to die
and save his city so . . .

but he was mastered by loving folly   750
and begot for himself a doom,
father-murdering Oedipus,
who sowed his mother's sacred womb,
whence he had sprung himself,
with bloody root, to his heartbreak.
Madness was the coupler
of this distracted pair.

Now, as it were, a sea
drives on the wave:
one sinks, another rises,   760
triple-crested around the prow
of the city, and breaks in foam.
Our defense between is but a little thing
no bigger than a wall in width.
I fear that with our princes
our city be subdued.

For heavy is the settlement
of ancient curses, to fulfilment brought.
That evil when fulfilled
passes not away.

Prosperity grown over fat
of men, gain seeking,   770
compels jettisoning
of all goods, utterly.

What man has earned such admiration
of Gods and men that shared his city
and of the general throng of mortal men,
as Oedipus—who ever had such honor
as he that from his land had banished
the Sphinx, that ate men up?

But when in misery he knew
the meaning of his dreadful marriage,
in pain distraught, in heart distracted   780
he brought a double sorrow to fulfilment.
With patricidal hand
he reft himself of eyes
that dearer to him were than his own children.
And on those children savage
maledictions he launched
for their cruel tendance of him
and wished they might divide
with iron-wielding hand his own possessions.
And now I fear   790
that nimble-footed Fury bring those wishes to fulfilment.

Messenger

Take heart, you mother's darlings, this your city
has escaped the yoke of slavery. Fallen
are the vauntings of the monstrous men.
Our city is in smooth water and though many
the assaults of the waves, has shipped no sea.
Our wall still stands protecting us, our gates
we barricaded with trustworthy champions.
For the most part all is well—at six of the gates.
The seventh the Lord Apollo, Captain of Sevens,*   800

* "Captain of Sevens" is an ancient cult title of Apollo.

took to himself: on Oedipus' race
he has fulfilled Laius' ancient follies.

Chorus
What new and evil thing concerns the city?

Messenger
The city is saved, but the twin princes—

Chorus
Who? What do you mean? Through fear of your words I am
frantic.

Messenger
Get your wits and hear. Oedipus' two sons—

Chorus
Alas, alas, the ills I prophesied.

Messenger
In very truth, crushed to the ground.   810

Chorus
They lie there? Bitter though it be, yet speak.

Messenger
The men have fallen, one another's killers.

Chorus
Did brother's hands achieve a mutual murder?

Messenger
The ground has drunk the blood shed each by each.

Chorus
So all too equal was their guiding spirit.

Messenger
Surely he destroys this most unlucky race.
Here is store of sorrow and joy at once.
The city has good fortune, but its lords,
the two generals, have divided the possessions
with hammered steel of Scythia. They shall have
what land suffices for a grave, swept thither
down the wind of their father's ill-boding curses.   820

Chorus

O great Zeus and Spirits that guard
the city, you Protectors
that guard our walls:
shall I rejoice, shall I cry aloud
for our city's safety?
or for those wretched ones, luckless and childless,
our generals, shall I lament?
They have earned their name too well
and "men of strife" they have perished   830
through impious intent.

O black curse consummated
on the race, the curse of Oedipus!
An evil chill assails my heart.
I raise the dirge at the tomb
like a Bacchanal, hearing
of their blood-dripping corpses,
of their ill-fated death.
Ill-omened indeed
is this melody of the Spear.

It has worked to an end, not failed,   840
the curses called on them by their father of old.
The decisions of Laius, wanting in faith,
have had effect till now.
My heart is troubled for the city;
divine warnings are not blunted.
O full of sorrows, this you have done
a deed beyond belief.
Woes worthy of groaning
have come in very truth.

> (*The bodies of the princes are carried in, escorted*
> *by their two sisters, Ismene and Antigone.*)

Here is visible evidence of the messenger's tale.
Twofold our griefs and double

the ills these two men wrought;
double the fated sorrow
now brought to fulfilment.   850
What shall I say but that
here sorrows, sorrows' children,
abide at the hearth of the house?
But, my friends, down the wind of groans
with hands that beat the head
ply the speeding stroke
which sends through Death's waters
the dark-sailed ship of mission
to the shore, untrodden by Apollo, and sunless,
the shore unseen, that welcomes all at last.   860
Here they come to their bitter task,
Ismene and Antigone,
to make the dirge for their brothers.
With true sincerity, I think,
from their deep bosoms,
they shall utter a song of grief that fits the cause.
Us it concerns to sing,
before their song,
the ill-sounding Furies' dirge,
and the hateful Hades paean.   870

O most luckless of all women
that fasten the girdle about their robes,
I cry, I groan: there is no guile
in my heart to check my true dirge.

Antigone (speaking over the bodies)
    O you misguided ones,
faithless to friends, unwearied in evil,
you who plundered your father's house
to your misery, with the spear.

Chorus
    Wretched indeed those who wretched death
have found to the ruin of their house.   880

Ismene

    O you that tore the roof
    from our house, you that glimpsed
    the bitter sovereignty, at last
    you are reconciled—by the sword.

Chorus

    Too truly has that dread spirit,
    the Fury of Oedipus,
    brought all this to fulfilment.

Antigone

    Stricken through the left sides
    stricken indeed,
    through sides born of a common mother.   890
    Alas, strange ones,
    alas for the curse
    of death that answered death!

Chorus

    A straight thrust to house and body
    delivered by unspeakable wrath,
    by the doom invoked by a father's curse,
    which they shared without discord.

Ismene

    Through the city the cry of weeping;
    the walls groan aloud;   900
    the plain that loved them groans aloud.
    There abide for their descendants
    the possessions for which
    their bitter fate was paid,
    for which their strife arose,
    for which they found the end of death.

Chorus

    In bitterness of heart they shared
    their possessions in equality:
    no blame from friends
    has their arbitrator,
    Ares, impartial to both sides.   910

Antigone

By the stroke of the sword they are as they are
By the stroke of the sword there awaits them—what?
The share in their ancestral tomb, says someone.

Chorus

A shrill cry escorts them from their house,
a cry heartrending,
a cry for its own griefs, its own woes,
in anguish of mind with no thought of joy,   920
weeping tears from a heart that breaks,
for these our two princes.

Ismene

One may say over the bodies
of this unhappy pair:
much they have done to their fellow citizens,
and much to all the ranks of foreigners
who died in this destructive war.

Chorus

Unlucky she that bore them
above all womankind
that are called by a mother's name.
She took as husband her own child
and bore these who have died   930
their brotherly hands working each other's murder.

Antigone

Brotherly indeed in utter destruction
in unkindly severance,
in frantic strife,
in the ending of their quarrel.

Chorus

Their enmity is ended, in the earth
blood-drenched their life is mingled.
Very brothers are they now.   940
Bitter the reconciler of their feud,
stranger from over the sea,

sped hither by the fire,
whetted steel.
A bitter and evil divider of possessions,
Ares, who made their father's curse
a thing of utter truth.

Ismene

They have their share, unhappy ones
of Zeus given sorrows:
beneath their bodies, earth
in fathomless wealth shall lie. 950

Chorus (speaking over the bodies)

You who have made your race
blossom with many woes:
over you at last have cried
the Curses their shrill lament,
and the race is turned to confusion and rout.
The trophy of Destruction stands
at the gates where they were smitten
and conqueror of the two
the Spirit at last has come to rest. 960

(The dirge proper. The sisters stand each at the head
of one of the corpses.)

Antigone

You smote and were smitten.

Ismene

You killed and were slain.

Antigone

By the spear you killed.

Ismene

By the spear you died.

Antigone

Wretched in acting.

Ismene

Wretched in suffering.

Antigone
Let the groans go forth.

Ismene
Let the tears fall.

Antigone
You lie in death—

Ismene
having killed—

Antigone and Ismene
Woe, woe.

Antigone
My mind is distraught with groans.

Ismene
With groans my heart is full.

Antigone
Alas, alas, creature of tears.

Ismene
Alas, again, all-miserable.   970

Antigone
By a loving hand you died.

Ismene
And killed one that loved you.

Antigone
A double sorrow to relate.

Ismene
A double sorrow to see.

Antigone
Two sorrows hard by one another.

Ismene
Brother's sorrow close to brother's.

Chorus
O wretched Fate, giver of heaviness,
awful shade of Oedipus,

black Fury,
verily a spirit mighty in strength!

Ismene and Antigone
Woe, woe.

Antigone
Evils unfit to look upon—

Ismene
have you shown after banishment.

Antigone
He came not back when he had slain.   980

Ismene
This one saved, lost his own life.

Antigone
This one died—

Ismene
and killed the other.

Antigone
Race unhappy.

Ismene
Deed unhappy.

Antigone
Grievous sorrows of kindred.

Ismene
Grievous, thrice grievous sorrow.

Chorus
O wretched Fate, giver of heaviness,
awful shade of Oedipus,
black Fury,
verily a spirit mighty in strength.

Antigone
You have learned the lesson by experience.

Ismene
And you have learned it, no whit later.   990

Antigone
  When you returned to the city—

Ismene
  yes, to face him with your spear.

Antigone
  Deadly to tell.

Ismene
  Deadly to see.

Antigone
  Pain—

Ismene
  Ill—

Antigone
  To house and land—

Ismene
  and most of all to me.

Antigone
  O unhappy king of sorrow!

Ismene
  O of all most rich in pain!   1000

Antigone
  Where shall we lay them in the earth?

Ismene
  Where their honor is greatest.

Antigone
  O brothers possessed by evil spirits, in doom—

Ismene
  that will sleep by the side of their father to his hurt.

Herald
  It is my duty to declare to you,
  counselors of the people, the resolves
  already taken and the present pleasure
  of this Cadmaean city. . . .

Our Lord Eteocles for his loyalty
it is determined to bury in the earth
that he so loved. Fighting its enemies
he found his death here. In the sight
of his ancestral shrines he is pure and blameless   1010
and died where young men die right honorably.
These are my instructions to communicate
with respect to him. His brother Polyneices,
or rather his dead body, you must cast out
unburied, for the dogs to drag and tear
as fits one who would have destroyed our country
had not some God proved obstacle to his spear.
Even in death he shall retain this guilt
against his Gods ancestral whom he dishonored
when he brought his foreign host here for invasion
and would have sacked the city. So it is resolved
that he shall have, as his penalty, a burial   1020
granted dishonorably by the birds of the air
and that no raising of a mound by hand
attend him nor observance of keening dirge.
Unhonored shall his funeral be by friends.
This is the pleasure of the Cadmaean state.

Antigone

So I to the Cadmaean magistrates
declare: if no one else will dare to join me
in burying him, yet will *I* bury him
and take the danger on my head alone
when that is done. He is my brother. I
am not ashamed of this anarchic act   1030
of disobedience to the city. Strange,
a strange thing is the common blood we spring from—
a mother wretched, a father doomed to evil.
Willingly then with one that would not will it,
live spirit with dead man in sisterhood

I shall bear my share. His flesh
the hollow-bellied wolves shall never taste of.
Let that be no one's "pleasure or decree."
His tomb and burying place I will contrive
though but a woman. In the bosom folds
of my linen robe I shall carry earth to him.
And I shall cover him: let no one determine
the contrary. Be of good cheer (*to her sister*), I shall   1040
find means to bring my will to pass.

Herald
                            I forbid
this act, defiance of the city's pleasure.

Antigone
I forbid you your superfluous proclamations.

Herald
Harsh is the people now that danger's past.

Antigone
Harsh truly. But *he* shall not go unburied.

Herald
Him the state hates, will you grace with a tomb?

Antigone
Long since the Gods determined of his honor.

Herald
Not till he cast in peril this land of ours.

Antigone
He suffered ill and gave back what he suffered.

Herald
This deed of his was aimed at all, not one.   1050

Antigone
Last of the Gods Contention ends her tale.
But I shall bury him: spare me long speech.

Herald
Have your own way: but I forbid the act.

Chorus

Alas, alas.
O high-vaunting, ruin to the race
fatal Furies, who have destroyed
the race of Oedipus so utterly—
What will happen me? What shall I do?
What shall I plan?
How shall I be so heartless,
not to mourn for you,
not to give escort to your funeral?
But I fear the dreadful authority   1060
of the people: I am turned from my purpose.

(*To the body of Eteocles*)

Many mourners you shall win:

(*To the body of Polyneices*)

But this poor wretch unwept
save for his sister's single dirge
shall go his road. Who would yield
so much obedience as this?

                               (*The Chorus divides in two.*)

First Half-Chorus

Let the state do or not
what it will to the mourners of Polyneices.
We will go and bury him;
we will go as his escort.
This grief is common to the race   1070
but now one way and now another
the city approves the path of justice.

Second Half-Chorus

But we will go with the other, as the city
and Justice jointly approve.
For after the Blessed Ones and the strength of Zeus
he is the one who saved the city
from utter destruction, from being overwhelmed
by the wave of foreign invaders.

PROMETHEUS
BOUND

Translated and with an Introduction by

DAVID GRENE

INTRODUCTION TO
PROMETHEUS BOUND

IN THE eighteenth century the critics knew what they thought about the *Prometheus* of Aeschylus and knew why they thought it. It was a bad play because the structure was episodic, the characters extravagant and improbable, the diction uncouth and wild. Their handbook of criticism was the *Poetics* of Aristotle, either directly or indirectly drawn upon. And it is plain that the Aeschylean play does not measure up to Aristotelian standards. Since the eighteenth-century critics believed there was only one canon for drama, rooted in the principles of Aristotle, they quite reasonably judged the *Prometheus* a bad play. During the nineteenth century, with the Romantic revival and the breakdown of the so-called "classical" rules of the drama, the *Prometheus* was acclaimed by the critics as a great work of art. But they so acclaimed it entirely in terms of its theme or its poetry and in the same breath spoke of the greatness of Sophocles' *Oedipus*, Shakespeare's *Hamlet*, and Goethe's *Faust*. There was no effort to discover what in the nature of Aeschylus' dramatic method set him so apart from Sophocles that the eighteenth-century critics had refused to recognize his merit. Nor did they sift the striking differences which exist between the *Prometheus* and any of the Shakespearean tragedies or *Faust*. They contented themselves with vague and not entirely satisfied references to the *Prometheus* as a study-drama rather than a play for the theater.

Of the three dramatists, Aeschylus perhaps appears for a modern reader the most provocative and the most enigmatic. There is so much in the *Oresteia*, for instance, and particularly in the *Agamemnon*, which appeals directly to our sense of the theater and dramatic poetry. And yet the conclusion with its stress on an obscure theological point and its very local emphasis on the court of the Areopagus baffles our awakened interest. But in no play of Aeschylus is a reader today so aware at the same time of the directness and universality of the theme and also of the purely Greek, and indeed purely fifth-century, implications of it as in the *Prometheus*. The remarks that follow constitute only one more attempt among many to assist readers who are not classical scholars to a more complete understanding of a very great and very puzzling play.

For Aeschylus the myth is the illustration of a great permanent truth that he finds at the heart of man's activity. His dramatic imagination seizes on such truths as are most frequently a compromise between two opposites, and consequently the myths he uses most are those which tell of conflict on a cosmic scale and conflict ultimately laid by some concessions on the part of both combatants. To make myth universally significant, both characters and plot must correspond symbolically with characters and plot on one or more levels in addition to the myth in which they are imbedded.

In the *Prometheus*, the probability is not in the action or the conditions the dramatist has stated for us before the play commences. It consists in setting forth a very simple story, one which comes from a common stock of mythological stories known to almost all, and fusing this with a number of other patterns known to almost all. Everybody in Greece knew the legend of the Titan who stole fire from heaven to give it to man. But everybody in Greece also knew the story of Peisistratus, the tyrant of Athens, or Lygdamis, the tyrant of Naxos, or Polycrates, the tyrant of Samos. They knew the kind of outrage citizens had suffered at their hands, the innovations in established custom and ritual and in the conventional governmental attitudes of mercy, the "unwritten laws." Thus when the Prometheus-Zeus conflict is represented also as the rebel versus tyrant conflict, it has been invested with a new probability. And men everywhere have felt, some obscurely and some clearly, an opposition between the animal and the spirit in man, between violence and persuasion, between might and intellect. So when the Zeus-Lygdamis versus Prometheus-rebel struggle is represented as another facet of the conflict between the two most powerful factors in human life —brute force and mind—the story has been invested with a new probability drawn from the community of man's experience. And men everywhere have known the torture of subjugation to a stronger force than themselves, have known the helplessness of persuasion against force, and yet have believed in the ultimate triumph of persuasion. And so, when the suffering Prometheus cries out in his helplessness and his knowledge, and doubts yet feels certain of the outcome, the story has been invested with a new probability drawn from the community of man's experience. The original story of Zeus and Prometheus is like a stone thrown into a quiet pool, where the ripples spread in wider and wider circles.

Methods like the Aeschylean, developed to varying degrees of complexity, are familiar in other forms of literature. The degree of complexity is determined by the number of levels of meaning involved. For instance, in the *Pilgrim's Progress*, there is only one meaning in the tale apart from the highly dramatic story of Christian's journey, and that is the progress of the Christian soul toward the Eternal City. But, in the *Prometheus*, Aeschylus has made his story significant on a number of different levels, though each level involves the conflict of two opposing principles. For Prometheus is, politically, the symbol of the rebel against the tyrant who has overthrown the traditional rule of Justice and Law. He is the symbol of Knowledge against Force. He is symbolically the champion of man, raising him through the gift of intelligence, against the would-be destroyer of man. Finally, there is a level at which Prometheus is symbolically Man as opposed to God.

We are never told in this play why Zeus wished to destroy man. There is no indication what sort of animal he wished to put in his place; but, insofar as Prometheus in disobedience to Zeus enlightened man by the gift of intelligence, it may be assumed that Zeus's creation would have had no such dangerous potentialities of development. This first attempt to destroy mankind is almost certainly the flood of Deucalion, of which we hear elsewhere, and there is a tradition to the effect that Prometheus counseled Deucalion to the building of the ark which preserved him and his family. The second action in Prometheus' rescue of man from the enmity of the world in which he found himself is even more significant. "I stopped mortals from foreseeing doom," says Prometheus.

> *Chorus:* What cure did you provide them with against that sickness?
> *Prometheus:* I placed in them blind hopes.
> *Chorus:* That was a great gift you gave to men.

As the rest of his gifts to man are all concerned with enlightenment, and, indeed, as fire itself becomes a symbol of that enlightenment, this gift of "blind hopes" seems at first strange. Yet it is quite consistent. There is a passage in the *Gorgias* which is illuminating here. We are told that in the days of Kronos and *when Zeus was newly king*, men were informed as to the day of their death and were judged alive, with all their clothes on and their possessions about them, by live judges. This was a practice which brought much injustice, says Plato, and Zeus ultimately ordered it otherwise. Plato is using the myth for the illustration of his own theme, and we must not be surprised that his picture of the development of man when this was the state of things does not accord with that of Aeschylus. But the dating in the case of Plato shows either that he and Aeschylus were drawing on the same myth or else that Plato is borrowing from Aeschylus: "In the days of Kronos and when Zeus was newly king." What, then, is the meaning of the blind hopes which were the compensation for man's loss of knowledge of his death and yet left him able to use his reason to build houses and yoke horses and invent cures for sickness?

Prometheus is wise in the wisdom of his mother Themis, or Earth, and consequently wise in the knowledge of destiny. This is not reason. It is absolute knowledge. The knowledge of the day of a man's death partakes of that quality, for it is in the province of destiny. Thus man at the beginning had an infinitely small particle of the *same kind of knowledge* which Prometheus enjoyed in large measure. Just as animals today seem to have a curious intuition of the coming of their death and crawl away into hiding to face it, so primitive man had this knowledge. And Prometheus caused them to cease to foreknow the day of their death. For the gift of reason, the supreme ally in their struggle against nature, made them fight on against death in "blind hope," even when the day of their death had come. It is worth noticing here that, of the two accounts of man's origins in the world—the one that of a golden age of material and moral perfection and the other of miserable ignorance and helplessness—Aeschylus has preferred the scientific tradition. But he has chosen to incorporate in his account a grain of the truth of the former. The very small particle of absolute knowledge which man possessed was a spark of the divine. The fire itself, Prometheus' greatest and most celebrated gift to man, is a symbol of practical, not speculative, reason. And nowhere does Aeschylus assert that such speculative reason in its full will ever be in man's possession.

There is a sense in which Prometheus in this play appeals directly to the human sympathies of his audience because though a Titan and a God his helplessness before Zeus places him on the same level with mortals. It is the story of the man-god who must suffer for his kindness to man by having his state equated with theirs. In the case of Prometheus the good achieved for man is achieved before the suffering—which comes in the nature of a punishment. The cry of Prometheus—

> I knew when I transgressed nor will deny it.
> In helping man I brought my troubles on me;
> but yet I did not think that with such tortures
> I should be wasted on these airy cliffs—

is the cry of one who is man enough to be weak under pain. Prometheus, though possessed of a knowledge of destiny and therefore of victory in the end, is for the present at the mercy of a brutal and ignorant opponent. So, too, is the mortal Io. So are all the mortals over whom Death holds power against which they fight with "blind hopes." Finally, Prometheus' deliverance by Heracles, who is part god and part man, once again binds his fate to the creature whom he has helped to survive in the teeth of the opposition of the supreme god.

PROMETHEUS BOUND

CHARACTERS

Might

Violence (muta persona)

Hephaestus

Prometheus

Oceanos

Io

Hermes

Chorus of daughters of Oceanos

PROMETHEUS BOUND

SCENE: *A bare and desolate crag in the Caucasus. Enter Might and Violence, demons, servants of Zeus, and Hephaestus, the smith.*

Might

This is the world's limit that we have come to; this is the Scythian country, an untrodden desolation. Hephaestus, it is you that must heed the commands the Father laid upon you to nail this malefactor to the high craggy rocks in fetters unbreakable of adamantine chain. For it was your flower, the brightness of fire that devises all, that he stole and gave to mortal men; this is the sin for which he must pay the Gods the penalty—that he may learn to endure and like the sovereignty of Zeus and quit his man-loving disposition.

Hephaestus

Might and Violence, in you the command of Zeus has its perfect fulfilment: in you there is nothing to stand in its way. But, for myself, I have not the heart to bind violently a God who is my kin here on this wintry cliff. Yet there is constraint upon me to have the heart for just that, for it is a dangerous thing to treat the Father's words lightly.

High-contriving Son of Themis of Straight Counsel: this is not of your will nor of mine; yet I shall nail you in bonds of indissoluble bronze on this crag far from men. Here you shall hear no voice of mortal; here you shall see no form of mortal. You shall be grilled by the sun's bright fire and change the fair bloom of your skin. You shall be glad when Night comes with her mantle of stars and hides the sun's light; but the sun shall scatter the hoarfrost again at dawn. Always the grievous burden of your torture will be there to wear you down; for he that shall cause it to cease has yet to be born.

10

20

Such is the reward you reap of your man-loving disposition. For you, a God, feared not the anger of the Gods, but gave honors to mortals beyond what was just. Wherefore you shall mount guard on this unlovely rock, upright, sleepless, not bending the knee. Many a groan and many a lamentation you shall utter, but they shall not serve you. For the mind of Zeus is hard to soften with prayer, and every ruler is harsh whose rule is new. 30

Might

Come, why are you holding back? Why are you pitying in vain? Why is it that you do not hate a God whom the Gods hate most of all? Why do you not hate him, since it was your honor that he betrayed to men?

Hephaestus

Our kinship has strange power; that, and our life together.

Might

Yes. But to turn a deaf ear to the Father's words—how can that be? Do you not fear that more? 40

Hephaestus

You are always pitiless, always full of ruthlessness.

Might

There is no good singing dirges over him. Do not labor uselessly at what helps not at all.

Hephaestus

O handicraft of mine—that I deeply hate!

Might

Why do you hate it? To speak simply, your craft is in no way the author of his present troubles.

Hephaestus

Yet would another had had this craft allotted to him.

Might

There is nothing without discomfort except the overlordship of the Gods. For only Zeus is free. 50

Hephaestus

I know. I have no answer to this.

Might
Hurry now. Throw the chain around him that the Father may not
look upon your tarrying.

Hephaestus
There are the fetters, there: you can see them.

Might
Put them on his hands: strong, now with the hammer: strike.
Nail him to the rock.

Hephaestus
It is being done now. I am not idling at my work.

Might
Hammer it more; put in the wedge; leave it loose nowhere. He's a
cunning fellow at finding a way even out of hopeless difficulties.

Hephaestus
Look now, his arm is fixed immovably!   60

Might
Nail the other safe, that he may learn, for all his cleverness, that
he is duller witted than Zeus.

Hephaestus
No one, save Prometheus, can justly blame me.

Might
Drive the obstinate jaw of the adamantine wedge right through
his breast: drive it hard.

Hephaestus
Alas, Prometheus, I groan for your sufferings.

Might
Are you pitying again? Are you groaning for the enemies of
Zeus? Have a care, lest some day you may be pitying yourself.

Hephaestus
You see a sight that hurts the eye.

Might
I see this rascal getting his deserts. Throw the girth around his   70
sides.

Hephaestus

I am forced to do this; do not keep urging me.

Might

Yes, I will urge you, and hound you on as well. Get below now, and hoop his legs in strongly.

Hephaestus

There now, the task is done. It has not taken long.

Might

Hammer the piercing fetters with all your power, for the Over-seer of our work is severe.

Hephaestus

Your looks and the refrain of your tongue are alike.

Might

You can be softhearted. But do not blame my stubbornness and harshness of temper.   80

Hephaestus

Let us go. He has the harness on his limbs.

Might (to Prometheus)

Now, play the insolent; now, plunder the Gods' privileges and give them to creatures of a day. What drop of your sufferings can mortals spare you? The Gods named you wrongly when they called you Forethought; you yourself *need* Forethought to extri-cate yourself from this contrivance.

(*Prometheus is left alone on the rock.*)

Prometheus

Bright light, swift-winged winds, springs of the rivers, number-less

laughter of the sea's waves, earth, mother of all, and the all-seeing   90
circle of the sun: I call upon you to see what I, a God, suffer
at the hands of Gods—
see with what kind of torture
worn down I shall wrestle ten thousand
years of time—

such is the despiteful bond that the Prince
has devised against me, the new Prince
of the Blessed Ones. Oh woe is me!
I groan for the present sorrow,
I groan for the sorrow to come, I groan
questioning when there shall come a time
when He shall ordain a limit to my sufferings.
What am I saying? I have known all before,   100
all that shall be, and clearly known; to me,
nothing that hurts shall come with a new face.
So must I bear, as lightly as I can,
the destiny that fate has given me;
for I know well against necessity,
against its strength, no one can fight and win.

I cannot speak about my fortune, cannot
hold my tongue either. It was mortal man
to whom I gave great privileges and
for that was yoked in this unyielding harness.
I hunted out the secret spring of fire,
that filled the narthex stem, which when revealed   110
became the teacher of each craft to men,
a great resource. This is the sin committed
for which I stand accountant, and I pay
nailed in my chains under the open sky.

Ah! Ah!
What sound, what sightless smell approaches me,
God sent, or mortal, or mingled?
Has it come to earth's end
to look on my sufferings,
or what does it wish?
You see me a wretched God in chains,   120
the enemy of Zeus, hated of all
the Gods that enter Zeus's palace hall,
because of my excessive love for Man.

What is that? The rustle
of birds' wings near? The air whispers
with the gentle strokes of wings.
Everything that comes toward me is occasion for fear.

(The Chorus, composed of the daughters of Oceanos, enters,
the members wearing some formalized representation of
wings, so that their general appearance is birdlike.)

Chorus

Fear not: this is a company of friends
that comes to your mountain with swift
rivalry of wings.   130
Hardly have we persuaded our Father's
mind, and the quick-bearing winds
speeded us hither. The sound
of stroke of bronze rang through our cavern
in its depths and it shook from us
shamefaced modesty; unsandaled
we have hastened on our chariot of wings.

Prometheus

Alas, children of teeming Tethys and of him
who encircles all the world with stream unsleeping,
Father Ocean,   140
look, see with what chains
I am nailed on the craggy heights
of this gully to keep a watch
that none would envy me.

Chorus

I see, Prometheus: and a mist of fear and tears
besets my eyes as I see your form
wasting away on these cliffs
in adamantine bonds of bitter shame.
For new are the steersmen that rule Olympus:
and new are the customs by which Zeus rules,
customs that have no law to them,   150
but what was great before he brings to nothingness.

Prometheus

>Would that he had hurled me
>underneath the earth and underneath
>the House of Hades, host to the dead—
>yes, down to limitless Tartarus,
>yes, though he bound me cruelly
>in chains unbreakable,
>so neither God nor any other being
>might have found joy in gloating over me.
>Now as I hang, the plaything of the winds,
>my enemies can laugh at what I suffer.

Chorus

>Who of the Gods is so hard of heart   160
>that he finds joy in this?
>Who is that that does not feel
>sorrow answering your pain—
>save only Zeus? For he malignantly,
>always cherishing a mind
>that bends not, has subdued the breed
>of Uranos, nor shall he cease
>until he satisfies his heart,
>or someone take the rule from him—that hard-to-capture rule—
>by some device of subtlety.

Prometheus

>Yes, there shall come a day for me
>when he shall need me, me that now am tortured
>in bonds and fetters—he shall need me then,
>this president of the Blessed—   170
>to show the new plot whereby he may be spoiled
>of his throne and his power.
>Then not with honeyed tongues
>of persuasion shall he enchant me;
>he shall not cow me with his threats
>to tell him what I know,

until he free me from my cruel chains
and pay me recompense for what I suffer.

Chorus

You are stout of heart, unyielding
to the bitterness of pain.
You are free of tongue, too free.
It is my mind that piercing fear has fluttered;
your misfortunes frighten me.
Where and when is it fated
to see you reach the term, to see you reach
the harbor free of trouble at the last?
A disposition none can win, a heart
that no persuasions soften—these are his,
the Son of Kronos.

Prometheus

I know that he is savage: and his justice
a thing he keeps by his own standard: still
that will of his shall melt to softness yet
when he is broken in the way I know,
and though his temper now is oaken hard
it shall be softened: hastily he'll come
to meet my haste, to join in amity
and union with me—one day he shall come.

Chorus

Reveal it all to us: tell us the story of what the charge was on
which Zeus caught you and punished you so cruelly with such dishonor. Tell us, if the telling will not injure you in any way.

Prometheus

To speak of this is bitterness. To keep silent
bitter no less; and every way is misery.

When first the Gods began their angry quarrel,
and God matched God in rising faction, some
eager to drive old Kronos from his throne
that Zeus might rule—the fools!—others again

earnest that Zeus might never be their king—
I then with the best counsel tried to win
the Titans, sons of Uranos and Earth,
but failed. They would have none of crafty schemes
and in their savage arrogance of spirit
thought they would lord it easily by force.   210
But she that was my mother, Themis, Earth—
she is but one although her names are many—
had prophesied to me how it should be,
even how the fates decreed it: and she said
that "not by strength nor overmastering force
the fates allowed the conquerors to conquer
but by guile only": This is what I told them,
but they would not vouchsafe a glance at me.
Then with those things before me it seemed best
to take my mother and join Zeus's side: 220
he was as willing as we were:
thanks to my plans the dark receptacle
of Tartarus conceals the ancient Kronos,
him and his allies. These were the services
I rendered to this tyrant and these pains
the payment he has given me in requital.
This is a sickness rooted and inherent
in the nature of a tyranny:
that he that holds it does not trust his friends.

But you have asked on what particular
charge he now tortures me: this I will tell you.
As soon as he ascended to the throne   230
that was his father's, straightway he assigned
to the several Gods their several privileges
and portioned out the power, but to the unhappy
breed of mankind he gave no heed, intending
to blot the race out and create a new.
Against these plans none stood save I: I dared.

I rescued men from shattering destruction
that would have carried them to Hades' house;
and therefore I am tortured on this rock,
a bitterness to suffer, and a pain
to pitiful eyes. I gave to mortal man   240
a precedence over myself in pity: I
can win no pity: pitiless is he
that thus chastises me, a spectacle
bringing dishonor on the name of Zeus.

Chorus

He would be iron-minded and made of stone, indeed, Prometheus, who did not sympathize with your sufferings. I would not
have chosen to see them, and now that I see, my heart is pained.

Prometheus

Yes, to my friends I am pitiable to see.

Chorus

Did you perhaps go further than you have told us?

Prometheus

I caused mortals to cease foreseeing doom.   250

Chorus

What cure did you provide them with against that sickness?

Prometheus

I placed in them blind hopes.

Chorus

That was a great gift you gave to men.

Prometheus

Besides this, I gave them fire.

Chorus

And do creatures of a day now possess bright-faced fire?

Prometheus

Yes, and from it they shall learn many crafts.

Chorus

Then these are the charges on which—

Prometheus

Zeus tortures me and gives me no respite.

Chorus

Is there no limit set for your pain?

Prometheus

None save when it shall seem good to Zeus.   260

Chorus

How will it ever seem good to him? What hope is there? Do you
not see how you have erred? It is not pleasure for me to say that
you have erred, and for you it is a pain to hear. But let us speak no
more of all this and do you seek some means of deliverance from
your trials.

Prometheus

It is an easy thing for one whose foot
is on the outside of calamity
to give advice and to rebuke the sufferer.
I have known all that you have said: I knew,
I knew when I transgressed nor will deny it.
In helping man I brought my troubles on me;
but yet I did not think that with such tortures   270
I should be wasted on these airy cliffs,
this lonely mountain top, with no one near.
But do not sorrow for my present suffering;
alight on earth and hear what is to come
that you may know the whole complete: I beg you
alight and join your sorrow with mine: misfortune
wandering the same track lights now upon one
and now upon another.

Chorus

             Willing our ears,
that hear you cry to them, Prometheus,   280
now with light foot I leave the rushing car
and sky, the holy path of birds, and light
upon this jutting rock: I long
to hear your story to the end.

       (*Enter Oceanos, riding on a hippocamp, or sea-monster.*)

Oceanos

                              I come
on a long journey, speeding past the boundaries,
to visit you, Prometheus: with the mind
alone, no bridle needed, I direct
my swift-winged bird; my heart is sore
for your misfortunes; you know that. I think   290
that it is kinship makes me feel them so.
Besides, apart from kinship, there is no one
I hold in higher estimation: that
you soon shall know and know beside that in me
there is no mere word-kindness: tell me
how I can help you, and you will never say
that you have any friend more loyal to you
than Oceanos.

Prometheus

What do I see? Have you, too, come to gape   300
in wonder at this great display, my torture?
How did you have the courage to come here
to this land, Iron-Mother, leaving the stream
called after you and the rock-roofed, self-established
caverns? Was it to feast your eyes upon
the spectacle of my suffering and join
in pity for my pain? Now look and see
the sight, this friend of Zeus, that helped set up
his tyranny and see what agonies
twist me, by his instructions!

Oceanos

                              Yes, I see,
Prometheus, and I want, indeed I do,
to advise you for the best, for all your cleverness.   310
Know yourself and reform your ways to new ways,
for new is he that rules among the Gods.
But if you throw about such angry words,

words that are whetted swords, soon Zeus will hear you,
even though his seat in glory is far removed,
and then your present multitude of pains
will seem like child's play. My poor friend, give up
this angry mood of yours and look for means
of getting yourself free of trouble. Maybe
what I say seems to you both old and commonplace;
but this is what you pay, Prometheus, for   320
that tongue of yours which talked so high and haughty:
you are not yet humble, still you do not yield
to your misfortunes, and you wish, indeed,
to add some more to them; now, if you follow
me as a schoolmaster you will not kick
against the pricks, seeing that he, the King,
that rules alone, is harsh and sends accounts
to no one's audit for the deeds he does.
Now I will go and try if I can free you:
do you be quiet, do not talk so much.
Since your mind is so subtle, don't you know   330
that a vain tongue is subject to correction?

Prometheus

I envy you, that you stand clear of blame,
yet shared and dared in everything with me!
Now let me be, and have no care for me.
Do what you will, Him you will not persuade;
He is not easily won over: look,
take care lest coming here to me should hurt you.

Oceanos

You are by nature better at advising
others than yourself. I take my cue
from deeds, not words. Do not withhold me now
when I am eager to go to Zeus. I'm sure,
I'm sure that he will grant this favor to me,   340
to free you from your chains.

Prometheus

    I thank you and will never cease; for loyalty
    is not what you are wanting in. Don't trouble,
    for you will trouble to no purpose, and no help
    to me—if it so be you want to trouble.
    No, rest yourself, keep away from this thing;
    because I am unlucky I would not,
    for that, have everyone unlucky too.
    No, for my heart is sore already when
    I think about my brothers' fortunes—Atlas,   350
    who stands to westward of the world, supporting
    the pillar of earth and heaven on his shoulders,
    a load that suits no shoulders; and the earthborn
    dweller in caves Cilician, whom I saw
    and pitied, hundred-headed, dreadful monster,
    fierce Typho, conquered and brought low by force.
    Once against all the Gods he stood, opposing,
    hissing out terror from his grim jaws; his eyes
    flashed gorgon glaring lightning as he thought
    to sack the sovereign tyranny of Zeus;
    but upon him came the unsleeping bolt
    of Zeus, the lightning-breathing flame, down rushing,   360
    which cast him from his high aspiring boast.
    Struck to the heart, his strength was blasted dead
    and burnt to ashes; now a sprawling mass
    useless he lies, hard by the narrow seaway
    pressed down beneath the roots of Aetna: high
    above him on the mountain peak the smith
    Hephaestus works at the anvil. Yet one day
    there shall burst out rivers of fire, devouring
    with savage jaws the fertile, level plains   370
    of Sicily of the fair fruits; such boiling wrath
    with weapons of fire-breathing surf, a fiery
    unapproachable torrent, shall Typho vomit,
    though Zeus's lightning left him but a cinder.

But all of this you know: you do not need me
to be your schoolmaster: reassure yourself
as you know how: this cup I shall drain myself
till the high mind of Zeus shall cease from anger.

Oceanos

Do you not know, Prometheus, that words are healers of the
sick temper?   380

Prometheus

Yes, if in season due one soothes the heart with them, not tries
violently to reduce the swelling anger.

Oceanos

Tell me, what danger do you see for me in loyalty to you, and
courage therein?

Prometheus

I see only useless effort and a silly good nature.

Oceanos

Suffer me then to be sick of this sickness, for it is a profitable
thing, if one is wise, to seem foolish.

Prometheus

This shall seem to be my fault.

Oceanos

Clearly your words send me home again.

Prometheus

Yes, lest your doings for me bring you enmity.   390

Oceanos

His enmity, who newly sits on the all-powerful throne?

Prometheus

His is a heart you should beware of vexing.

Oceanos

Your own misfortune will be my teacher, Prometheus.

Prometheus

Off with you, then! Begone! Keep your present mind.

Oceanos

These words fall on very responsive ears. Already my four-legged
bird is pawing the level track of Heaven with his wings, and he
will be glad to bend the knee in his own stable.

Chorus

STROPHE

I cry aloud, Prometheus, and lament your bitter fate,
my tender eyes are trickling tears: 400
their fountains wet my cheek.
This is a tyrant's deed; this is unlovely,
a thing done by a tyrant's private laws,
and with this thing Zeus shows his haughtiness
of temper toward the Gods that were of old.

ANTISTROPHE

Now all the earth has cried aloud, lamenting:
now all that was magnificent of old
laments your fall, laments your brethren's fall   410
as many as in holy Asia hold
their stablished habitation, all lament
in sympathy for your most grievous woes.

STROPHE

Dwellers in the land of Colchis,
maidens, fearless in the fight,
and the host of Scythia, living
round the lake Maeotis, living
on the edges of the world.

ANTISTROPHE

And Arabia's flower of warriors   420
and the craggy fortress keepers
near Caucasian mountains, fighters
terrible, crying for battle,
brandishing sharp pointed spears.

One God and one God only I have seen
before this day, in torture and in bonds
unbreakable: he was a Titan,
Alas, whose strength and might
ever exceeded; now he bends his back
and groans beneath the load of earth and heaven.   430

ANTISTROPHE

The wave cries out as it breaks into surf;
the depth cries out, lamenting you; the dark
Hades, the hollow underneath the world,
sullenly groans below; the springs
of sacred flowing rivers all lament
the pain and pity of your suffering.

Prometheus

Do not think that out of pride or stubbornness I hold my peace;
my heart is eaten away when I am aware of myself, when I see
myself insulted as I am. Who was it but I who in truth dispensed
their honors to these new gods? I will say nothing of this; you   440
know it all; but hear what troubles there were among men, how
I found them witless and gave them the use of their wits and made
them masters of their minds. I will tell you this, not because I
would blame men, but to explain the goodwill of my gift. For
men at first had eyes but saw to no purpose; they had ears but did
not hear. Like the shapes of dreams they dragged through their
long lives and handled all things in bewilderment and confusion.
They did not know of building houses with bricks to face the sun;
they did not know how to work in wood. They lived like swarming ants in holes in the ground, in the sunless caves of the earth.   450
For them there was no secure token by which to tell winter nor
the flowering spring nor the summer with its crops; all their doings were indeed without intelligent calculation until I showed
them the rising of the stars, and the settings, hard to observe. And
further I discovered to them numbering, pre-eminent among

subtle devices, and the combining of letters as a means of re- 460
membering all things, the Muses' mother, skilled in craft. It was
I who first yoked beasts for them in the yokes and made of those
beasts the slaves of trace chain and pack saddle that they might be
man's substitute in the hardest tasks; and I harnessed to the carriage, so that they loved the rein, horses, the crowning pride of the
rich man's luxury. It was I and none other who discovered ships,
the sail-driven wagons that the sea buffets. Such were the con-
trivances that I discovered for men—alas for me! For I myself am 470
without contrivance to rid myself of my present affliction.

Chorus

What you have suffered is indeed terrible. You are all astray and
bewildered in your mind, and like a bad doctor that has fallen sick
himself, you are cast down and cannot find what sort of drugs
would cure your ailment.

Prometheus

Hear the rest, and you will marvel even more at the crafts and
resources I contrived. Greatest was this: in the former times if a
man fell sick he had no defense against the sickness, neither healing food nor drink, nor unguent; but through the lack of drugs 480
men wasted away, until I showed them the blending of mild
simples wherewith they drive out all manner of diseases. It was
I who arranged all the ways of seercraft, and I first adjudged
what things come verily true from dreams; and to men I gave
meaning to the ominous cries, hard to interpret. It was I who set
in order the omens of the highway and the flight of crooked-
taloned birds, which of them were propitious or lucky by na- 490
ture, and what manner of life each led, and what were their
mutual hates, loves, and companionships; also I taught of the
smoothness of the vitals and what color they should have to
pleasure the Gods and the dappled beauty of the gall and the lobe.
It was I who burned thighs wrapped in fat and the long shank
bone and set mortals on the road to this murky craft. It was I who
made visible to men's eyes the flaming signs of the sky that were

before dim. So much for these. Beneath the earth, man's hidden 500
blessing, copper, iron, silver, and gold—will anyone claim to
have discovered these before I did? No one, I am very sure, who
wants to speak truly and to the purpose. One brief word will tell
the whole story: all arts that mortals have come from Prometheus.

Chorus

Therefore do not help mortals beyond all expediency while neg-
lecting yourself in your troubles. For I am of good hope that once
freed of these bonds you will be no less in power than Zeus. 510

Prometheus

Not yet has fate that brings to fulfilment determined these things
to be thus. I must be twisted by ten thousand pangs and agonies,
as I now am, to escape my chains at last. Craft is far weaker than
necessity.

Chorus

Who then is the steersman of necessity?

Prometheus

The triple-formed Fates and the remembering Furies.

Chorus

Is Zeus weaker than these?

Prometheus

Yes, for he, too, cannot escape what is fated.

Chorus

What is fated for Zeus besides eternal sovereignty?

Prometheus

Inquire of this no further, do not entreat me. 520

Chorus

This is some solemn secret, I suppose, that you are hiding.

Prometheus

Think of some other story: this one it is not yet the season to give
tongue to, but it must be hidden with all care; for it is only by
keeping it that I will escape my despiteful bondage and my agony.

Chorus

STROPHE

May Zeus never, Zeus that all
the universe controls, oppose
his power against my mind:
may I never dallying
be slow to give my worship at   530
the sacrificial feasts
when the bulls are killed beside
quenchless Father Ocean:
may I never sin in word:
may these precepts still abide
in my mind nor melt away.

ANTISTROPHE

It is a sweet thing to draw out
a long, long life in cheerful hopes,
and feed the spirit in the bright
benignity of happiness:
but I shiver when I see you   540
wasted with ten thousand pains,
all because you did not tremble
at the name of Zeus: your mind
was yours, not his, and at its bidding
you regarded mortal men
too high, Prometheus.

STROPHE

Kindness that cannot be requited, tell me,
where is the help in that, my friend? What succor
in creatures of a day? You did not see
the feebleness that draws its breath in gasps,
a dreamlike feebleness by which the race   550
of man is held in bondage, a blind prisoner.
So the plans of men shall never
pass the ordered law of Zeus.

ANTISTROPHE

This I have learned while I looked on your pains,
deadly pains, Prometheus.
A dirge for you came to my lips, so different
from the other song I sang to crown your marriage
in honor of your couching and your bath,
upon the day you won her with your gifts
to share your bed—of your own race she was,
Hesione—and so you brought her home.   560

(Enter Io, a girl wearing horns like an ox.)

Io

What land is this? what race of men? Who is it
I see here tortured in this rocky bondage?
What is the sin he's paying for? Oh tell me
to what part of the world my wanderings have brought me.
O, O, O,
there it is again, there again—it stings me,
the gadfly, the ghost of earth-born Argos:
keep it away, keep it away, earth!
I'm frightened when I see the shape of Argos,
Argos the herdsman with ten thousand eyes.   570
He stalks me with his crafty eyes: he died,
but the earth didn't hide him; still he comes
even from the depths of the Underworld to hunt me:
he drives me starving by the sands of the sea.

The reed-woven pipe drones on in a hum
and drones and drones its sleep-giving strain:
O, O, O,
Where are you bringing me, my far-wandering wanderings?
Son of Kronos, what fault, what fault
did you find in me that you should yoke me
to a harness of misery like this,
that you should torture me so to madness   580
driven in fear of the gadfly?

« 331 »

Burn me with fire: hide me in earth: cast me away
to monsters of the deep for food: but do not
grudge me the granting of this prayer, King.
Enough have my much wandering wanderings
exercised me: I cannot find
a way to escape my troubles.
Do you hear the voice of the cow-horned maid?

Prometheus

Surely I hear the voice, the voice of the maiden, gadfly-haunted,
the daughter of Inachus? She set Zeus's heart on fire with love   590
and now she is violently exercised running on courses overlong,
driven by Hera's hate.

Io

How is it you speak my father's name?
Tell me, who are you? Who are you? Oh
who are you that so exactly accosts me by name?
You have spoken of the disease that the Gods have sent to me
which wastes me away, pricking with goads,
so that I am moving always
tortured and hungry, wild bounding,
quick sped I come,   600
a victim of jealous plots.
Some have been wretched
before me, but who of these
suffered as I do?
But declare to me clearly
what I have still to suffer: what would avail
against my sickness, what drug would cure it:
Tell me, if you know:
tell me, declare it to the unlucky, wandering maid.

Prometheus

I shall tell you clearly all that you would know, weaving you no
riddles, but in plain words, as it is just to open the lips to friends. 610
You see before you him that gave fire to men, even Prometheus.

Io

O spirit that has appeared as a common blessing to all men, unhappy Prometheus, why are you being punished?

Prometheus

I have just this moment ceased from the lamentable tale of my sorrows.

Io

Will you then grant me this favor?

Prometheus

Say what you are asking for: I will tell you all.

Io

Tell who it was that nailed you to the cliff.

Prometheus

The plan was the plan of Zeus, and the hand the hand of Hephaestus.

Io

And what was the offense of which this is the punishment? 620

Prometheus

It is enough that I have told you a clear story so far.

Io

In addition, then, indicate to me what date shall be the limit of my wanderings.

Prometheus

Better for you not to know this than know it.

Io

I beg you, do not hide from me what I must endure.

Prometheus

It is not that I grudge you this favor.

Io

Why then delay to tell me all?

Prometheus

It is no grudging, but I hesitate to break your spirit.

Io

Do not have more thought for me than pleases me myself.

Prometheus

Since you are so eager, I must speak; and do you give ear. 630

Chorus

Not yet: give me, too, a share of pleasure. First let us question her concerning her sickness, and let her tell us of her desperate fortunes. And then let you be our informant for the sorrows that still await her.

Prometheus

It is your task, Io, to gratify these spirits, for besides other considerations they are your father's sisters. To make wail and lament for one's ill fortune, when one will win a tear from the audience, is well worthwhile.

Io

I know not how I should distrust you: clearly 640
you shall hear all you want to know from me.
Yet even as I speak I groan in bitterness
for that storm sent by God on me, that ruin
of my beauty; I must sorrow when I think
who sent all this upon me. There were always
night visions that kept haunting me and coming
into my maiden chamber and exhorting
with winning words, "O maiden greatly blessed,
why are you still a maiden, you who might
make marriage with the greatest? Zeus is stricken
with lust for you; he is afire to try 650
the bed of love with you: do not disdain him.
Go, child, to Lerna's meadow, deep in grass,
to where your father's flocks and cattle stand
that Zeus's eye may cease from longing for you."
With such dreams I was cruelly beset
night after night until I took the courage
to tell my father of my nightly terror.

He sent to Pytho many an embassy
and to Dodona seeking to discover
what deed or word of his might please the God,   660
but those he sent came back with riddling oracles
dark and beyond the power of understanding.
At last the word came clear to Inachus
charging him plainly that he cast me out
of home and country, drive me out footloose
to wander to the limits of the world;
if he should not obey, the oracle said,
the fire-faced thunderbolt would come from Zeus
and blot out his whole race. These were the oracles
of Loxias, and Inachus obeyed them.   670
He drove me out and shut his doors against me
with tears on both our parts, but Zeus's bit
compelled him to do this against his will.
Immediately my form and mind were changed
and all distorted; horned, as you see,
pricked on by the sharp biting gadfly, leaping
in frenzied jumps I ran beside the river
Kerchneia, good to drink, and Lerna's spring.
The earth-born herdsman Argos followed me
whose anger knew no limits, and he spied   680
after my tracks with all his hundred eyes.
Then an unlooked-for doom, descending suddenly,
took him from life: I, driven by the gadfly,
that god-sent scourge, was driven always onward
from one land to another: that is my story.
If you can tell me what remains for me,
tell me, and do not out of pity cozen
with kindly lies: there is no sickness worse
for me than words that to be kind must lie.

Chorus

Hold! Keep away! Alas!
never did I think that such strange

words would come to my ears:
never did I think such intolerable   690
sufferings, an offense to the eye,
shameful and frightening, so
would chill my soul with a double-edged point.
Alas, Alas, for your fate!
I shudder when I look on Io's fortune.

Prometheus

You groan too soon: you are full of fear too soon: wait till you
hear besides what is to be.

Chorus

Speak, tell us to the end. For sufferers it is sweet to know before-
hand clearly the pain that still remains for them.

Prometheus

The first request you made of me you gained   700
lightly: from her you wished to hear the story
of what she suffered. Now hear what remains,
what sufferings this maid must yet endure
from Hera. Do you listen, child of Inachus,
hear and lay up my words within your heart
that you may know the limits of your journey.
First turn to the sun's rising and walk on
over the fields no plough has broken: then
you will come to the wandering Scythians
who live in wicker houses built above
their well-wheeled wagons; they are an armed people,   710
armed with the bow that strikes from far away:
do not draw near them; rather let your feet
touch the surf line of the sea where the waves moan,
and cross their country: on your left there live
the Chalybes who work with iron: these
you must beware of; for they are not gentle,
nor people whom a stranger dare approach.
Then you will come to Insolence, a river
that well deserves its name: but cross it not—

it is no stream that you can easily ford—
until you come to Caucasus itself,
the highest mountains, where the river's strength   720
gushes from its very temples. Cross these peaks,
the neighbors of the stars, and take the road
southward until you reach the Amazons,
the race of women who hate men, who one day
shall live around Thermodon in Themiscyra
where Salmydessos, rocky jaw of the sea,
stands sailor-hating, stepmother of ships.
The Amazons will set you on your way
and gladly: you will reach Cimmeria,
the isthmus, at the narrow gates of the lake.   730
Leave this with a good heart and cross the channel,
the channel of Maeotis: and hereafter
for all time men shall talk about your crossing,
and they shall call the place for you Cow's-ford.*
Leave Europe's mainland then, and go to Asia.

(*To the Chorus*)
Do you now think this tyrant of the Gods
is hard in all things without difference?
He was a God and sought to lie in love
with this girl who was mortal, and on her
he brought this curse of wandering: bitter indeed
you found your marriage with this suitor, maid.
Yet you must think of all that I have told you
as still only in prelude.   740

Io
O, O

Prometheus
Again, you are crying and lamenting: what will you do when you
hear of the evils to come?

* Cow's-ford: Bosporus.

Chorus

Is there still something else to her sufferings of which you will speak?

Prometheus

A wintry sea of agony and ruin.

Io

What good is life to me then? Why do I not throw myself at once from some rough crag, to strike the ground and win a quittance of all my troubles? It would be better to die once for all than suffer all one's days.

Prometheus

You would ill bear my trials, then, for whom Fate reserves no death. Death would be a quittance of trouble: but for me there is no limit of suffering set till Zeus fall from power.

Io

Can Zeus ever fall from power?

Prometheus

You would be glad to see that catastrophe, I think.

Io

Surely, since Zeus is my persecutor.

Prometheus

Then know that this shall be.

Io

Who will despoil him of his sovereign scepter?

Prometheus

His own witless plans.

Io

How? Tell me, if there is no harm to telling.

Prometheus

He shall make a marriage that shall hurt him.

Io

With god or mortal? Tell me, if you may say it.

Prometheus

Why ask what marriage? That is not to be spoken.

Io

Is it his wife shall cast him from his throne?

Prometheus

She shall bear him a son mightier than his father.

Io

Has he no possibility of escaping this downfall?

Prometheus

None, save through my release from these chains. 770

Io

But who will free you, against Zeus's will?

Prometheus

Fate has determined that it be one of your descendants.

Io

What, shall a child of mine bring you free?

Prometheus

Yes, in the thirteenth generation.

Io

Your prophecy has now passed the limits of understanding.

Prometheus

Then also do not seek to learn your trials.

Io

Do not offer me a boon and then withhold it.

Prometheus

I offer you then one of two stories.

Io

Which? Tell me and give me the choice.

Prometheus

I will: choose that I tell you clearly either what remains for you 780
or the one that shall deliver me.

Chorus

Grant her one and grant me the other and do not deny us the tale.
Tell her what remains of her wanderings: tell us of the one that
shall deliver you. That is what I desire.

Prometheus

    Since you have so much eagerness, I will not
refuse to tell you all that you have asked me.
First to you, Io, I shall tell the tale
of your sad wanderings, rich in groans—inscribe
the story in the tablets of your mind.   790
When you shall cross the channel that divides
Europe from Asia, turn to the rising sun,
to the burnt plains, sun-scorched; cross by the edge
of the foaming sea till you come to Gorgona
to the flat stretches of Kisthene's country.
There live the ancient maids, children of Phorcys:
these swan-formed hags, with but one common eye,
single-toothed monsters, such as nowhere else
the sun's rays look on nor the moon by night.
Near are their winged sisters, the three Gorgons,
with snakes to bind their hair up, mortal-hating: 800
nor mortal that but looks on them shall live:
these are the sentry guards I tell you of.
Hear, too, of yet another gruesome sight,
the sharp-toothed hounds of Zeus, that have no bark,
the vultures—them take heed of—and the host
of one-eyed Arimaspians, horse-riding,
that live around the spring which flows with gold,
the spring of Pluto's river: go not near them.
A land far off, a nation of black men,
these you shall come to, men who live hard by
the fountain of the sun where is the river
Aethiops—travel by his banks along   810
to a waterfall where from the Bibline hills
Nile pours his holy waters, pure to drink.
This river shall be your guide to the triangular
land of the Nile and there, by Fate's decree,
there, Io, you shall find your distant home,
a colony for you and your descendants.

If anything of this is still obscure
or difficult ask me again and learn
clearly: I have more leisure than I wish.

Chorus

If there is still something left for you to tell her of her ruinous
wanderings, tell it; but if you have said everything, grant us the   820
favor we asked and tell us the story too.

Prometheus

The limit of her wanderings complete
she now has heard: but so that she may know
that she has not been listening to no purpose
I shall recount what she endured before
she came to us here: this I give as pledge,
a witness to the good faith of my words.
The great part of the story I omit
and come to the very boundary of your travels.
When you had come to the Molossian plains
around the sheer back of Dodona where   830
is the oracular seat of Zeus Thesprotian,
the talking oaks, a wonder past belief,
by them full clearly, in no riddling terms,
you were hailed glorious wife of Zeus that shall be:
does anything of this wake pleasant memories?
Then, goaded by the gadfly, on you hastened
to the great gulf of Rhea by the track
at the side of the sea: but in returning course
you were storm-driven back: in time to come
that inlet of the sea shall bear your name
and shall be called Ionian, a memorial   840
to all men of your journeying: these are proofs
for you, of how far my mind sees something farther
than what is visible: for what is left,
to you and you this I shall say in common,
taking up again the track of my old tale.
There is a city, furthest in the world,

Canobos, near the mouth and issuing point
of the Nile: there Zeus shall make you sound of mind
touching you with a hand that brings no fear,
and through that touch alone shall come your healing.   850
You shall bear Epaphos, dark of skin, his name
recalling Zeus's touch and his begetting.
This Epaphos shall reap the fruit of all
the land that is watered by the broad flowing Nile.
From him five generations, and again
to Argos they shall come, against their will,
in number fifty, women, flying from
a marriage with their kinsfolk: but these kinsfolk
their hearts with lust aflutter like the hawks
barely outdistanced by the doves will come
hunting a marriage that the law forbids:
the God shall grudge the men these women's bodies,
and the Pelasgian earth shall welcome them   860
in death: for death shall claim them in a fight
where women strike in the dark, a murderous vigil.
Each wife shall rob her husband of his life
dipping in blood her two-edged sword: even so
may Love come, too, upon my enemies.
But one among these girls shall love beguile
from killing her bedfellow, blunting her purpose:
and she shall make her choice—to bear the name
of coward and not murder: this girl,
she shall in Argos bear a race of kings.
To tell this clearly needs a longer story,   870
but from her seed shall spring a man renowned
for archery, and he shall set me free.
Such was the prophecy which ancient Themis
my Titan mother opened up to me;
but how and by what means it shall come true
would take too long to tell, and if you heard
the knowledge would not profit you.

Io

Eleleu, eleleu
It creeps on me again, the twitching spasm,
the mind-destroying madness, burning me up
and the gadfly's sting goads me on—
steel point by no fire tempered—   880
and my heart in its fear knocks on my breast.
There's a dazing whirl in my eyes as I run
out of my course by the madness driven,
the crazy frenzy; my tongue ungoverned
babbles, the words in a muddy flow strike
on the waves of the mischief I hate, strike wild
without aim or sense.

Chorus

STROPHE

A wise man indeed he was
that first in judgment weighed this word
and gave it tongue: the best by far
it is to marry in one's rank and station: 890
let no one working with her hands aspire
to marriage with those lifted high in pride
because of wealth, or of ancestral glory.

ANTISTROPHE

Never, never may you see me,
Fates majestic, drawing nigh
the bed of Zeus, to share it with the kings:
nor ever may I know a heavenly wooer:
I dread such things beholding
Io's sad virginity
ravaged, ruined; bitter wandering
hers because of Hera's wrath.   900

EPODE

When a match has equal partners
then I fear not: may the eye

inescapable of the mighty
Gods not look on me.
That is a fight that none can fight: a fruitful
source of fruitlessness: I would not
know what I could do: I cannot
see the hope when Zeus is angry
of escaping him.

Prometheus

Yet shall this Zeus, for all his pride of heart
be humble yet: such is the match he plans,
a marriage that shall drive him from his power
and from his throne, out of the sight of all.   910
So shall at last the final consummation
be brought about of Father Kronos' curse
which he, driven from his ancient throne, invoked
against the son deposing him: no one
of all the Gods save I alone can tell
a way to escape this mischief: I alone
know it and how. So let him confidently
sit on his throne and trust his heavenly thunder
and brandish in his hand his fiery bolt.
Nothing shall all of this avail against   920
a fall intolerable, a dishonored end.
So strong a wrestler Zeus is now equipping
against himself, a monster hard to fight.
This enemy shall find a plan to best
the thunderbolt, a thunderclap to best
the thunderclap of Zeus: and he shall shiver
Poseidon's trident, curse of sea and land.
So, in his crashing fall shall Zeus discover
how different are rule and slavery.

Chorus

You voice your wishes for the God's destruction.

Prometheus

They are my wishes, yet shall come to pass.

Chorus

Must we expect someone to conquer Zeus?   930

Prometheus

Yes; he shall suffer worse than I do now.

Chorus

Have you no fear of uttering such words?

Prometheus

Why should I fear, since death is not my fate?

Chorus

But he might give you pain still worse than this.

Prometheus

Then let him do so; all this I expect.

Chorus

Wise are the worshipers of Adrasteia.

Prometheus

Worship him, pray; flatter whatever king
is king today; but I care less than nothing
for Zeus. Let him do what he likes,
let him be king for his short time: he shall not   940
be king for long.
                        Look, here is Zeus's footman,
this fetch-and-carry messenger of him,
the New King. Certainly he has come here
with news for us.

Hermes

                        You, subtle-spirit, you
bitterly overbitter, you that sinned
against the immortals, giving honor to
the creatures of a day, you thief of fire:
the Father has commanded you to say
what marriage of his is this you brag about
that shall drive him from power—and declare it   950

in clear terms and no riddles. You, Prometheus,
do not cause me a double journey; these

(Pointing to the chains.)

will prove to you that Zeus is not softhearted.

Prometheus

Your speech is pompous sounding, full of pride,
as fits the lackey of the Gods. You are young
and young your rule and you think that the tower
in which you live is free from sorrow: from it
have I not seen two tyrants thrown? the third,
who now is king, I shall yet live to see him
fall, of all three most suddenly, most dishonored.
Do you think I will crouch before your Gods,   960
—so new—and tremble? I am far from that.
Hasten away, back on the road you came.
You shall learn nothing that you ask of me.

Hermes

Just such the obstinacy that brought you here,
to this self-willed calamitous anchorage.

Prometheus

Be sure of this: when I set my misfortune
against your slavery, I would not change.

Hermes

It is better, I suppose, to be a slave
to this rock, than Zeus's trusted messenger.

Prometheus

Thus must the insolent show their insolence!   970

Hermes

I think you find your present lot too soft.

Prometheus

Too soft? I would my enemies had it then,
and you are one of those I count as such.

Hermes

Oh, you would blame me too for your calamity?

Prometheus

In a single word, I am the enemy
of all the Gods that gave me ill for good.

Hermes

Your words declare you mad, and mad indeed.

Prometheus

Yes, if it's madness to detest my foes.

Hermes

No one could bear you in success.

Prometheus

Alas!

Hermes

Alas! *Zeus* does not know that word.   980

Prometheus

Time in its aging course teaches all things.

Hermes

But you have not yet learned a wise discretion.

Prometheus

True: or I would not speak so to a servant.

Hermes

It seems you will not grant the Father's wish.

Prometheus

I should be glad, indeed, to requite his kindness!

Hermes

You mock me like a child!

Prometheus

And are you not
a child, and sillier than a child, to think
that I should tell you anything? There is not
a torture or an engine wherewithal
Zeus can induce me to declare these things,   990
till he has loosed me from these cruel shackles.
So let him hurl his smoky lightning flame,

and throw in turmoil all things in the world
with white-winged snowflakes and deep bellowing
thunder beneath the earth: me he shall not
bend by all this to tell him who is fated
to drive him from his tyranny.

Hermes

Think, here and now, if this seems to your interest.

Prometheus

I have already thought—and laid my plans.

Hermes

Bring your proud heart to know a true discretion—
O foolish spirit—in the face of ruin.   1000

Prometheus

You vex me by these senseless adjurations,
senseless as if you were to advise the waves.
Let it not cross your mind that I will turn
womanish-minded from my fixed decision
or that I shall entreat the one I hate
so greatly, with a woman's upturned hands,
to loose me from my chains: I am far from that.

Hermes

I have said too much already—so I think—
and said it to no purpose: you are not softened:
your purpose is not dented by my prayers.
You are a colt new broken, with the bit   1010
clenched in its teeth, fighting against the reins,
and bolting. You are far too strong and confident
in your weak cleverness. For obstinacy
standing alone is the weakest of all things
in one whose mind is not possessed by wisdom.
Think what a storm, a triple wave of ruin
will rise against you, if you will not hear me,
and no escape for you. First this rough crag
with thunder and the lightning bolt the Father

shall cleave asunder, and shall hide your body
wrapped in a rocky clasp within its depth;
a tedious length of time you must fulfil   1020
before you see the light again, returning.
Then Zeus's winged hound, the eagle red,
shall tear great shreds of flesh from you, a feaster
coming unbidden, every day: your liver
bloodied to blackness will be his repast.
And of this pain do not expect an end
until some God shall show himself successor
to take your tortures for himself and willing
go down to lightless Hades and the shadows
of Tartarus' depths. Bear this in mind
and so determine. This is no feigned boast   1030
but spoken with too much truth. The mouth of Zeus
does not know how to lie, but every word
brings to fulfilment. Look, you, and reflect
and never think that obstinacy is better
than prudent counsel.

Chorus
       Hermes seems to us
to speak not altogether out of season.
He bids you leave your obstinacy and seek
a wise good counsel. Hearken to him. Shame
it were for one so wise to fall in error.

Prometheus
Before he told it me I knew this message: 1040
but there is no disgrace in suffering
at an enemy's hand, when you hate mutually.
So let the curling tendril of the fire
from the lightning bolt be sent against me: let
the air be stirred with thunderclaps, the winds
in savage blasts convulsing all the world.
Let earth to her foundations shake, yes to her root,
before the quivering storm: let it confuse

the paths of heavenly stars and the sea's waves
in a wild surging torrent: this my body
let Him raise up on high and dash it down   1050
into black Tartarus with rigorous
compulsive eddies: death he cannot give me.

Hermes

These are a madman's words, a madman's plan:
is there a missing note in this mad harmony?
is there a slack chord in his madness? You,
you, who are so sympathetic with his troubles,
away with you from here, quickly away!   1060
lest you should find your wits stunned by the thunder
and its hard defending roar.

Chorus

                  Say something else
different from this: give me some other counsel
that I will listen to: this word of yours
for all its instancy is not for us.
How dare you bid us practice baseness? We
will bear along with him what we must bear.
I have learned to hate all traitors: there is no
disease I spit on more than treachery.   1070

Hermes

Remember then my warning before the act:
when you are trapped by ruin don't blame fortune:
don't say that Zeus has brought you to calamity
that you could not foresee: do not do this:
but blame yourselves: now you know what you're doing:
and with this knowledge neither suddenly
nor secretly your own want of good sense
has tangled you in the net of ruin, past
all hope of rescue.

Prometheus

    Now it is words no longer: now in very truth   1080
the earth is staggered: in its depths the thunder
bellows resoundingly, the fiery tendrils
of the lightning flash light up, and whirling clouds
carry the dust along: all the winds' blasts
dance in a fury one against the other
in violent confusion: earth and sea
are one, confused together: such is the storm
that comes against me manifestly from Zeus
to work its terrors. O Holy mother mine,   1090
O Sky that circling brings the light to all,
you see me, how I suffer, how unjustly.

PRINTED IN U.S.A.